Handbook of Training and Development

Handbook of Training and Development

Edited by Steve Truelove

Copyright © Fielden House, 1992

First published 1992

Blackwell Publishers
108 Cowley Road,
Oxford, OX4 1JF,
UK

238 Main Street, Suite 501
Cambridge, Massachusetts 02142,
USA

British Library Cataloguing in Publication Data
A CIP catalogue record for this book is available from the British Library.

Library of Congress Cataloging in Publication Data
Handbook of training and development/edited by Steve Truelove.
     p.   cm.
   Includes bibliographical references and index.
   1. Employees—Training of—Handbooks, manuals, etc.   2. Employees—
Training of—Great Britain—Handbooks, manuals, etc.
HF5549.5.T7H2956   1992
658.3′124—dc20   92–8831
ISBN 0–631–18227–6 (alk. paper)

Typeset in 11 on 13 pt Ehrhardt
by Hope Services (Abingdon) Ltd.
Printed in Great Britain by
T.J. Press (Padstow) Ltd, Padstow, Cornwall.

This book is printed on acid-free paper

Contents

List of Figures

List of Tables

About the Contributors

Malcolm Craig Originally an engineer in the Merchant Navy, Malcolm is now based in Cambridge as an Independent Consultant and Researcher in the development of customized selection and training systems, in particular fault diagnosis training. He currently tutors on Open University Undergraduate and Business School programmes. He is a Chartered Psychologist and has published numerous articles based on applied research in the field of training.

Sylvia Downs Sylvia gained her degree in 1950 from University College, London. She stopped work as a research assistant in 1953 to have her three children and joined ITRU in 1961. Her main research interests covered training methods for the older worker, trainability assessments (later known as trainability tests) and learning to learn. In 1982 she set up the Occupational Research Unit at UWIST and continued her researches into learning to learn in the YTS and for adults, funded by the then MSC. Latterly, she has applied the findings in New Zealand, South Africa and within large organizations in the UK.

She is a Chartered Psychologist, Fellow of the British Psychological Society and Fellow of the Institute of Training and Development. She has published widely both academically and to a wider training market.

Bob Hamlin Bob is a Principal Lecturer within the Wolverhampton Business School at Wolverhampton Polytechnic, and is Divisional Manager of its Management Development Division. Prior to joining the Business School, he worked for over 20 years within the Chemicals, Plastics, Machine Tool and Engineering Industries, during which time he gained extensive experience as a professional trainer, training manager and management trainer. He has over 7 years experience in the trainer training field and in the provision of management training and consultancy services to client organizations both in the private and public sectors. His research interests are concerned primarily with identifying the criteria of managerial effectiveness and management competencies through empirical studies, the results of which have been published widely.

John Roscoe John has been training trainers with the Polytechnic of West London (formerly Thames Valley College) for over 15 years. His experience includes training all levels of trainers, from instructors to training managers. Face-to-face training has been conducted throughout the UK and internationally in open and tailor-made courses. He has also contributed to the development of open learning provision for the ITD Certificate and Diploma. In addition to facilitating trainer training, he undertakes training consultancy projects for a variety of clients.

Gill Sanderson Gill spent 7 years lecturing on organizational behaviour in the Department of Management of Manchester Polytechnic. Prior to that she was a work-study engineer on the shop floor of a steel works, taught rockclimbing to young people in industry, and lectured in science and liberal studies at High Peak College of Further Education. She has worked for Fielden House for 8 years, most of which she has spent managing their Merseyside Centre. She has a degree in Psychology from Sheffield University.

Jim Stewart Currently Senior Lecturer teaching HRM and HRD on both undergraduate and post-graduate/professional courses at Nottingham Polytechnic, he was previously Senior Lecturer at Wolverhampton Business School, where he was very actively involved in consultancy work, involving design and delivery of in-house management development programmes.

Author of numerous articles in professional and academic journals on HRD related subjects, he has written one book titled *Managing Change Through Training and Development* (November 1991, Kogan Page).

Jim previously spent 7 years as an OD and MD consultant within local government. He started his career in the retail industry with 10 years in management positions and 2 years in the training function.

Steve Truelove Steve gained a degree in Occupational Psychology from UWIST, Cardiff, in 1974. He worked in the engineering industry as a personnel officer, later moving into the papermaking industry where his experience broadened to include responsibility for the training function. He joined Fielden House as a Tutor/Consultant in 1987 and is now manager of its HRD Division, specializing in the training of trainers.

Rosemary Winter   Rosemary, a graduate from Durham University, had a first career as a geography teacher. In 1988 she left her job as Head of Department to work in industry as Deputy Manager of Courtaulds' Coventry site training centre. The centre concentrated on open learning and Rosemary specialized in technology based training. This included introducing interactive video to Courtaulds and involved her in research work in justifying the benefits of interactive video. The results of some of this work were published in the ITD journal in May 1991. Rosemary is now employed at Birmingham Training and Enterprise Council as a Training and Development Co-ordinator.

Preface

The original idea for this book came out of meetings between Don Halpin, Managing Director of Fielden House Limited, George Webster, Executive Director of the Institute of Training and Development and Richard Burton, of Blackwell Publishers. It was agreed that, despite the range of books now available on subjects within the training field, there was a need for a single volume that would support students of the ITD's Certificate in Training and Development programme.

When discussing the content of the book with other providers of the certificate programme, it became obvious that it would be impossible to provide a truly comprehensive coverage of all the subject matter areas of the certificate syllabus. Additionally, it was recognized that the needs of the students of the programme vary considerably. Although some are absolutely new to the training function, many already have considerable experience in the field before they undertake the course.

We also recognized the opportunity to include chapters which would be of value to trainers who were operating, or seeking to operate, at a fairly advanced level, and who wanted information on specific techniques not readily found elsewhere. The book, therefore, comprises both highly original contributions – particularly with regard to the process of Diagnosis – and a selection of overviews of topics which have been widely written about by others. The influence of previous writers is readily acknowledged.

The book is arranged in three sections: Section 1 deals with the process of Diagnosis. Specific techniques of analysis and investigation, the analysis of organizational training needs, the diagnosis of learning blockages and a way of categorizing learning are given; Section 2 looks at the implementation of training. It covers the process of setting objectives, designing learning events, methods of evaluation, and both traditional (tutor delivered) and new (open and distance) methods of delivery; Section 3 deals with some of the Strategic Considerations of training. The administration of training is discussed, and the influence of national policies is described in relation both to historical developments and the current situation in the UK. Ways in which employees develop are also considered.

The chapters are presented in self-contained units and readers may choose to start almost anywhere, depending on their particular needs.

I would like to thank Fiona Sewell for the fine work she did in copyediting this book.

Steve Truelove

1
Techniques for Investigation

MALCOLM CRAIG

Knowledge is of two kinds.
We know a subject ourselves,
or we know where we can find
information upon it.

Samuel Johnson, 1775

Introduction

The overall objective of any investigation is to gather information. This subject of investigation is not to be confused with analysis; there are techniques of investigation and when the information has been produced we can use techniques of analysis, some of which, relevant to the trainer, are covered in the next chapter.

The Oxford English Dictionary (2nd edition, 1989) defines 'investig-ate' as follows: 'to search or inquire into, to examine (a matter) systematically or in detail; to make an inquiry or examination into. To make search, to reconnoitre, to scout, to inquire systematically.' The common picture we have of people who investigate does not normally include trainers. Investigations are typically carried out by specialists at the scene of transport disasters, by journalists prowling in the corridors of power, by detectives in trench coats or by independent consultants. The theme of this chapter is that the role of investigator can be usefully adopted by people who work in the field of training. This applies in particular where the proportion of time spent on direct training has declined, to be replaced with tasks associated with an internal training consultant role. External independent consultants operate by using a selection of favourite techniques carried around in the head, or in a shiny black 'toolbox' with combination locks. It is argued here that training practitioners within organizations also need access to such techniques.

There are at least three strong reasons for the free dissemination of investigative techniques. First, traditionally training processes have, in the past, been reactive to changing circumstances in the workplace and there is now a need for trainers to anticipate change and to plan accordingly. Information from well-executed investigation is crucial for tasks which require planning. Secondly, any assessment of the contribution made by training to overall productivity or service must be based on sound, well-founded information. Thirdly, the practising of investigative techniques helps develop in people a more searching, inquisitive approach. Whether training responsibility includes the practical detail of instruction or the conceptual thinking of training policy formulation, a searching, inquisitive approach is of value to the trainer.

Before going on further with this subject it will be helpful if you reflect upon your own current involvement in work that could be described as 'investigative'.

Self-diagnosis

To set the scene, you are asked to consider how far you take an investigative role. Look at the list below and from this, not untypical, outline of training functions say which of these: (a) has demanded investigative work by you; and (b) you see as needing some investigation. You may like to make a note of functions not on this list, and consider these too.

- Interpreting business plans to identify future skill needs
- Planning future training initiatives
- Identifying present skill needs
- Analysing present skill use
- Analysing abilities
- Analysing tasks
- Analysing functions
- Instructing/tutoring
- Designing training material
- Choosing methods of training delivery
- Calculating training cost pay-back
- Predicting employee ability to learn new skills

- Training evaluation
- Designing and/or using training simulation
- Writing training plans.

As can be seen from inspection of this list, this self-diagnosis section is relevant also to analysis, and can be referred back to when reading the next chapter, substituting 'investigative' with 'analytical' and 'investigation' with 'analysis' in the introduction to the exercise.

Given that you have carried out investigation of some kind, what technique did you use? Put another way, what did you do that could be described as a technique? If Agatha Christie's Poirot had been asked these questions he would probably have replied, 'observation, questioning, and most important listening'. All three are techniques which require a high level of skill if they are to be used effectively. Poirot might also have added thinking or deductive reasoning, which is a technique for analysis of the information collected using the three investigative techniques just mentioned.

If you have not done what can be called investigation but you recognize that a potential need exists, now is the time to think about how you would go about it.

Purpose

Before describing investigative techniques in more detail it is necessary to think first about our purpose for doing investigation. Purpose must be clear to you, the investigator, and to those who cooperate in providing information. There must be no hidden agendas or secrecy; openness is vital to any investigation in the place of work.

The identification of purpose is the first step in an investigation, which in turn must always be part of a process leading to results. This process is illustrated in figure 1.1.

With regard to training, the purpose for investigation normally comes from one of three possible sources: (a) some kind of problem exists (problem solving); (b) everything seems all right but some independent assurance is needed (assurance); or (c) there is a need to plan effectively, to avoid being caught out by changes to plant, markets, processes or policy (planning). Here are three examples, each of which could provide the purpose for carrying out an investigation.

- Why do younger people do less well on this training programme than older people? (Problem)

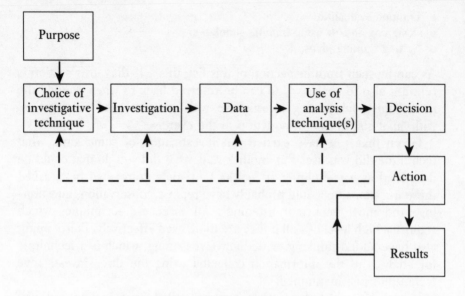

Figure 1.1 The investigative process

- There is little scope for further improvement to our training performance in terms of training productivity, or is there? (Assurance)
- Who could be most quickly retrained for this new process, and how? (Planning)

Being clear about the purpose of investigation fulfils or helps fulfil five essential requirements:

1 It allows others to appreciate the reason for investigation.
2 It helps identify who should be involved.
3 It helps identify whether quantitative or qualitative data is needed.
4 It provides a reference point if the investigation appears to be going astray.
5 It helps decide whether groups of people or individuals would be the best source of information.

Clarity of purpose also guides us in choosing an investigative technique. For example, if the purpose of an investigation is to contribute to a problem-solving exercise then a technique is needed which, as far as possible, allows equal involvement by every participant, such as a brainstorming, a delphi or a survey questionnaire technique. If on the other hand the purpose is to provide assurance then a preferred technique may be one that allows for control and interpretation by an independent individual, such as critical incident, questioning/listening

Table 1.1 Investigative techniques for different purposes

Technique	Purpose		
	Planning	Assurance	Problem solving
Brainstorming	*		*
Critical incident technique	*	*	*
Listening and questioning	*	*	*
Repertory grid	*		*
Survey questionnaire	*	*	
Delphi	*		*
Structured observation			*

and/or structured observation. The various options are illustrated in Table 1.1.

You may find it useful to refer back to this table as you read through the various techniques, described below.

Investigative Techniques

The techniques listed in Table 1.1 have been chosen for inclusion here because each is capable, in different ways, of making a contribution to the investigation of training-related processes.

There is not space in this chapter, or indeed in this book, to provide all that can be said about these techniques. For this reason, additional sources of information and guidance are given in each case.

Brainstorming technique

Background
This technique was developed by Alex Osborn in the late 1930s. There are two broad principles which underpin the use of brainstorming; one is the suspension of judgement and the other is that quantity breeds quality. We are conditioned by our upbringing and especially our education to judge events and ideas at first hearing or seeing. In this act of judgement we tend to react by looking for difficulties; why something will not be possible or feasible. This behaviour blocks or certainly hinders the production of creative ideas. Therefore, an important

principle in brainstorming use is the suspension of judgement. The second principle is quite straightforward; it is that the greater the number of ideas that can be generated, the more chance there is of finding a solution to a problem.

The technique can only be used to address problems where a number of possible solutions are possible. Trainers who have attended an Open University systems summer school will recall that the brainstorming of a problem such as 'how many ways can we think of to reduce road accidents' can produce more than two hundred ideas from twelve people. The technique is not suitable where, for example, existing ideas have been used and it is wished to assess or evaluate what has been done. Brainstorming exercises are essentially problem-solving oriented; brainstorming is commonly referred to as a problem-solving technique. However, at the end of a brainstorming exercise the result is a mass of information, which must be categorized and analysed before a problem-solving stage is reached. The actual process of brainstorming is an act of investigation, to see how many ways we can think of to provide the path to a solution.

Using the Technique
First, the setting or general environment is important. There must be no group members armed with a filofax or mobile phone ready to leap off to some world-saving mission; it is essential that a period of at least 45 minutes is allocated by everyone to this task and that no interruptions are possible. This has to be made clear to each brainstorming group member at least two days before the event, along with details of where, when, who will be there and the problem to be addressed, as well as a statement about brainstorming, its purpose, the rules and what the hoped-for outcome is likely to be. This is particularly important for those who have not been involved in the technique before. In the case of companies where it is part of on-going practice it is hoped that this precaution becomes accepted automatically. Ideally the group should sit in a semi-circle, not blocked by tables or desks.

The composition of the group is important. Research has shown that cohesive groups perform better than non-cohesive groups in this situation. Also, the 'status' held by various members needs to be suspended during the session. It is unhelpful if some people in the group are reluctant to provide ideas due to the presence of more senior people; there has to be an understanding from the beginning that everyone is there as an equal partner.

There are four rules to be observed when brainstorming:

1 Ideas are to be freely expressed without any questioning about feasibility or usefulness; anything and everything is accepted.
2 Discussion, categorizing and rejection/acceptance of ideas are done only when the actual brainstorming exercise is at an end, and this end must be made clear to the group by the leader.
3 Members are to be encouraged to build on ideas already expressed or to modify these ideas with further ideas.
4 Quantity is asked for, the aim being to get as many ideas as possible.

In preparing for a brainstorming exercise the leader can encourage the flow of ideas by stating to the group that they must avoid criticism and instead use their imagination.

The verbal and non-verbal behaviour of the leader can bring a brainstorming exercise to a premature end before all possible ideas have come from the group. This can be avoided by noting the following points:

● Never say, 'Is there anything else?' or 'We have a lot of ideas now'. The expectation must always be for more ideas.
● Never refer to the time passing, or to being 'near the end of our time'.
● Never look exhausted or limp during the exercise. An energetic appearance must be maintained.
● Never be discouraged by silence. In brainstorming, seconds of silence seem like minutes, but allow for thinking time.

At the end of the idea-generation session, the leader, with the help of the group, categorizes all the ideas into three types: (a) good workable ideas; (b) ideas worthy of consideration; and (c) weirdo ideas. The group then addresses each of the three types, to focus in on possible ways forward; what can and what cannot be used. It is important that all categories are discussed, in particular the weirdo, because it is common for creative, innovative ideas to come out of this category. Here lies the strength of brainstorming: that creative ideas are not discouraged as is typical with business meeting practice and general work-related communication.

This description of brainstorming use is that of classical brainstorming in which there is a structure to the exercise. There is also unstructured brainstorming where ideas, any ideas, are asked for. This last version is not seen as of value to the trainer. There is, too, a variation on the technique known as brain writing, and as the name implies this involves people writing down ideas, either independently to be considered later in a group or as part of a group from the beginning. This approach avoids the leader influence on the process but also demands that members are able to record thoughts quickly and fluently on paper. On balance it can be said that it is classical, structured, brainstorming that has been most proven as a technique for generating possible problem-solving ideas.

Typical uses for the technique

- To generate ideas for means to overcome the problem of workflow stoppages
- To generate ideas for ways to encourage people to learn new techniques/ skills
- To generate ideas for ways to increase motivation
- To encourage ideas for ways to introduce a new process.

Learning the technique
This is a funny one; it is the act of 'learning' that contributes to our lack of creativeness. We learn rules, order and 'accepted' ways of doing things until we reach a strait-jacketed state. Only certain people will readily think of new ideas or ways of doing things differently. The act of brainstorming is to encourage more people to break out of their learned behaviour or instant reactions. So learning is confined to the leader and is minimal. There are simply the rules to be followed in order to conduct the session, and the need to note the points about verbal and non-verbal behaviour shown towards the group. A useful reference is Osborn 1941.

Critical incident technique (CIT)

Background
This technique was developed by John Flanagan, an American psychologist, during the Second World War to investigate bombing missions over Germany. The purpose was to discover why errors were made and subsequently to discover ways of improving flight-crew training.

The technique can be described quite simply; its effective use, however, requires a good deal of practice. The aim is to gather information, from practitioners, about job behaviour which has a significant influence on the success or failure of the outcome. All jobs contain a certain amount of what can be called 'padding', tasks which are done for one reason or another but which do not seriously influence eventual outcome. The highlighting of critical incidents and identification of actual behaviour which leads to either success or failure is fundamental to the design and evaluation of training processes.

When people first practise this technique they soon realise the extent to which we talk in sweeping generalities. The technique forces you to be quite specific when discussing skills, performance standards or attitudes. For example, an investigator using CIT may be told by a supervisor that critical to a certain task is 'initiative'. In terms of information to aid training this word is meaningless; that is, unless a trainer picks it up and goes running off to some outdoor activities course to teach so-called 'initiative'. In contrast, the CIT user goes on to say, 'What does the person *do* that makes you say initiative is critical?'. When this line of investigation is followed by probing actual critical behaviour, the outcome is often to think again about the use of a word like 'initiative'. Realization dawns that it is not really initiative at all, or that if the task were organized differently, initiative would not be needed. Sometimes, however, genuine acts of initiative critical to the work may be uncovered, and the behaviours – rather than 'initiative' – can be accommodated in training. Getting away from the habit of talking in generalities, which are not always well founded, is probably the biggest obstacle to be overcome when learning this technique.

Using the technique

The technique can be used in three ways: (a) by one-to-one critical incident interview; (b) by group questioning with up to six participants; or (c) by critical incident questionnaire. There is some debate among researchers whether the quality of information is improved or diminished by using group participation in place of one-to-one interviews. Where time for investigation is scarce the second option is to be preferred, and in certain circumstances can provide richer information than a series of one-to-one contacts. The questionnaire option is always third and last, even though information is gathered quickly and at less expense than by the first two methods. This economy, as with all questionnaire use, is achieved at the cost of losing spontaneous and possibly very relevant information that comes from face-to-face contact.

What makes face-to-face CIT use such a powerful investigative tool is that a balance is achieved between the too-structured questionnaire or structured interview, and the open, unstructured interview or question-naire. There are specific points to note when conducting a critical incident interview whether in the one-to-one situation or in a group.

1 When CIT is used among a homogeneous group of people who discover what can be almost called a law. For example, imagine you were interviewing, one by one, a group of people who operate a new version of the point-of-sale

terminal in a large retail store with the purpose of improving the training programme. The second operator would give you incidents not given by the first operator and possibly miss some that the first operator provided. The third may well provide new incidents. The fourth is unlikely to add new information; certainly by the fifth interview the description of critical skilled behaviour will be exhausted; no other person could add anything to what is known. Even in the most complex of jobs seven 'experts' will exhaust what can be said about skilled behaviour. The skilled CIT interviewer will maintain enthusiasm and interest in what is being said, even if it is the eighth person being spoken to and he or she has heard it all before during the previous seven interviews. This is a crucial requirement in CIT use.

2 The CIT interviewer *never* asks leading questions. When the interviewer is an 'expert' in the particular subject there is a temptation to introduce ideas into the discussion; this must be avoided.

3 When asking for another incident the interviewer never says 'Is there anything else?' or 'Have you any more examples?'. This is an invitation for the interviewee to bale out and say 'No'. Instead this line must be taken: 'You have given me three very good examples of critical behaviour, now I would like you to give me another', or 'You referred to right attitude. Can you say what this person does that demonstrates right attitude?'. In this way, the flow of incidents is maintained until the interviewee cannot possibly offer more.

4 In CIT use it is essential that only incidents relating to one quite specific situation are talked about. For example, the interpersonal behaviour involved in dealing with customers at the point-of-sale terminal, referred to earlier, would generate critical incidents, and behaviour that is typical of a competent, skilled person – as well as the behaviour typical of a less than competent, unskilled person – would be described. Another vital point relevant here is that only one particular person at a time is considered. A false name may be used to preserve anonymity, but the interviewee must think only of that person's behaviour when describing behaviours to the interviewer. In group application of CIT it is possible to consider a skilled operation overall irrespective of who performs. A critical incident is identified and then contributions are collected from group members about that incident – and only that incident – before moving on to consider a further incident.

The critical incident questionnaire is of the semi-structured type and close to being 'open'. The respondents are asked to name a situation, such as the experience leading up to a plane crash; the experience of getting out and surviving a plane crash; preparing a newspaper printing console; preparing instruments for an operation in a theatre. There are typical specific situations for which critical incidents could be provided. Then respondents are asked to name a critical incident, following questionnaire guidance notes, and then to describe effective behaviours that contributed to a successful outcome or to skilled performance.

Particularly ineffective behaviours that contributed to unsuccessful outcome or unskilled performance are also asked for. When this incident has been exhausted, further incidents are requested, all relating to the identified situation.

In most cases, the one-to-one CIT interview is to be preferred. The questionnaire produces much less valuable data, but if a quick, cheap overview of a skilled occupation is needed the CIT questionnaire will perform better than other designs of forms. No direct questions are asked; therefore this type of questionnaire does not prejudge the outcome.

Typical uses for the technique

- For describing skilled performance in terms of effective and less than effective behaviour – used in the setting of standards for highways national vocational qualifications
- To generate information about effective behaviour that can be incorporated into a training programme – used in the development of various training programmes
- To provide data about errors made in learning a task that can be used in the design of a trainability test – used in the development of all trainability tests
- To identify behaviour critical to the learning of a new process, as with new technology – used during the introduction of new technology in the newspaper industry
- Gathering information about behaviour from critical incidents where customers are pleased or not pleased – used to good effect with both the police and the health service.

The United States Personnel Research and Development Centre, Washington, lists over seven hundred studies in which the CIT has been used for investigation purposes.

Learning the technique

At the time of this book going to press there is no standard manual or guide to this technique. The one main reference is John Flanagan's paper (Flanagan 1954). People interested in using the technique are recommended to study this carefully. Courses offered from time to time to teach the design of trainability tests devote a major part of the time to learning and practising the technique.

When used well, CIT is one of thhe most powerful and reliable information-gathering methods available. Learning opportunities are scarce; the best option is John Flanagan's paper plus practice with someone familiar in the use of the technique.

Listening and questioning techniques

Background

These two investigative skills are inseparable; one supports and reinforces the other. Both skills are largely neglected in schools, colleges and universities despite the fact that it is through these skills that learning takes place. The same statement is true in the field of training. For the trainer who wishes to promote learning, a high level of listening and questioning skills is crucial, yet how many trainers would claim to have a high degree of skill in this area? The ability of hearing is sometimes confused with the skill of listening; hearing is difficult to change but, with training, listening can show considerable improvement. Questioning is one of the earliest verbal activities of the child, so we tend to think that everyone is well practised. Unfortunately practice does not make perfect; it only reinforces effective or non-effective behaviour.

Listening and questioning differ from the other techniques described here in that they are not optional; they are essential to nearly all investigations.

Using the techniques

The skills of listening and questioning are used in four main ways: (a) in one-to-one communication; (b) in groups; (c) to oneself; and (d) as an outside observer. The way they are utilised can determine the kind of listening and questioning put to use.

One-to-one is the most used in work and in everyday life. Here, the skilled listener and questioner will:

- Make good use of silence, allowing the other person time to think and reply
- Use signs of listening to encourage the other person, such as 'Yes', 'I see', 'Then?' and so on
- Check out any terms or phrases that are unfamiliar or unclear, demonstrating, in this way, listening and questioning skill
- Ask again for any word or name that has been missed, especially when being first introduced to someone
- Maintain a distance between him or herself and the other person that is appropriate to the situation
- Use appropriate questions from a range of types: semi-closed, open, comparison, mirror, what if, value, reflective, etc.
- Avoid lengthy questions, questions loaded with jargon, negative questions and trick questions.

These positive listening and questioning behaviours can be learned and practised to good effect by trainers.

The act of listening and questioning in groups presents particular problems. Possibly the most significant to be overcome is that when someone wishes to ask a question of a group of people, the chances of that person listening effectively to what is being said immediately preceding his or her asking the question is poor. This applies not only to meetings but to trainers with a group of trainees. A first step in correcting this situation is to be aware of our natural behaviour in this respect. It is hardly necessary to stress that a group of effective listeners and questioners will perform rather better than a group where the importance of these techniques goes unrecognized.

The importance of listening to your own deliberations can be overlooked. We speak to ourselves either outwardly or inwardly. In each case there is value in reflecting upon how we question the various assumptions made and the conclusions we arrive at. This self-listening and self-questioning is used with protocol analysis, a technique described in the next chapter.

Trainers can find themselves in the role of outside observers, invited to sit in on departmental meetings, observing a new process for which training is going to be needed or watching a demonstration of a 'new' piece of training technology that someone wishes to sell. In such situations it is often difficult to question directly but the skill of using summarizing questions, to demonstrate that you have both listened and understood the meaning of what was said, is important.

Typical uses for the techniques
As pointed out earlier, the skills of listening and questioning are crucial to nearly all investigation, the one exception being the routine search for information in books, journals etc. More specifically, the techniques are used in a wide range of one-to-one situations which demand shifts in the types of listening and questioning used. On the one hand, there might be a need to gather information from a machine operator about a recent safety training course attended; on the other hand, the need might be to gather information from a production manager about plans to introduce more flexible working arrangements. In one situation the most appropriate technique may be to use a set of pre-planned questions and, through effective listening to answers, to be prepared to ask further questions as necessary. In the other situation the approach may be to adopt an entirely open technique, beginning with the words, 'Tell me'. At other times a useful technique is to begin with an open approach, allowing the other person, or group of people, to give you information spontaneously while you use prompt questions and effective listening,

then follow this with pre-planned questions, using only those questions which gather information not given in the open response session.

The next time that you set out to gather information, by whatever method, say to yourself, 'How good are my listening and questioning techniques?'.

Learning the techniques
As stated at the beginning, these techniques and the skills used are seldom taught and, it must be said, are greatly underrated. Three excellent short guides, written by Ian Mackay and published by BACIE, are essential reading for trainers (Mackay 1980, 1984, 1989). There is scope for enterprising trainers out there to produce much-needed improvement upon what is currently available in the area of taught courses, or open learning for those who prefer this approach. The subject, however, is essentially a social process, so it is best learned in a social setting and not in front of a computer or training module.

Repertory grid technique

Background
This technique, which has many applications for trainers, came out of what is called personal construct theory (PCT), developed in the 1930s by the late George Kelly, a psychologist and also a clinician who wished to understand people as well as he could. The idea of personal construct theory is important to an understanding of the practical use of the grid. Associations of people exist to develop and promote this theory. Put simply, we all have our own way of using words to help make sense of the world around us: mountains described as beautiful by one person can be described by another as fearsome (in fact the idea of mountains being 'beautiful' began only in the late eighteenth century). The same development of view we hold is true of other objects, people and events. We 'construct' our views of surroundings by the words we use to describe them. There is, for example, an argument that if we did not have the element 'God' to apply constructs to, a view about this subject could not exist. In more practical terms, the comparison between three employees on a measure of how they each describe quality can tell us a good deal about their respective views on this subject.

As with all techniques there are advantages and disadvantages with the use of the grid. However, it has had more than its fair share of detractors over the years. The two main criticisms are, first, that it forces people into an unrealistic comparison between three chosen elements (see below), and second, that for adequate information gathering there is reliance upon a reasonable level of verbal fluency on the part of respondents. This said, the practical application of the grid in the workplace has proved to be a most useful investigative tool.

Using the technique
For someone coming to the technique for the first time the jargon associated with it can seem rather confusing: triads, constructs, elements and networks. In practice non-psychologists soon adjust to the language and learn to use the grid without too much difficulty.

In any one situation there are elements, which in the use of the repertory grid are either nouns or verbs. The nouns must be specific objects or people; the verbs must be events or activities. Once the elements are established for a particular subject – say, customer attitude to a training programme – it is then possible to design a grid so that each person involved in the investigation can be asked to apply their own personal constructs to a selected triad of elements. Possibly the simplest way for you to grasp this process is for you to think of three people – yourself plus two others you know well; we will call the two John and Mary. You would be asked to say which two are most alike. If you replied 'Myself and Mary', you would then be asked to say on what basis you are alike. When this answer has been given you are asked to say if this applied to John as well. It may well be that it does not, and you go on to say in what way John is different in this respect, and so on. As the process continues a considerable amount of information builds up about agreement and differences between the chosen elements (in this example the elements are people – yourself, John and Mary).

The steps in using a grid are little different from the steps in any investigation. First, be clear about the purpose of the technique in use, and make this known to all who take part or are otherwise involved. Second, decide upon method of delivery, whether by interviewer questioning by manual questionnaire, or by computer software program (the Open University makes use of a repertory grid program). Third, decide on the way that analysis is to be performed – on the content of the replies or on the structure of the data. This has to be decided before you begin so that the information you collect can fit the programme you have for analysis purposes. Fourth, choose the relevant elements. Fifth, gather constructs from people who participate, then rank responses with the help of participants to achieve higher-order constructs for the grid. Finally analyse the results.

For people unfamiliar with repertory grid use this may read as somewhat technical; however, reference to manuals and guides on the subject will provide a more thorough step-by-step description than space allows here (see 'Learning the technique' below).

Typical uses for the technique
There are a number of uses relevant to the field of training:

- Gathering information from practitioners about issues, in preparation for the design of a questionnaire
- Gathering constructs that people use to describe the climate of an organization
- Tailoring the provision of training to meet the actual needs of employees by gathering information about what is important to them
- As a counselling method to elicit information relevant to the development of staff
- To evaluate a method of training by gathering and comparing information from trainees
- To identify what quality means to different people

These are only a selection of practical uses for the grid. As trainers become practised in its use, wider areas of application will be recognized.

Learning the technique
One of the most practical industry-related guides to the technique is Valerie and Andrew Stewart's book (Stewart and Stewart 1981). The manual from Fay Fransella and the late Donald Bannister also provides a sound guide to the practical use of the grid (Fransella and Bannister 1977). Both sources provide all that a trainer in industry needs to know about the subject. As a means of developing the technique and sharing ideas with others it is a good plan to make use of a standard course in the subject. Details of programmes in personal construct theory and use of the repertory grid are available from the Centre for Personal Construct Psychology, 132 Warwick Way, London SW1 4SD.

Survey questionnaire technique

Background
Surveys are conducted most often by the use of questionnaires:

> The little men in untold legions
> Descend upon the private regions

Behold my child, the questionnaire
And be as honest as you dare.

Anon.

Possibly the most used in industry is the attitude questionnaire, to capture employee attitudes to various aspects of work. The so-called evaluation questions asked at the close of a training programme represent what is essentially an attitude questionnaire; they elicit attitudes towards the course rather than providing the hoped-for objective assessment. Attempting to 'measure' attitudes by questionnaire provides a minefield of contradictions, to the point of asking whether attitudes can in fact be measured.

The trainer who considers the use of a survey questionnaire needs to be aware that design, piloting, implementation and analysis are a highly skilled process. Done badly by unskilled personnel, it leads inevitably to a costly waste of time and resources and can be seriously counterproductive. When a questionnaire is administered to a group of people – and for trainers this normally means employees – the investigator gets only one chance to make a success of the venture. If the questions are seen as ambiguous or ill-considered and, most important, there is no feedback and action as a result of the employee's participation, any further attempts to use questionnaires are doomed before starting.

Having given this warning, it must be said that in large organizations the survey questionnaire can, if well done, provide large amounts of valuable investigative data.

Using the technique

All questionnaires fall into one of three types: (a) structured; (b) semi-structured; and (c) open. The structured questionnaire leads the respondent to give a specific answer to each question. The format is usually of the multiple-choice kind, where one or more boxes have to be ticked in answer to the question. The most important part in the design of such a questionnaire is the piloting stage. It is essential that structured questionnaires are piloted using a representative sample from the planned respondents in order to get their reactions. A process of iteration takes place; the trainer must go back to square one and amend or change what has already been done. If major changes are needed a second pilot becomes necessary. This must be done before using the questionnaire in investigation. Piloting helps overcome a serious weakness in the use of structured questionnaires; the weakness is that the survey designer largely determines the outcome of the survey rather than, as should be the case, the population of respondents doing so. There needs to be an independent check on the type of questions asked. 'If you do not have an answer you do not have a question'; therefore in asking a question we largely predetermine the answer. Overcoming this problem is a major issue in questionnaire use, and seldom is it fully resolved.

Semi-structured questionnaires, where set questions are followed by the opportunity to provide further spontaneous comment and/or answers, provide more qualitative data than the structured type. (The critical incident questionnaire reverses this by asking for spontaneous reactions to critical incidents first, and only when this has been done are set questions asked.) Piloting of the semi-structured questionnaires is necessary too; the opening questions need to be checked independently.

The open questionnaire uses only key reference points of areas to be covered in the investigation. The most powerful words in such investigation are 'Tell me'; for example: 'So you are having difficulty with this new instruction sheet, tell me about it', or, 'This statistical process control system has been in use by you for two months now after the training, tell me about it.' These are examples of the open-question alternative to asking specific questions. Specific, closed questions are simply those that you, the trainer, feel are important in these situations.

It is common practice for organizations to design questionnaires to elicit customer attitudes to the service provided. The questions in such a survey reflect what is seen as important to the organization, not what is important to the customer. The open alternative is simply to say, 'Tell me what particularly pleases you about our service.' By using only probe and prompt questions a large amount of data can be collected on the basis of this one lead-off question. Then comes, 'Tell me what particularly displeases you about our service.' Again, a considerable amount of data can be collected. It is of interest that responses to the 'pleases' question provides most useful data for the design of customer care training programmes. At times training is designed in response to things going wrong and tends to be based on negative-type information. It is positive, effective behaviour which needs to be captured instead.

When making a choice of which type of questionnaire to use, a trade-off has to be considered between quantity and quality of data. To achieve both using a questionnaire involves considerable cost in terms of time and resources. If a general overview of employees' attitudes is required, a well-piloted closed questionnaire may well provide valid results. If a long-running problem is being resolved and views are needed, a semi-structured or preferably an open method is needed. The structured questionnaire provides quantity of data and, given the help of the computer, is quickly analysed. Quality of data, however, is sacrificed. The semi-structured, and particularly the open, method are time-consuming and hence costly to analyse; quantity has to be limited, but quality of data is enhanced. When using survey questionnaires you pay your money and take your choice.

The key skill used in questionnaire design is formulation of each question. The most common error, which seems endemic in question-naires, is the asking of two questions in one. Another is the answer of one question being dependent upon the answer given to an earlier question, and this can lead to difficulty, especially if the context has been changed in between. Then there are questions too long to grasp; use of jargon, abbreviations or acronyms is to be avoided too. Leading questions should be avoided at all times, and this also applies to hidden agenda questions – those that are there for reasons known only to the survey designer.

Before questions are formulated it is necessary to be clear about:

• The purpose of the survey
• How the answers are to be analysed
• The reading age of the population to be surveyed
• The issues involved in the area being surveyed
• The sensitivity of questions in relation to the type of respondent
• The culture of the population.

Checking through these points, formulating valid questions, structuring the questionnaire and piloting are tasks which the trainer should attempt only after developing the necessary skills.

Typical uses for the technique

• To survey employee attitudes in medium to large organizations
• To elicit views about a situation prior to making changes or introducing a training programme, to be followed by a second survey after the event for evaluation purposes
• To gather data for a skill audit
• To gather views about quality control or quality assurance issues
• To assess the value of a training programme by eliciting course members' perception of training relevance, effectiveness and usefulness.

Learning the technique

A good practical guide to this subject is provided by Reeves and Harper (Reeves and Harper 1981). The trainer may also need to call on expertise in the personnel area for guidance on questionnaire design.

Delphi technique

Background

This technique was developed by the Rand Corporation in the United States. The first reported work was in 1949; however, the technique was not used elsewhere until the mid-1960s. Early application was in the area of business forecasting, using the collected judgement of experts. Over the years the technique has been used for many other purposes, including planning, evaluation, programme development and policy making.

'delphi is a systematic method of collecting opinions from a group of experts through a series of questionnaires, in which feedback of the group's opinion distribution is provided between question rounds while preserving the anonymity of the responses' (Helmer 1972). The technique makes use of questionnaires, so the comments made about survey questionnaire methods in this chapter apply equally to the delphi technique. It is designed to gather information from experts independently and to feed back the resulting collective responses, again independently and anonymously. At this feedback stage, each person is asked to reconsider her or his initial responses by taking into account what has been written by others.

This is a group information-collecting exercise which avoids the problems inherent in groups, such as members being unduly influenced by more outgoing characters, or by people who are particularly verbose in the group situation. It also avoids the group-chair-directed influence. Meetings, though common in industry, normally provide a poor, ineffective means of investigation, analysis or decision making. The value of meetings appears to be mainly in providing social interaction. The delphi technique is worthy of more attention in the United Kingdom, to match the important place it holds in business in the United States.

Using the technique

As with many investigative techniques, the basic description of delphi is simple. This apparent simplicity has led to examples of badly done delphi investigations, where investigators overlooked important steps in the technique or included too much interpretation of their own about how the technique should be used. The steps are as follows:

1 Identify the group of people who will be involved, and make clear to each person the reasons for using this technique; for example:

- It avoids excessive influence from one or more outspoken individuals, commonly found in meetings.
- It overcomes the problem of having individuals unwilling to take up a position before facts are known.
- It avoids 'group think' – the tendency of decisions to be taken on the basis of instant group pressure.
- It overcomes the problem some individuals have of bringing up a point in meetings for fear of ridicule or loss of face; the fate, unfortunately, of some innovative ideas.
- It overcomes the problem of individuals being unwilling to question or contradict those in higher positions during meetings.

Each person in the delphi group must feel that she or he is free to comment as she or he wishes, and contributing as little or as much as is necessary.

2 Design a questionnaire of the semi-structured or open type. This form of questionnaire is chosen because group members must have the opportunity to give their ideas and opinions.
3 Gather in the questionnaires and put together the responses in order of the questions, not indicating who said what.
4 Feed back this collective information to the individual members with a copy of their initial completed questionnaire. Each person is asked if he or she would change one or more parts of his or her questionnaire responses as a result of seeing the collective results.
5 Collect the questionnaires, whether revised or unchanged.
6 Design a more structured questionnaire, listing questions according to the opinions gathered from the initial open questionnaire. This again is administered independently and a collective response is produced.
7 Attempt the reporting of a consensus on the subject; that is, to produce information and data that can contribute to sound decision making. It is possible, however, that widely divergent ideas and/or opinions exist within the group. In the event of this occurring three things can be done. One is to present these differences and go through another delphi cycle, asking for further comments. The second is to see if extreme opinions are being given by a minority of members, in which case the delphi coordinators can ask them to elaborate on their non-conforming opinions. The third is to accept the information as making a valid contribution despite the lack of consensus; you should still be a good deal better informed than when you began the project. The number of questionnaire rounds will depend upon the kind of subject. A normal minimum is two rounds, but over four may begin to try the patience of most people.

These steps can be conducted for a range of training-related tasks. One of the most useful for the trainer is to adopt the delphi technique for forecasting. This is the original purpose of the technique and has been its main application over the years.

In industry, whether manufacturing, service or financial, a reasonable time-span for forecasting purposes is up to two years. The trainer who aims to be proactive rather than reactive needs to have some information and data about possible, likely or planned development. The delphi technique is a useful technique for gathering such information. A group of people is identified who should be aware of developments in their respective areas. For example, a stores controller may be able to indicate the amount and extent of information technology to be introduced, and may well have views about resulting training needs; the same could be true of a production manager who is aware of the impending introduction of statistical process control and the planned development of stronger links with marketing, and so on. Again, these experts in their own field, though not training professionals, may well have a valuable contribution to make if asked about the implication for training of these new developments.

The use of this technique also allows the information/data-gathering net to be spread widely; that is, to customers and suppliers if necessary; distance or location is no bar to the use of delphi and advantage should be taken of this fact.

Typical uses for the technique

- As described above, to help in the process of forecasting training need
- To gather information from related and relevant areas of expertise about the design of a training programme, an example being operator training, where information/data from personnel in quality assurance, inspection, marketing, maintenance, stores and buying can be of value
- To gather customer, supplier and internal views about a planned change in the method or type of training in use.

Learning the technique

First it is necessary to be skilled in questionnaire use (see the questionnaire survey section in this chapter). The most comprehensive guide to the delphi technique is the book by Linstone and Turoff (Linstone and Turoff 1977), and another useful guide is that from Mullen (Mullen 1983). As Mullen recounts, health service managers were asked to give, independently, three problems or difficulties relating to information in the NHS. Then they were asked for three changes or improvements in information. From this data a more structured questionnaire was designed that used a scoring system. This report demonstrates practical use of the technique, and discusses problems encountered.

Not directly related to training but offering a very good description of the delphi technique in practice is Foley's paper (Foley 1984).

Structured observation technique

Background

There are times when most trainers need to observe the use of a skill or a process. This is done either to gather information in preparation for the design of some training or to check on the effects of training.

In years gone by, when many skills were mainly of the manual variety – carpentry, centre lathe turning, hot metal printing etc. – a considerable amount of information could be gathered from the technique of structured observation. The time-and-motion figure with a clipboard and a stopwatch was a common sight. Increasingly, the use of cognitive (mental) skills are replacing traditional manual skills. For example, the newspaper printer has become a monitor and supervisor of a new process that is near to being fully automatic. The traditional skills of printing, which required seven years of apprenticeship, are now largely obsolete. In such situations it is still possible to use structured observation of skill use, but now this approach must be backed up with at least one other technique such as critical incident, protocol analysis or basic interview. The reason for this is that the increase in monitoring, checking, fault recognition etc. requires perceptual and problem-solving skills not available to observation. Investigation by observation must now be supported by a record of what can be said about a skill or a process.

Using the technique

Seeing is not observing; taking a video is not recording observation. To observe effectively is a skill. This skill of observing fine and distinct differences, as well as activities, is necessary in structured observation. The following step-wise approach is recommended for the use of the structured observation technique.

1 Map out the area of activity to be observed: check that you will be observing a precise use of skill or activities in a particular process, and not a whole system of stores sales or microchip production. Structured observation, used to collect worthwhile data, must be clearly targeted at a specific area.

2 Identify the people who will be observed and get their willingness to participate by having a discussion with them about the purpose of the

investigation. There is an investigative technique known as participant observation, of which there are three levels. At the first level, the investigator is concealed as part of the working group. At the second, the investigator is slightly more open but still part of the group. At the third, the role of the investigator is totally open; she or he collects the information that the other group members give while still within the group. It is unlikely that trainers would wish to use the first or second levels but they may on occasion consider the third level. Structured observation, however, is at none of these levels; the relationship is one of job participants and investigator as observer. This must be made clear to the people being observed.

3 Prepare for the structured observation. Possibly the best way to do this is to conduct a critical incident interview with the person or people who are to be part of the investigation. The aim here is to highlight the sequence and type of activities which are critical to the job. From this information, divide a large sheet of paper up into boxes for recording detail about what is observed in the order it is to happen.

4 Observe and record. There is debate about the use of on-site or off-site observation recording. In most cases the best plan is not to use on-site recording. Taking notes almost inevitably has a strong influence on the person being observed; also, the act of recording interrupts the observation. For this reason it is wise to limit any observation to no more than 30 minutes. Then go off site to record immediately what you have observed. Any job or process may require a series of such observation 'windows' of 30 minutes during the course of an investigation.

5 Check out your completed observation recording with the job participants. It is on this step that you can say, 'What is critical at this point when you closed the hopper down?', and so on. What is looked for here is cognitive skills – usually the reasoning behind specific acts.

6 Put your investigation findings together in the form of a description of what was observed, together with a description of cognitive skills being used with each activity. Any act of observation can only be valid when it is composed of at least two points of view, one from the outside and one from the inside.

The actual task of observation is always subjective. We interpret what we see, and it is not necessarily what is seen by someone else: eye-witness reports in criminal courts are notoriously varied and unreliable for this reason. However, with the double checking described here and practice in acute observation, a good deal of reliable and valuable data for training purposes can be gathered. When observing skilled behaviour one main approach is needed, that of inquisitiveness; you need to note every detail. For example, if you observe someone learning to blow glass using a foot-operated mould, the practised glass-blower will tell you that it is all down to experience and a 'feel' for the glass and for the right time to release the mould. This is only partly true. When observing, the number of times the rod is turned can be noted both when collecting glass and when blowing. The manipulation of fingers is critical but could be taught separately and much more quickly on a simulator. How far is body position critical? What is the effect of right-handedness or left-handedness? Left-handedness is discouraged in some parts of the glass industry for equipment reasons, when in fact left-handers, because they are normally more dextrous with both hands, are more suited to this kind of work, where two-handedness is vital. It is this kind of curiosity that is required of the investigator who uses observation. At all times you must have an open, receptive mind.

Typical uses for the technique

- To observe non-verbal behaviour used by skilled and less skilled service providers when talking to customers
- To monitor and observe problems of line balancing in a continuous manufacturing process, in order to identify areas of weakness that may be corrected by suitable training
- To observe the skilled sequence of movements when a manufacturer's expert is demonstrating the use of a new piece of equipment or machine (done for the purpose of designing suitable training for operators new to the system)
- To observe and record instructional technique during a training session.

Learning the technique

There are no formal methods of learning structured observation. Textbooks on the subject have been written primarily for the social scientist and are difficult to relate to the field of training. What can be said about learning this technique is that we practise observation anyway. The learning begins when we recognize that looking and seeing are not observation. Then we need to recognize that in the context of work we can make a better job of observation if we structure what is to be observed. Finally we have to recognize that reports of observation are seldom enough to make a contribution to training; it is necessary to support observation with another technique such as critical incident or the standard interview. From this starting point it is necessary to practise observation for a fixed period of time. A good idea is to focus on a television interview being done with two or more people (typical examples can be found on BBC's *Newsnight*) and make a point of observing as much as you can about behaviours that you see; then immediately after the interview record all your observations. If the programme can be recorded you may like to check on your observations during a re-run; how accurate, how comprehensive, how useful; realizing no doubt that improvements could be made.

Two references useful for conducting structured observation of behaviour in groups are Rackham and Morgan 1977 and Bales 1979. Generally, the more we make a conscious effort to get more out of the observations the better will be our findings.

Summary

In this chapter, a range of investigative techniques has been reviewed, the aim being to raise awareness about the use of investigation as a means of generating information useful to training. Seven techniques have been described, with references to sources of further guidance. Each technique is simply a means to an end; that is, the production of reliable, accurate information. This information can be acted upon, as in the creation or modification of training programmes, or can be analysed to present data to guide action, particularly in decision making.

A general conclusion, after examining the typical uses listed for each technique, is that periodically during the working life of a trainer there must be occasions when the application of at least one investigative technique would be of value to his or her organization. Knowing what is available and where to find guidance is a sound beginning.

Further reading

Adams-Webber, J. R. and Jack, R. (1979) *Personal Construct Theory*. Chichester: Wiley.

Bales. R. F. (1979) *SYMLOG: A System for the Multiple Level Observation of Groups*. London: Collier Macmillan.

Bannister, D. (1985) *Issues and Approaches in Personal Construct Theory*. London: Academic Press.

Flanagan, J. (1954) The Critical Incident Technique. *Psychological Bulletin*, 51, no. 4.

Foley, P. (1984) *The Future of the Sheffield Economy, An Investigation Using the Delphi Method*. Sheffield: University of Sheffield.

Fransella, F. and Bannister, D. (1977) *A Manual for Repertory Grid Technique*. London: Academic Press.

Helmer, O. (1972) Cross Impact Gaining. *Futures*, 4 (1–2), 149–67.

Kelly, G. A. (1955) *The Psychology of Personal Constructs*. New York: W. W. Norton & Co.

Kerry, T. (1982) *Effective Questioning*. Basingstoke: Macmillan Education.

Linstone, H. A. and Turoff, M. (1977) *The Delphi Method, Techniques and Applications*. Reading, Mass.: Addison-Wesley.

Mackay, I. (1980) *A Guide to Asking Questions*. London: BACIE.

Mackay, I. (1984) *A Guide to Listening*. London: BACIE.

Mackay, I. (1989) *Expecting Answers*. London: BACIE.

Mullen, P. M. (1983) *Delphi-Type Studies in the Health Service*. Birmingham: University of Birmingham, Health Service Management Centre.

Osborn, A. (1941) *Applied Imagination*. New York: Scribners.

Rackham, N. and Morgan, T. (1977) *Behaviour Analysis in Training*. Maidenhead: McGraw-Hill.

Reeves, T. K. and Harper, D. (1981) *Surveys at Work, A Practitioner's Guide*. London: McGraw-Hill.

Stewart, V. and Stewart, A. (1981) *Business Applications of Repertory Grid*. London: McGraw-Hill.

2
Techniques for Analysis

MALCOLM CRAIG

If you do not know where you are going, any road will take you there.

Anon.

Introduction

First and foremost, the reason given for trainers to use techniques of analysis is to provide direction – 'Where are we at the moment, and what is the best way forward?'. Analysis is the resolution or breaking up of anything complex into various simple elements, the opposite of synthesis; it is the exact determination of the elements or component parts of anything complex. Edward Caird said in 1877 that 'analysis is simply going back on the path which the mind has already travelled, proceeding from the more to the less determined'.

In the preceding chapter, the theme was the trainer as investigator in an internal consultant role: the theme of this chapter follows on from that, being the trainer as analyst of complex situations where individuals interact in the workplace. You may like to use the self-diagnostic section near the beginning of the previous chapter by simply substituting the word 'investigative' with 'analytical' and 'investigation' with 'analysis' in the introduction to the exercise.

Increasingly, trainers in the course of their work need to reduce complex situations to a manageable size and to identify the various elements which must be considered. A lack of training, or lack of relevant training, may be an issue which is targeted during an investigation of company ills. A first step in reaction to this could be a training audit, using an investigative technique such as a questionnaire to establish the current state of play of training practice. From this investigation, one or more techniques of analysis could be used to reduce this information to a number of component parts. For example, how far is it possible to identify training productivity (achieving greater benefit from less cost) or training effectiveness (achieving greater benefit at the same cost) or training efficiency (maintaining consistent results at less cost)? Given a thorough breakdown into component parts, how relevant to a production or a service process is the training as represented by these parts?

This example of training as it affects company fortunes is a corporate issue, but the same principle applies at the shop-floor level. In the situation, for instance, where operators experience difficulty in using a new piece of control equipment fitted to a machine, the elements of the total machine system need to be considered and not simply the control alone. This is necessary in order to establish all possible changes which could affect operator behaviour. An end result of such analysis may be that the cause of the problem lies not in the way the operators were trained to use the new control, nor in the operators' ability to learn, but in the way the job is organized; this may not have been changed in response to the new technology. In such circumstances, any efforts made by the trainer to improve operator training would be largely redundant, and without some investigation this might well have been the response.

When trainers are called upon to analyse a situation it is almost certain that, in the words of Edward Caird, they will be going back on a familiar path but with a different purpose in mind, and hopefully carrying at least one technique of analysis. The trainer is most likely to be involved in analysis as it applies to four areas of company activity:

1 Job analysis – various techniques for analysing jobs, functions, tasks, skills and abilities
2 Analysis for setting of standards – functional job analysis and functional analysis
3 Analysis of training effectiveness – cost/benefit analysis, a systems approach
4 Training and the organization – a systems approach.

The first, job analysis in its various forms, has been done over many years. Between 1911, the start of serious work in this area, and 1941 there were 401 job analysis studies in print, an average of roughly ten per month. Since 1911, there has been a stream of 'new' job analysis techniques (though in reality each one is a variation on basic principles used from the beginning). There is little that can be called truly new in the field of training, and this applies to job analysis, standard setting or evaluation of training.

The second area, standard setting, is also called competencies, though here it is worth recalling the words of Laurence Peter (of the Peter Principle) that, 'Competence, like truth, beauty and contact lenses, is in the eye of the beholder.' There are as many definitions of competencies and competence as there are people who write on this subject. Analysis of standards, to be meaningful, must go beyond simply statements of competence. The practical tests used over the years by Worshipful Companies and by the City and Guilds of London Institute were models for this type of activity; the challenge now is to apply these well-proven principles to jobs where cognitive rather than motor skills have become dominant.

The analysis of training effectiveness, the third area, is one where the trainer can have enormous scope to demonstrate the worth of training to an organization. This is also one area where the trainer can put a numerical value on pay-off from training input.

The task of relating training activity to the organization in which it takes place can be valuable for the trainer who wishes to use training flexibly across the company, taking account of the many interactions between employees and between departments, with the aim of building the results of such analysis into training programmes.

The next part of this chapter considers some techniques of analysis relevant to the four areas summarized above.

The Techniques

Job analysis

Background

An analogy of digging a hole can well be applied to the task of job analysis. Both the area to be covered and the depth are arrived at by knowing the purpose of the hole. This analogy goes further in that the task can be both tedious and messy. The area of a particular job to be analysed and the depth are arrived at by knowing the purpose of the analysis exercise. There are four levels of any job that can be analysed:

1 This is at the surface of the job and somewhat superficial from a trainer's point of view. It is the level known as job functions. Each job consists of a number of functions, of which there are broadly three types. One is managing/supervising, such as planning, directing, developing or organizing.

The second is direct work, such as operating, maintaining, selling or marketing. The third is specialist work, such as consulting, advising, researching or analysing. As can be seen here, functions are described using verbs or action words ending in 'ing'. A job at this level is a collection of functions. When people perform the same set of functions as each other it can be said that they do the same job. It is at this level that standards are typically set, and there are appropriate analysis techniques for this purpose.

2 We are now below the surface and have reached the collection of tasks which are done in any job. Each function consists of one or more tasks. A task is defined as a discrete unit of work that has a clearly identified beginning and end, which also has input(s), a process and output(s). A task can be short and repetitive, such as a two-minute assembly task on a production line, or longer and non-repetitive, such as a ten-hour scheduling task done once a month. It is at this level that, typically, respective jobs are compared.

3 At this level, interest builds up for the trainer, because we are now considering skills. Each task consists of one or more skills, which are classified as being either motor, cognitive or perceptual, even though in most jobs there is an interaction between all three in carrying out skilled tasks. It is at this level that, typically, training is designed.

4 The bottom at last, and seldom do trainers, or anyone else, dig this far. This is the level of abilities. Each skill consists of one or more abilities. Weakness in abilities largely explains lack of progress in learning a skill. At the last count (Fleishman 1984), there are thirty-seven abilities. Unless impaired physically or mentally in some way we can use all thirty-seven abilities, and each of us can use some well and others not so well. It is at this level that, typically, we can identify learning difficulties and aid transfer between jobs, because it is essentially abilities which transfer rather than skills.

This dividing of a job up into levels and identifying the component parts at each level is an example of a broad job analysis technique. It can be appreciated from looking at a job in this way that the levels become wider as the analysis becomes deeper; we have a pyramid-shaped hole, and there is more to consider as we move from functions through tasks and skills to abilities (see figure 2.1). When using a job analysis technique it is important to appreciate whether it is functional job analysis (Fine and Wiley 1971) and/or task analysis (Annette et al. 1971) and/or skills analysis (Singleton 1978, 1989) and/or abilities analysis (Fleishman 1984) that will prove to be most appropriate for your purpose. There are also some techniques which attempt to cut across all components of a job, such as job components inventory (Banks et al. 1979) or position analysis questionnaire (PAQ: McCormick 1976) or work performance survey system (WPSS: Gael 1983).

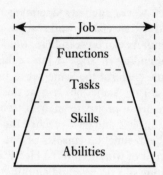

Figure 2.1   The four levels of any job

Functional job analysis and functional analysis

Background

Now we will consider some of the more specialist techniques. The technique of functional job analysis as developed by Fine (Fine and Wiley 1971) relies upon a description of task statements which go towards each function. The description goes no further than the level of tasks.

Using the technique

Task information is gathered from job holders through interviews and checked out or verified by others who know the job well. The task information is analysed by using three categories – reasoning, mathematics and use of language – to provide an educational development scale. Then there are three further categories – data, people and things – to provide a worker function scale. Finally there is a worker instruction scale which is from a category describing the amount of discretion and prescription there is in the worker's job. Each of these scales is broken down further into levels in which each statement within a 'task bank' is given a figure that represents the percentage of worker involvement.

As can be appreciated from this summary of the analysis method, this technique involves a good deal of time and effort from a number of people in the organization. The general response from users of this analysis is that the effort is well worthwhile. The data bank, once established, can provide valuable information for a range of uses: setting standards, contributing to training planning and design, designing recruitment and selection systems, and job movement/career progression decisions.

There is some confusion among users in the analysis of functions. For trainers who are also mathematicians there is possibly a mental block to be overcome because 'functional analysis' is first and foremost a mathematical process, and they may take time to adjust to this use of the term in the context of training. We do have, however, not only functional job analysis (just described) but also functional analysis (mathematics) and functional analysis (competency-related). This last, a variation on the analysis of functions, considers whole work roles and measures only outcomes through purposes and functions rather than the process of doing a job or the inputs that go into a job. It is described as a 'top-down' rather than a 'bottom-up' approach. Going back to our analogy, whoever heard of digging a hole by starting at the bottom? All jobs by their nature can only be analysed by considering the sequence of levels. Functions can only be meaningful as they relate to jobs; tasks can only be meaningful as they relate to functions and skills. There is little option but to use a top-down approach when analysing jobs; in many cases analysis only to the level of outcomes is totally inadequate as a means of gaining information with which anything worthwhile can be done. Functional analysis is effectively task description rather than task analysis. Task description (Miller 1962), is a description of what has to be accomplished in operational, real work terms. Task analysis, on the other hand, is a behavioural understanding of the actual tasks.

This is not to say that job analysis must always go to the deepest depths. One skill of the analyst is in judging the appropriate level, given knowledge about the job and why the analysis is needed. For example, in setting standards for highways reinstatement work, the performance measure must come from an analysis of outcome, of process tasks and skills, and of work organization tasks and skills (this last is needed for reasons of economy). The level of abilities analysis need not be used here. There does, however, need to be a measure of process as well as outcome.

Typical uses for the technique

● To make a comparison between jobs on the basis of shared functions
● To make a comparison between jobs on the basis of unlike functions
● To set standards based on outcomes from functions.

Learning the technique
The book by Fine and Wiley (1971) is recommended as a guide to functional job analysis. There is also a specialized approach to functional

analysis from Schafer (1988). For other information on functional analysis see Training Agency 1989.

Task analysis

Background

Moving now to task analysis: when functions have been identified it is possible to analyse the tasks which make up a particular function. Possibly the best known form is hierarchical task analysis (HTA). This technique was developed with training specifically in mind. As Annette (Annette et al. 1971) wrote, 'too many task analysis techniques seem to stop short at an attempt to describe the task without going on to examine the training required'. This technique breaks down tasks by levels, hence the 'hierarchy'. The first level is to state the overall objective of the task, the next to state the overall objective of each operation within the task. These objectives sum up to represent the overall objectives of the task.

It is worth noting that more in-depth work at this point, on these objectives, could help produce standards for this task. Each task we do consists of a series of what can be called sub-operations. For the basic task of putting sugar into a cup of tea a sub-operation is picking up the spoon; it is difficult to break down this task to a level lower than this or of scooping sugar from a bowl as a second sub-operation. In more complex tasks than this, such as one used by Annette in his studies of operating an acid purification plant, it is possible to generate many layers of analysis, or breaking down into component parts. The solution of when to stop for the trainer lies in him or her asking about training. For example, at any stage in HTA it is possible to ask training-related questions:

- How critical to the whole process is this sub-operation?
- Is any special skill involved?
- Could additional/different training improve this skill?
- What are the benefits and pay-off of training input at this stage? Then return to the first question.

If, after questioning the sub-operation and returning to the first question, the outcome is that it is critical and has scope for the improvement of skills through training, the information can be included in a training plan along with the stated benefits.

The analysis can proceed until the trainer and clients within the company are satisfied that every case where training can make a contribution towards a task has been identified.

AET and task analysis

Background

A neglected aspect of task analysis is that of ergonomics, the study of human movement. This applies in particular to areas of work where training can make a contribution to health and safety. Training in the correct way to control the environment, move, and handle equipment can prevent loss of time through injury or sickness at all levels of the workforce. One method that includes this aspect of work is described fully by Rohmert and Landau (1983). This is *Arbeitswissenschaffliches Erhebungsuerfahren zur Tatigkeitsanalyse* (AET) or ergonomic job analysis procedure. In Germany, this method has been used to analyse around 4,000 shop-floor and managerial jobs.

Using the technique

There are three parts to this analysis. Part A covers a work system analysis, which consists of objects such as materials, information, equipment and other people, as well as the work environment and the influence of the environment. Part B covers task analysis; that is, relating tasks to abstract objects, material objects and person-related objects, as well as the number and repetitiveness of tasks. Part C is the job-demand analysis in terms of demands on perception, demands for decisions and demands for responses and activity. Each of these headings within the three parts is sub-divided into component parts. This AET method provides a more holistic approach than is achieved by most other task analysis techniques, and is more in keeping with current trends of recognizing the total involvement of people within the workplace, such as total quality initiatives. This is essentially a process-oriented approach as opposed to a product-oriented approach.

Typical uses for the technique

- To identify environmental influences on job holders, and job performance
- To identify resources and use of resources, including human resource, as they affect jobs
- To describe types of demands upon job holders
- To provide a holistic analysis of jobs.

Learning the technique
The book by Rohmert and Landau (Rohmert and Landau 1983) provides a comprehensive guide, in English, to this technique. There is also value in combining this technique with the systems approach (see below), as the two are complementary.

Skills analysis

Background
Although skills analysis has been practised since the turn of this century, there is not what can be called a comprehensive technique for aiding this kind of work. It is necessary to draw upon the techniques referred to in this chapter, or others not included here, to provide a method of skills analysis. A decision has to be made about choice of technique or techniques depending upon the skill to be analysed, and the purpose of the analysis.

'Skill' is practised effective performance of a particular activity in an optimum time. A person is said to be skilled when he or she performs to the standards required of a job and not necessarily when he or she has a qualification. Context is very important to the understanding of skilled performance. A fourth division footballer's skill should be appropriate to that context, as compared with someone in the first division. Any technique used must take context into account.

There has been a distinct shift in the practise of workplace skills over the past twenty years, since the introduction of the microprocessor in 1972. Traditional skills like welding and centre lathe turning could be analysed by careful structured observation. It also helped if the services of an occupational psychologist could be used. Now, the situation is quite different; not only are many skills more of the cognitive and perceptual kind but there is also a complex interaction between cognitive, perceptual and motor skills in a number of jobs. A further complication is that jobs themselves are now more interrelated, which in turn can affect skilled performance. There are many examples of work where skill is now difficult to analyse, whether for training design or recruitment and selection purposes: advanced word processing, office technology networking operation, data input and processing for newspaper production, CNC control of manufacturing processes, or retail point-of-sale operation. There does not appear to be an available method of analysis for dealing adequately with this development. The

AET technique, which considers broad holistic aspects of tasks, is possibly the nearest to a solution in this respect.

Using the techniques

1 Ask of any skilled activity, 'What type of skill or skills are involved?'. The skill could be almost totally perceptual as in the case of a repetitive quality-checking task, or almost totally cognitive as in the case of a problem-solving task. Few jobs are totally of one type. The welder is close to practising a motor skill exclusively, yet the really skilled welder is the one who has an acute visual perception of changes in the shape and colour of the weld pool; in this particular case cognitive skills are normally minimal. This analysis into types of skill is a vital first step, and includes identification of the type of skill which is dominant. Structured observation and AET could be used at this stage.
2 Discover the type of behaviour which is vital to skilled performance; what is it that very skilled people *do* that has the greatest influence on outcome? For this step, use of the critical incident technique is essential (see the previous chapter). Basic statements of what is done, or standards, are largely meaningless; it is only through knowing what the skilled person does, how she or he actually behaves, that we can analyse skill.
3 Discover what less skilled people do in performing a task; it is only through a comparison between most skilled and less skilled that we can highlight the essential behaviours which contribute to skilled performance. Again, critical incident technique is used here.
4 Verify – check out with independent skilled people not involved in the analysis. They are challenged to identify anything missing, incorrect or misleading.

In cases where complex information processing, problem solving, decision making or fault diagnosis is involved, probably the most effective technique is protocol analysis (see below). The analysis of skill is now more complex and demands the use of more than one technique; that is, until someone comes up with a comprehensive system.

Typical uses for the techniques

• To aid the design of training programmes
• To highlight differences between effective and less than effective job performance
• To help identify the amount of overlap between skills, to aid multi-skilling or job transfer decisions.

Learning the techniques
See the analysis techniques in this chapter, and Singleton 1989.

Protocol analysis

Background

People who, in the course of their work, must solve problems will sometimes talk out loud; not through dementia, loneliness or insanity but to indulge in protocol analysis, though they do not call it by this name. An analysis of recorded speech when solving a problem can reveal a good deal about the particular strategy used. This approach can also be used to analyse a number of cognitive tasks, other than problem solving; for example, how an operator follows a particular sequence of events, why particular decisions are taken or why certain changes are made to the process or the equipment. It is probably true to say that skilled people are not always the best at articulating exactly how they use a particular cognitive skill. Protocol analysis, when combined with another technique such as structured observation, can provide a powerful means of analysing tasks where cognitive skills play a strong part.

Using the technique

There are two broad approaches to the use of this technique. One is to use instant, on-site recordings of the spoken reasoning as the problem is being worked on, or a sequence of events is being followed. The other is to record thoughts retrospectively, as soon after the event as possible. A good deal of debate goes on between field researchers about the value of each approach. Doing instant recording can interfere with the job in hand and possibly distort the outcome; on the other hand, retrospective recording can lead to people changing what they actually thought in order to justify their actions, especially if the outcome was unfavourable. On balance it can be said that on-site instant recording can be done effectively, particularly with the use of a professional standard personal tape recorder; this small piece of equipment can be overlooked by the person doing the work, and spontaneous thoughts are usually gathered quite well.

The usefulness of this type of analysis can be best appreciated when two troubleshooters or problem solvers record their thoughts in a situation where one is known to be highly effective at this kind of task, and the other is less than effective. A comparison of protocols, the distinct sequence of procedure taken, will show clear differences between the two sets of recording. This essential reasoning of the effective troubleshooter, or more than one if possible, can be built into a training programme.

Typical uses for the technique

- To identify the thought processes which are used by effective operators who must follow a complex sequence of operations
- To identify the problem-solving skill of a manager who is recognized as being effective in this area, or more than one manager if possible
- To identify the diagnostic skill of a troubleshooter on a specific complex task – in this case the 'troubleshooter' can be an electronics technician, a chef, a medical practitioner or an insurance claims analyst.

Learning the technique
There is only one major textbook on the subject (Ericsson 1984). This book also contains a list of references to cases where protocol analysis has been used.

The mechanics of collecting the data are straightforward. The process of analysing the data needs to be done by using the recommended book as a guide. There is no known formal training in this technique.

Abilities analysis

Background
Although Edwin Fleishman has been working on human abilities for more than twenty years, the results of this work are almost unknown in the United Kingdom. If someone has difficulty in learning a skill it is almost certain that one or more abilities essential to that skill are weak (not lacking, because we all have these abilities). The million dollar question for trainers is, 'Which abilities can be strengthened through training and which cannot?'. For example, a skill, such as draughtsmanship, requires the ability of visualization; that is, being able to picture clearly in the mind a concrete object from schematic information on paper. Some people have strong visualizing ability while that of others can be weak or almost non-existent. There are no known ways of improving this ability through training, so what does the trainer do? Sometimes the response is to use the work 'thick' or say 'she will never learn this job', without knowing the reason why.

A knowledge of the thirty-seven abilities revealed from the work of Fleishman (Fleishman 1984) is essential to a deeper understanding of how people learn or do not learn skills.

Using the technique

The use of ability rating is done with a scale which consists of a list of the thirty-seven abilities and a rating system for each one. For example, having read the description above of the ability 'visualization', the job holder would be asked to indicate on a scale, ranging from 'highly critical' to 'not used', to what extent this ability is critical. For a design engineer or a hairdresser visualization would be 'highly critical'; on the other hand, a clerical officer or bus driver might well record 'not used' in the job. Ability scales can be used at various stages. The main use is to analyse a particular skill in terms of abilities; another way is to analyse a job or a specific task in terms of abilities. Finally, people can be asked to provide self-analysis of their strengths and weaknesses with regard to the thirty-seven abilities. This scale goes from 'highly developed' to 'weak' and then 'no opportunity to discover'. It is possible to establish an ability profile for a job, a task or a skill.

Suppose we wished to know which abilities were critical for a senior nurse in an acute ward. The ability scales would be given to at least forty such job holders and their responses to the scales compared. In analysing the results, the expectation would be for a significant level of agreement between the forty nurses. In the case of no significant agreement there would need to be an investigation into reasons for the discrepancy; does the role vary with context or does nurses' perception of the job vary? For example, if one nurse recorded for mathematical reasoning 'highly critical' and another recorded 'not used' there would be a basis for some debate.

This type of analysis helps to highlight the true requirements of a job. If an analysis of this kind revealed that mathematical reasoning was not used in a job for which GCSE mathematics was required, there would be a need to question the requirement for the qualification.

Typical uses for the technique

- To provide a deeper insight into how people learn or do not learn skills
- To compare respective jobs in terms of abilities used; where two jobs share common abilities, transfer of people between them should provide few problems, in terms of skill learning and use
- To identify the true ability needs of a job in order to establish qualification requirements.

Learning the technique

The most comprehensive coverage of this technique is provided through the work of Fleishman (1984). The writer is currently developing an instrument for the analysis of abilities to be used in-house.

Training benefits analysis

Background

Benefits to be derived from training are of two broad kinds. One is the tangible measurable benefits, and the other is non-tangible benefits that come mainly from the views of those who are trained and those who do the training. Possibly the most reliable method of establishing the tangible benefits is to use the technique of cost benefit analysis. The purpose of this technique is to balance training costs, in all their forms, against training results. This provides a measure of the relationship between effectiveness of training and the cost of providing that training, in short the pay-off. The subjective or non-tangible results typically come from end-of-training-course assessment reports or follow-up assessments some time after training has taken place. These results can also be balanced against the cost of providing the training but this is somewhat more difficult, due to the problem of assigning value to this type of perceived benefit.

Using the technique

There are five steps to conducting a cost benefit analysis:

(1) State quite clearly the problem area. Here are some examples of such statements:

The introduction of this new printing press will involve the learning of new skills by both operators and maintenance personnel. What are our options, how do we proceed, what are the respective costs and the possible benefits?

Training that we do may be described as overkill and seems excessively costly. What would the effect be on outcome (benefit) if we (a) removed the training input; or (b) reduced the training input?

The chairperson says our training could be better, and does not compare well with competitors. Is 'better' going to be achieved at the same or greater cost? Is our information on training cost/benefit adequate for meaningful comparisons to be made with the training provided by other companies in our field?

(2) Having stated the problem area to the satisfaction of ourselves and colleagues, the next step is to collect various assumptions that we make about problem areas. What is the general perception of the problem held by all those who could be involved? To get back to the printing press problem above, we can imagine some assumptions which could be forthcoming, such as:

The age profile of the staff is too high for the effective introduction of new skills.

The new equipment is so complex that a different type of person is needed.

The manufacturer's course cannot be relied upon to deliver the training.

There are no suitable skills in the local labour market, we must train.

Such assumptions provide a base-line from which to work. During analysis, these assumptions can be either confirmed or refuted, but it is important that they are recorded at the beginning of analysis. This helps to provide a model or at least a perception of where you are at the present time.

(3) This step takes you back to the use of investigative techniques, described in the previous chapter. Cost benefit analysis cannot be done effectively without sound information. You need to know for both costs and for benefits the following:

- Who?
- When?
- Where?
- Why?
- How?
- What cost?
- For how long?
- How do we measure?

Brainstorming or questioning can be used. Where, for example, more than one method of training delivery is possible you will need to repeat this information gathering for each one.

After this step you will have broken the problem area into its component parts.

(4) This information is now compared, first that on the difference between costs of training input and benefits from output. The accountant mind wishes to see numerical data attached to such comparison; for example, a figure that shows a return on investment (ROI). Kearsley (1982) points out, 'If a sales training programme costs $100,000 but increases sales by $1 million its ROI would be $1,000,000 ÷ $100,000 = 10 times. Similarly if a safety training programme cost $25,000 and it resulted in $100,000 less in accident payments, its ROI would be $100,000 ÷ $25,000 = 4. Obviously, any ROI greater than 1 is worth looking at.'

An important part of such analysis is that the problem area is one that can be controlled during the period of the analysis. In other words, it is unrealistic to look for large company corporate benefits from training, no matter how well planned and executed this has been in a department. The area has to be of such a size that monitoring can be done to check for what are called extraneous variables; that is, events or new initiatives which could also explain the increased benefits. Use of the systems approach technique (see below) is useful in this respect. Training can be shown to have a pay-off providing the choice of problem area is not over-ambitious. For an example of this, consider another aspect of return on investment as it affects training. A particular robot costs £120,000 and payback on capital is questioned. This can be calculated by dividing the capital cost (£120,000) by labour-saving costs per year minus the cost of maintenance. In this case the robot works two shifts and in total replaces four people at a total cost of £48,000 per year. With zero maintenance costs, payback time would be 2½ years. However, maintenance costs are £12,000 per year; therefore the pay back time is increased to 3 years 4 months. After the introduction of robot maintenance training and fault diagnosis, downtime on the robot is reduced and maintenance costs are also reduced to £6,500, resulting in a pay-back time of just under 3 years. There is also the benefit of increased production from higher uptime of the robot. When conducted in controlled manageable problem areas of this kind, training can demonstrate significant pay-off.

The non-tangible or subjective benefits of training can also come into a cost benefit equation. Such benefits include increased confidence, increased sense of worth, exercised minds being more alert, sharing ideas and knowledge, facilitating career progression and so on. This type of benefit needs to be described in behavioural terms; for example, 'Increased confidence is demonstrated by . . .', 'Career progression has been facilitated by . . .'. It is important to state such benefits.

There is an interesting situation if a ROI calculation shows a negative or break-even result and the subjective outcome shows very positive results, or the reverse, if a high ROI on training has to be considered against a very negative set of subjective responses. Having done analysis of this kind it is always necessary to interpret the results. However, most of human activity is subject to interpretations, very little can be called truly objective, and figures merely give the appearance of objectivity. The aim of the trainer in analysing training benefit is to appear as objective as possible.

(5) Present the results of your analysis. This presentation needs to consist of:

- Your initial purpose in conducting the analysis
- A statement of the problem area
- Assumptions made about this problem from the beginning
- What information was collected, both objective and subjective
- Results coming from an analysis of the options available for training

- A statement of how these results compared with initial assumptions – whether these assumptions were refuted or supported
- Recommendations about the course of action to take.

Typical uses for the technique
- To analyse the cost and benefits of a new approach to training, such as interactive video or multi-media training
- To analyse the costs and benefits of training in an area of skill new to a company, such as office technology networking
- To analyse ways to improve training productivity, such as demonstrating how greater benefits can be achieved at less cost.

Learning the technique
As can be seen from the description of this technique, there is a reliance upon the use of investigative techniques for information gathering (see previous chapter). Chapter 5 is also relevant, and complementary, to this aspect of analysis. The book by Kearsley (1982) is strongly recommended as a comprehensive practical approach to this subject.

Systems approach to analysis

Background
Taking a systems approach provides the trainer with a technique for analysing in a broad, holistic way. Few trainers now operate on detailed, one-job-specific training activities. The general trend is for training roles to encompass a range of jobs and skills within the organization. For this reason, it is necessary to develop an approach that provides an overview of operations, and at the same time identifies the various interactions going on between people and between processes.

Some people who analyse, particularly independent consultants, have become what can be called 'systems people', and the study of systems becomes almost a way of life. It is not necessary for trainers to take on such commitment to systems thinking, but the learning and practice of a basic systems approach can be of great value in the field of training. For example, a health service trainer analysing skill use in a hospital may consider the operating theatre as a self-contained system bounded by the physical walls of the theatre. However, by adopting a systems approach he or she would draw systems diagrams to build up an overview of the various activities, and of the people involved. Often, surprising facts are discovered in this way, such as the surgeon not being a part of this system but someone who enters and leaves, and in fact works within his or her own system. Such insight provides a new perspective on skill use analysis. Also, the activity of nursing staff and porters outside the theatre has an influence on performance within the theatre. In this way boundaries are redrawn until all relevant skill use is included, and the interactions between skills are identified.

The trainer in an analyst's role must step back from the immediate area of concern and consider a wider perspective before making judgements or recommendations.

Using the technique
The tools are simple and basic: a large sheet of scrap paper, a pencil and a large eraser. The approach to be taken is simply that of an open mind, freed as far as possible of fixed ideas about the particular situation. Ask, 'What system am I looking at?'. Going back to the hospital, the trainer taking a systems approach to theatre work will have identified a patient identification system. All systems have inputs, activities (they must *do* something) and outputs. On the sheet of paper the trainer writes down all the inputs, and who and what are involved, not in a list but at random all over the sheet. Other people could be involved in the generation of ideas, ideally through the use of brainstorming (see chapter 1). When no more can be added, the 'who' from this data can be written down spread over the sheet in such a way that lines of influences can be drawn between them; who influences whom? At this stage you have used a tool that can generate discussion, making people think afresh about what they have considered to be a routine activity. (Unfortunately patient identification is a routine activity that can and sometimes does go disastrously wrong.) A diagram like that for the people involved can be drawn for activities, and again for skills used. When this information has been gathered it is possible to identify the boundary of the system, who and what acts within the boundary, and who and what acts outside the boundary of the system – that is, in the environment. In this case there are people and activities outside the hospital that influence patient identification without actually being part of this identification system; for example, activities outside the hospital such as those of the general practitioner.

Now the most important part of the analysis can be done; this is to ask who controls this system and how. For this task it is back to the sheet of paper, pencil and eraser. By drawing and redrawing a systems control diagram it is possible to come up with something like figure 2.2. As can be seen, it is possible to generate discussion about who actually controls and how. Within the box labelled 'Process' is the actual activity of

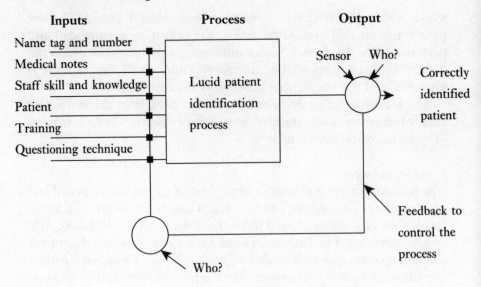

Figure 2.2   Systems analysis of a patient identification process

identification, where there is skill use which can be analysed separately. The key issue in this system is control. There needs to be a fail-safe mechanism for patient identification.

This and other examples of a systems approach to health care activities can be included in health service training programmes. The approach is relevant to all situations where people act together within systems at work.

Possibly the best way to get a feel for systems thinking is to consider your own body as a human system. Within this system there are a number of sub-systems: blood circulation system, respiratory system, bone structure system and nervous system. Each interacts with the other to provide the human activity system that is you. The doctor who adopts a systems approach will consider this 'whole body' system and in fact the environment of this system, your workplace and domestic position etc. The doctor who adopts a non-systems or reductionist approach will tend to get locked into one or two problem areas to the exclusion of all else. In the workplace, too, no doubt there are trainers who have a reductionist, narrow-vision approach and trainers who have a wider overview of events. The adoption of systems approach technique should encourage the former to take a broader view and will provide the latter with a tool to help improve performance.

Typical uses for the technique

- To analyse the cause of a particular failure; who and what were involved and to what extent training-related issues played a part
- To analyse the interactions between skills in a new process for which a training programme is to be designed, and to identify skills overlap between activities
- To establish how a training programme is to be controlled, including who relates inputs to the output (the criteria) and how this is controlled, and whether weaknesses are to be found in the inputs or in the actual training process ('Process' box) – standard measures of output are meaningless without reference to the process of getting there
- To identify influences upon a process; who and what needs to be considered to provide a complete picture for a training programme
- To describe organizational structure as it actually operates rather than as shown on an organizational chart.

Learning the technique

Possibly the most comprehensive means of learning the systems approach is through two Open University systems courses, T244 and T247. The first is mainly people or 'soft' systems oriented, and the second is process or 'hard' systems based. The two courses are complementary and can be done without necessarily taking an Open University degree. Such courses provide trainers with a valuable source of personal development.

There is also a need for a practical, vocational-oriented workbook for users of the systems approach. In the absence of such a guide you are referred to the further reading list at the end of the chapter.

Summary

In this chapter, some techniques of analysis which should be of interest and use to the trainer have been described. By this stage of the chapter it should be apparent that investigative techniques and analysis techniques go hand in hand. First get your information, then analyse, then decide what to do.

It must be said, in concluding, that these techniques are not set in stone. There can be value in a flexible approach to their use; even in combining techniques if this helps achieve your purpose. While not seeking the analysing discipline of the scientist, it is true to say that the skill to analyse at the level described here must be of value to the present-day trainer. The skills of both investigation and analysis can make a significant contribution to the work of a trainer who wishes to be more proactive in his or her work. The aim of these two chapters has been to act as a guide to the acquisition of these skills.

Further reading

Annette, J. and Duncan, K. D. (1967) Task Analysis and Training Design. *Occupational Psychology*, 41, 211–21.

Annette, J., Duncan, K. D., Stammers, R. B. and Gray, M. J. (1971) *Task Analysis*. London: HMSO.

Banks, M. H., Jackson, P. R., Stafford, E. M. and Warr, P. B. (1979) *Job Component Inventory*. Sheffield: Manpower Services Commission.

Diaper, D. (1989) *Task Analysis for Human–Computer Interaction*. Chichester: Horwood.

Ericsson, K. A. (1984) *Protocol Analysis*. Cambridge, Mass.: MIT Press.

Fine, S. A. and Wiley, W. (1971) *An Introduction to Functional Job Analysis*. Michigan: Upjohn Institute for Employment Research.

Flanagan, J. C. (1954) The Critical Incident Technique. *Psychological Bulletin*, 51, 327–58.

Fleishman, A. E. (1984) *Taxonomy of Human Performance*. Orlando: Academic Press.

Gael, S. (1983) *Job Analysis*. San Francisco: Jossey-Bass Inc.

Gael, S. (1988) *The Job Analysis Handbook for Business, Industry and Government*. New York: Wiley.

Helmer, O. (1972). Cross Impact Gaining. *Futures*, 4 (1–2), 149–67.

Kearsley, G. (1982) *Costs, Benefits, and Productivity in Training Systems*. Reading, Mass.: Addison-Wesley.

McCormick, E. J. (1976) Job and Task Analysis. In M. D. Dunnette (ed.), *Handbook of Industrial and Organisational Psychology*, Chicago: Rand McNally.

Miller, R. B. (1962) Task Description and Analysis. In R. M. Gagne (ed.), *Psychological Principles in Systems Development*, New York: Holt Rinehart and Winston.

Rackham, N. and Morgan, T. (1977) *Behaviour Analysis in Training*. London: McGraw-Hill.

Rohmert, W. and Landau, K. (1983) *Arbeitswissenschaffliches Erhebungsuerfahren zur Tatigkeitsanalyse, Ergonomic Job Analysis Procedure*. London: Taylor Francis.

Schafer, G. (1988) *Functional Analysis of Office Job Requirements*. Chichester: Wiley.

Singleton, W. T. (1978) *The Analysis of Practical Skills*. Lancaster: MTP Press.

Singleton, W. T. (1989) *The Mind at Work*. Cambridge: Cambridge University Press.

Training Agency (now Employment Department: TEED) (1989) *Competence and Assessment*. Special Issue 1. Sheffield: Standards Programme, The Training Agency.

3
Analysis of Organizational Training Needs

JOHN ROSCOE

All is change; all yields its place and goes.

Euripides

Introduction

Analysis of organizational training needs (AOTN) is a process of taking an overview of the performance of the organization. Its purpose is to identify where training can make major contributions to improving organizational performance. It sets out to ask the following questions about the way the organization is functioning now and will function in the future:

- What?
- When?
- Where?
- Why?
- Who?
- How?

In asking, and answering, these questions the process will allow issues and problems which the organization currently faces to be identified. Important issues need a planned response and the causes of problems need to be established and possible solutions identified. Training is just one possible response and should be selected only when it is most appropriate. AOTN also allows potential future problems to be identified and appropriate action to be taken.

The process of conducting an AOTN will allow decisions to be made, on the basis of evidence, about where training will offer the best investment. It will strengthen proposals for funding training and allow priorities between training needs to be established. It will also provide information upon which to judge whether resources currently employed in training could be better used elsewhere.

AOTN requires the collection, interpretation and analysis of information from across the organization. This information can be from access to existing records which often can only be reached by talking to people throughout the organization. In addition, the views and opinions of those in day-to-day contact with the various activities need to be sought, compared, interpreted and used.

Training needs eventually have to be dealt with at an individual level. The question that needs to be asked is whether this person's performance is satisfactory. If the answer is 'No' then some form of training may be considered. If the answer is 'Yes' then training for development may be worthwhile for those with potential. This is usually the responsibility of the line manager who can set the standard of performance required and judge whether it has been achieved.

A training gap (see figure 3.1) can be said to exist if the performance deficiency is due to lack of knowledge and skill. The limitation of this individual approach is that it can result in demands for training from every employee. These demands may be for training to improve current performance or develop the potential of the individual. A trainer responsible for making strategic decisions about the allocation of

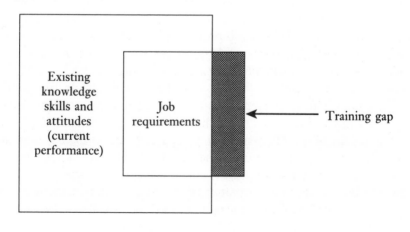

Figure 3.1   Identifying the training gap

training resources will find this level of detail unhelpful. Some training needs may also relate to the performance of groups rather than individuals. To establish the training needs of the organization a process needs to be adopted which allows a broad view to be taken of the performance of the groups or operating units of the organization.

The key focus of AOTN is the future. Otherwise investment may occur in training redundant skills; for example, production line welding skills training when industrial robots will be replacing welders on the line.

Organizations may have problems and challenges facing them. Everyone in the organization will have slightly different views of their nature and the solutions to them. The process of AOTN identifies those issues where training is part of the solution. Where training solutions are not appropriate the problem should not be ignored by the trainer. It is your responsibility, as part of the management team, to inform management that a problem exists, and what its probable causes and potential solutions are.

When carrying out an AOTN you may decide that solutions other than training are appropriate. You may have to convince others that training is not the best solution. As a training specialist you can develop training solutions and it is best to let other specialists develop alternate solutions. Very often a solution other than training will have some consequential training needs. When it is implemented you are likely to have a role in supporting any solution. It is therefore important to be involved with the development of alternate solutions.

The main benefit of AOTN is that it provides a perspective on individual training needs. It allows decisions to be made about where investment in training offers the best return to meet current and future needs. An effective AOTN will prevent waste of resources in doing job analysis and task analysis which is not necessary. It will also avoid using training where it is not justified. In addition, in the process of an AOTN contact is made with important and influential people across the organization. These contacts are useful for the trainer as informal ways into the organization and for building the credibility of training.

The results of AOTN need to be presented to senior management for approval and support. Resources may need to be allocated or reallocated to develop the training proposed. This is a further opportunity to build the credibility of training, establish relationships with management and put the case for investment in training. Evaluation will also be easier if needs are clearly identified and those judging performance are confident in the trainers.

The Process of Analysing Organizational Training Needs

The process of AOTN can be represented by a flowchart (see figure 3.2). Each stage will be examined in turn.

Appoint a responsible person

Carrying out an AOTN requires the commitment of resources. These need to be carefully planned to maximize the benefit to be gained. Before any further action is undertaken for an AOTN the purpose and clear terms of reference must be agreed. This should be undertaken by the responsible person. The usual justification for an AOTN is using limited training resources more effectively and 'building training into the business'.

AOTN requires the collection of information from across the organization about current performance problems and future needs and plans. Much of that information will be confidential within the organization and commercially sensitive outside. For training to be tied into the business the business plans must be made available from the start. To gain access to people and information an AOTN must have a high-powered and well-recognized source of authority leading it. This person may not carry out any of the detailed work. It is not necessary for this person to be a trainer; in some organizations it may even be preferable for her or him not to be, as then the results can be presented as having status independent from the training specialist.

For large organizations a project team may be set up to carry out an AOTN. Only through the use of a team can the information be collected, collated and analysed in a reasonable time period. A team can collect more information, from a wider base, more quickly. The information can be analysed more effectively when reviewed by a team with various specialists. The results of a team approach can be more of an overview of the current situation rather than a series of snapshots taken over an extended period of time. The responsible person leads the project team and gives authority to requests for information, meetings and access to people. This person can also act as a sounding board for the results being collected and the proposals prepared.

When this initial setting up is being undertaken it is also sensible to agree an informal mechanism for checking back the findings, as well as to agree a final report date by which the study is to be completed. When

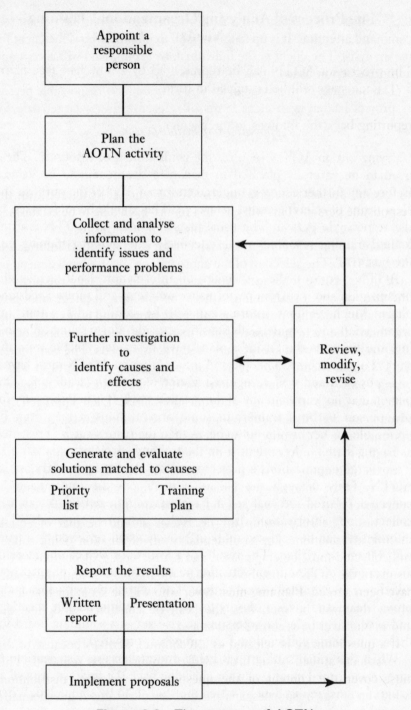

Figure 3.2   The process of AOTN

the findings are presented the authority of the responsible person will command attention. It is up to this person to identify who is the client for the analysis. The client is the individual, or group, who will accept and authorize action based upon the findings.

The outcome of this stage is the appointment of a responsible person as project leader, with clear terms of reference and a target date for reporting back the findings to the client.

Plan the AOTN activity

An overall project timetable for the AOTN should be agreed with the responsible person. This will enable a report-back date to be established and prevent the collection of data continuing without result.

There are many techniques which can be used to collect information in an AOTN. The selection of the approaches to be used will depend on such things as the time-scale, how many people are doing the analysis, the size of the organization, where people are located, and how information for other purposes is collected, stored and accessed. People are always the richest source of information on the performance of the organization and what are the perceived training needs. The plan for the AOTN must identify how it will tap this source. The ways in which people can provide information include the interview, telephone interview, group discussion and questionnaires. Each approach has advantages and disadvantages in terms of time, costs, quality of information, and quantity of people it is possible to consult.

Interviewing for AOTN uses the same skills as interviewing in other contexts, and these are discussed in chapter 1. The differences from other types of interviewing situation are the relationships between interviewer and interviewee, confidentiality and the expectations of the outcomes. The relationship for interviews should be that of equals sharing information. The confidentiality of information being sought and collected must be emphasized and maintained. Expectations of the results of the AOTN must be limited by the interviewer until the results have been agreed. Planning must cover who will be seen, for how long, where they will be met, how they can be contacted, and how the information will be recorded and stored.

If a questionnaire is selected as a technique, perhaps because of the geographical spread of staff, detailed planning will be required. This must cover the content of the questionnaire, piloting, distribution, follow-up of non-responses, analysis and use of results. A questionnaire has the potential to reach a wide audience at the same time. Its main weakness is interpreting the replies and being unable to ask follow-up questions.

The people to start with are managers of different operational functions of the organization. These people will allow an overview of the organization as a whole to be developed as well as of their parts of it. From there you may go down the organization as seems appropriate based on the information collected and how it fits in with where you are starting. Just asking the questions influences the situation and can create expectations of action which may prove unrealistic. This needs to be carefully managed by those undertaking the analysis.

A Delphi technique could be used to solicit the views of senior management. This should identify areas of focus and attention for the future which may have training implications now. This approach is developed in Chapter 1.

A second approach to be considered during planning is observation. This can be used to collect information about the workplace, the workforce and working processes. It allows those involved in the AOTN to develop a 'feel' for parts of the organization which have not been worked with in the past. Observation may generally be an unobtrusive way of collecting information. It depends upon the extent of openness and trust which exists. If the workforce is suspicious of management and concerned about potential threats to their livelihood then observation may be very intrusive. What will be observed is what they think you ought to see, or expect to see, rather than normal activity. Observation is probably not the primary source of information to be used, but it can certainly provide insights and the basis for 'hunches'. These can then be investigated further using questioning techniques and the third approach, which is using records.

The examination of records is a potentially very powerful source of information about organizational problems and possible training needs. The weakness is that all organizations have far too many records for all of them to prove useful in an AOTN.

In planning the analysis, thought needs to be given to what potentially available records will be helpful. These may be accessed centrally in some organizations, in others asked for locally. The collection of records should not be seen as a paper chase (or computer file chase). Everything collected should be worth looking at; the more that is collected the longer it will take to review and decide whether it is useful.

A well-planned AOTN will seek to use a variety of data-collection techniques. As much information as can be collected and used in the time available is wanted. This should come from a variety of sources to enable it to be cross-checked and provide confirmation. The plan must also allow for the collection of additional information to investigate further the problems, their causes and how training might help. Areas in which to collect information are shown in figure 3.3.

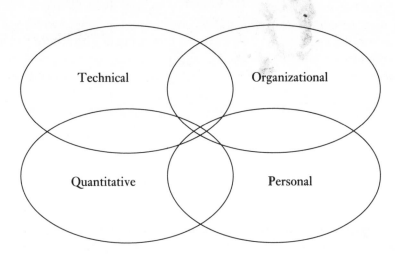

Figure 3.3   Outside influences on organizational training needs

The information collected and the analysis undertaken must be treated as confidential. Confidentiality must be assured to those providing information which is either sensitive internally or commercially sensitive. The storage of the information needs to be secure. Those providing information may naturally ask for access to the results. However, until the findings have been presented and accepted they must be treated as confidential. It will be up to your client to decide how, and to what extent, the results will be disseminated.

Planning for the analysis also requires the culture and politics of the organization to be taken into account. These factors will determine what are acceptable methods of collecting information, who can be contacted, how they should be contacted and when. Culture and politics will also shape what are the acceptable proposals and solutions to issues and problems identified.

Information about outside influences on the organization is required as well as internally generated data, because the organization does not operate in a vacuum (see figure 3.4).

The outcome of the planning phase is an action plan against an agreed time-scale, of who will do what within the project team.

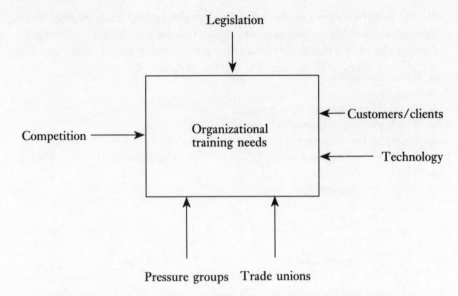

Figure 3.4   Outside influences on organizational training needs

Collect and analyse information to identify issues and performance problems

This is the point where the plan for the AOTN is implemented. Appointments are made, people seen, records accessed and question-naires prepared, sent out, collated, analysed and interpreted.

In collecting the information it is helpful to try and distinguish between fact and opinion. Both are a valuable part of the process; a lot can be learned about expectations, beliefs and values from opinions expressed. Often, however, opinions are presented as facts, and evidence needs to be sought to support them.

There are many useful documents which can contribute to analysing training needs. These, together with other potential sources of information on training needs, are listed in appendix A. These documents, and other information, may already exist for the whole or parts of the organization. If they do not, then they may be prepared from data collected. The use of such documents does not immediately identify training needs, or even issues and problems facing the organization. What they do provide is a basis for assessing the present position and preparing further questions. These can be explored through face-to-face meetings which will enable important issues and problems to be identified.

To help clarify which are the major issues and performance problems a series of questions may be asked of the information collected:

- Where is the pain?
- What is mentioned most, and what least?
- Can fact and opinion be separated?
- Which problems are worth solving?
- Are these key issues/problems for the organization?
- Do different sources identify different issues/problems?
- Who owns the problems?
- Who wants the problems solved?
- Is information about problems
  - valid?
  - consistent?
  - relevant?

The key question is 'Where is the pain?' when considering performance problems. If the organization feels no pain then can there be a real performance problem which needs solving? Without identifiable pain there is little incentive for applying resources to solve a problem.

Unless someone owns the problem and is committed to getting it resolved no further action can be justified. In some cases the trainer may decide the problem/issue is of such magnitude that it is worthwhile setting out to get someone to own it through influence and persuasion.

The recognition of key issues and performance problems will depend upon the expertise and experience of those carrying out the AOTN. In analysing the information collected, those involved in the analysis must be aware of their preconceptions. Evidence should exist for conclusions and any assumptions made should be challenged. This is another strength for a team approach with people from various disciplines bringing a variety of views to bear.

No individual or team will come up with exactly the same set of issues and performance problems to be addressed. However, this is not a weakness, as there is no idealized 'right' answer. What we want to achieve is the identification of areas where action can be taken to develop and improve organizational performance, through training. Other analytical techniques can be used to review the information collected and identify key issues and important performance problems (see chapters 1 and 2).

The outcome of this stage of the AOTN process is the identification of key issues and performance problems facing the organization. These are things which are judged to be important by responsible people in the organization and need to be resolved. This stage will also establish who owns the problems and how committed they are to finding and implementing solutions to solve them.

Further investigation to identify causes and effects

After the issues and problems facing the organization have been identified, attention must turn to causes. It is very easy to confuse symptoms with causes. This does not matter when investigating issues and problems; it becomes critical if the solution treats symptoms rather than causes. For the trainer this can mean training undertaken which fails because it addresses the symptoms of a problem, not the cause. Unless the cause can be treated resources will be wasted and the problem will continue unresolved. The reaction to a problem is often to treat the symptoms because it has been inadequately diagnosed: problems are often described in terms of symptoms, such as 'deadlines not met' or 'supply and demand difficulties'.

Further investigation will be focused on using the information already collected and obtaining more information to identify the contributory causes to problems. Detailed analysis which would be required for the development of training should not be undertaken until a training solution is clearly appropriate. Only those issues and problems which have been identified as important justify further investigation.

Causes of performance problems can be categorized into three broad areas (see figure 3.5):

- Environmental
- Motivation and incentive
- Lack of knowledge and skill.

Once a performance problem has been identified which justifies further investigation, the contributory causes need to be explored. There is rarely a single cause to a problem; usually there are several contributory ones.

A problem may present itself as 'no trained staff', which when investigated throws up 'high labour turnover'. Staff are not staying long enough in a job to become competent. The cause of the staff turnover may be poor recruitment and selection, lack of training opportunities, low pay or poor conditions. Unless the relative importance of these possible causes can be shown, poor decisions about solving the problem will result.

To help clarify the causes of a performance problem it can be useful

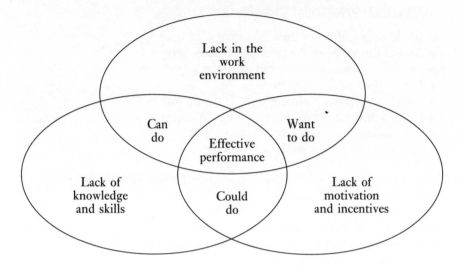

Figure 3.5   Causes of performance problems

to ask questions. The following are intended to indicate the sort of questions to ask.

Environmental deficiency
Job holders' performance is prevented or obstructed.
   Questions to consider include:

- Are job holders' roles clear?
- Is there role conflict with other job holders?
- Are job holders overloaded?
- Is the chain of command clear?
- Is the workflow well organized?
- Is there waiting time while others perform?
- Are adequate supplies of material available?
- Are the work processes adequate?
- Are tools and equipment adequate and appropriate?
- Does the product/service have a market?
- Does the product/service match the competition?
- Is changing technology undermining the position?
- Is the level of economic activity driving the problem?
- Does legislation bear upon the situation?

Motivation/incentive deficiency
Job holders are not encouraged to perform.

Questions to consider include:

- Could staff perform if their lives depended upon it?
- Are staff unaware of the value of products/services?
- Are there disagreements about how best to perform?
- Is the effort greater than the reward?
- Are there negative consequences of performing?
- Is the deficient area distasteful or socially negative?
- Is punishment used as a management tool?
- Are there unpleasant working conditions?
- Are there rewards for non-performance?
- Does the organization's culture support performance?
- Is there discontent and low morale?

Knowledge and skill deficiency
Job holders do not know how or when to perform.
   Questions to consider include:

- Are job holders new to the task(s)?
- Is/are the task(s) sequential or complex?
- Is decision making required in the task(s)?
- Do general principles need to be applied in the task(s)?
- Have job holders had guidance in how to perform well?
- Do job holders get feedback on performance?
- Has inadequate performance been directly observed?
- Have job holders been trained in the task(s)?
- Is there a history of inadequate training?
- Did job holders practise skills during training?
- Was the training group-paced or individually paced?
- Were staff unable to learn from training provided?

The outcomes from the further investigation phase are the identification of contributory causes for each performance problem identified. There will be supporting evidence which shows that they are causes rather than symptoms. In addition, the implications of the challenges and issues related to the future plans and expectations of the organization will be recorded. These results – the identification of contributory causes for key topics and performance problems – form the basis for the next stage, which is the generation of potential solutions.

Generate and evaluate solutions matched to causes

Every problem has more than one single cause; therefore multiple solutions need to be considered. Every situation has a range of possible responses to the contributory causes and influences which bear upon it (see figure 3.6). There is generally no single response which is appropriate on its own, neither is there a right answer.

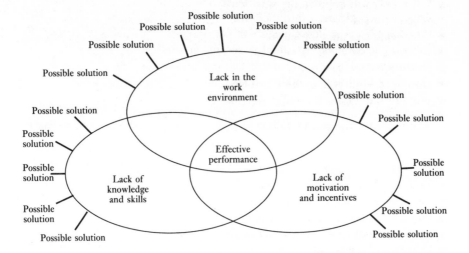

Figure 3.6   Range of possible solutions for a performance problem

Three areas of causes have been identified:

- Environmental
- Motivation and incentive
- Lack of knowledge and skill.

Generating possible solutions appropriate to problems requires considering changing the environment, changing the incentives and encouraging motivation, reducing the need for knowledge and skill and, finally, training for knowledge and skill. A checklist of possible responses to performance problems is shown in appendix B. Trainers should be committed to using the limited resources available for training to maximum effect. They will want to concentrate on those issues offering the best return on the resources employed.

Training is only an appropriate solution if the cause of the problem is associated with lack of knowledge and skill. In considering the best solution to a performance problem it is worthwhile considering all the possible solutions. Each of these can be considered in general terms and a decision made regarding which offers the best investment return.

The range of possible solutions must be evaluated to determine which are most appropriate to the issues and problems identified. The criteria for evaluation will be concerned with:

- Whether it will work
- Whether it will improve the situation
- Whether it is feasible
- Whether it can be afforded
- What the costs versus benefits are
- How timely the solution is
- How acceptable it is to those involved
- What resources are needed to develop it.

Think about the points below before deciding on the type of training intervention:

- Credibility of training proposed
- Value of closing the performance gap
- Focus on relevant knowledge and skills
- Power of intervention to overcome resistance
- Mass of people trained to maintain momentum
- Duration of intervention:
    – one shot for one-shot deficiency
    – on-going for long-term need.

When the solution proposed is training it is legitimate for the trainers to develop it further. The implications in terms of training resources required, detailed analysis to be undertaken, selection of strategies, design of training and production of training material can all be considered.

Those problems and issues without training solutions may be just as important as training problems. They too require action to resolve them or reduce their impact. It is the responsibility of the trainer, as a member of the management team, to share information on performance problems and issues facing the organization. Justifying investment in training requires results to be achieved and this is less likely for problems where training is not a preferred solution.

Even when a problem, or issue, facing the organization is linked to a lack of knowledge and skill, training may not be the preferred solution. Possible reasons to reject a training solution are:

- It will take too long.
- It will cost too much.
- Training resources are not available.
- It will stop/clash with other training.
- There is a lack of learning skills in those needing to learn.

- There is a lack of potential in those needing to learn.
- Training is rejected in this context by management, learners or the culture of the organization.

When a non-training solution seems the most appropriate response, trainers need to be careful not to overstep their areas of expertise and credibility. If a change in environment or incentives appears to be the best solution then it will require relevant specialists to work out the details. In this way the credibility and authority of the trainers and the process of AOTN can be enhanced.

A great deal of information is generated and processed during an AOTN. This needs to be organized and distilled into a form which can be managed and actioned. A way of organizing this material is to prepare a priority list and a training plan.

Priority list
A priority list can be prepared to help analyse and record the information collected. This includes all the major problems identified. Problems which do not have major training implications should be included as well as those where training offers a solution. This adds authority to the analysis and provides a useful input to the management team on key issues facing the organization. The credibility of training can be built up by acting responsibly as part of the management team.

The layout of a priority list, shown in appendix C, includes descriptions of the problems, what the training implications are, what other implications for action have been identified and an assessment of priority. The problems identified should be expressed in brief terms, preferably a single sentence. The cause(s) of the problem will be apparent from the problem statement when considered with the training implications and other implications. Training implications explain how training will help solve or reduce the problem; other implications indicate other action which is considered appropriate to help solve the problem, either instead of training or in conjunction with it. The implications may include the need for further analysis or for bringing in other specialists, as well as more specific solutions.

Every problem can be expected to have non-training implications. For those problems where non-training action is the key solution recommended, there may still be some training implications. Where a performance problem is traced to lack of supervision the main recommendation may be to reorganize the way the work is supervised. There may be a consequential need to train supervisors to operate within the new structure.

The priority list requires the problems identified to be prioritized. This is to help decide where to apply limited resources. All organizations face limitations upon the resources available. The identification of priority areas can help to make decisions about how to deploy scarce resources. Priorities try to distinguish the urgent from the important. The important things need to be done, sometimes at the expense of the urgent: if the urgent tasks always take priority the organization may lose long-term viability through short-term expediency.

Criteria for setting priorities for the problems identified will be influenced by:

- Legal requirements
- The needs of the business – future oriented
- The size of the pay-off – small investment offering large return
- Political considerations – internally and externally
- Staff morale
- Resources available
- Satisfying the management
- Meeting the expectations and aspirations of staff.

These are not listed in any rank order, and they are a guide to deciding priorities rather than a formula. Different individuals will arrive at their personal ranking of priorities.

The priority list is a working document for those undertaking the analysis of organizational training needs. It is intended to help draw together the findings and proposed action. In considering priorities, the issues examined provide a basis for discussing priorities with the 'client' and senior management.

Training plan

The second document it is helpful to produce during an AOTN is the training plan. This is another working document which is developed from the priority list. It is not a list of courses nor the detailed design of training proposed. What it provides is an outline of how the training implications identified in the priority list will be developed into viable training interventions. The training plan is not likely to replace existing training commitments, therefore it must fit within them.

It must be prepared in the context of the following:

- Line managements' continuing responsibility for training and development
- Organizational priorities and development plans
- Training resources available
- Existing training commitments

- Acceptable training strategies
- Cost-effectiveness considerations
- Requirements for job/task analysis
- Links with competences and NVQs.

One approach to a training plan is shown completed in appendix D. This layout has the following features:

1 Job title – of those it is proposed to train
2 Need – what need the proposed training will address
3 Proposed training – what form of training, and the strategy to be used
4 Proposed action – what need to be done to develop the training proposed
5 Time-scale – target time to complete proposed action
6 Responsibility – who is accountable for the proposed action

A checklist of training strategies which may be considered is included in appendix E. The selection of a particular strategy will be determined by the judgement of the trainer, the resources available, the expectations of staff and the culture of the organization.

The purpose of the training plan is to clarify how the training solutions will be developed. This will provide further information, in a structured form, which can be developed into the reporting of the AOTN findings.

The outcome of this stage in the AOTN process will be proposed solutions for the major issues and problems which have been identified. These proposals will need to be agreed by the client before resources are committed to implementing them.

Report the results

Having analysed the situation, identified challenges and problems facing the organization, pin-pointed contributory causes and identified solutions, we might consider the AOTN complete. In fact, all the work that has been undertaken will be wasted if no action is taken based upon the findings. Even where the trainer has authority to use resources and develop training solutions it is still wise to present the results. This gives an opportunity for confirmation from senior management that the results conform to their plans and expectations. Changes can be made before proceeding with implementation.

Gaining senior management agreement and commitment has a number of advantages for the trainer:

1 It gives authority in implementing the proposals. The cooperation of staff across the organization is likely to be greater when plans have senior management support.

2 The proposals provide an opportunity to discuss the resource implications. For example, will more money and staff be needed? What shall we stop doing if resources are to be redeployed? These questions can be very powerful in gaining resources.
3 It brings the trainer into contact with senior management. This provides opportunities to build the relationship between trainers and senior management and enhance the credibility of training.

There are two main ways of reporting the findings, a written report and an oral presentation. They should not be considered as alternatives because both are essential.

The report is essential because it provides a reference document for the proposals. It should be written to the intended audience, the decision makers, and provide detailed proposals for action with evidence to support the issues identified. It may be appropriate to include an edited version of the priority list and training plan.

The presentation is equally essential because reports, however good, often never get read. The report which lies unread never gets actioned. Therefore the purpose of the presentation is to gain commitment to action, to agree proposals in principle and ensure the report can be actioned in detail. To succeed in the presentation, emphasis must be placed on the benefits of the proposals. During the presentation a dialogue must take place to confirm agreements, clarify misunderstandings and counter objections. By the end of the presentation there should be agreement on the way forward, what action is to be taken and by whom. Further advice on presentations is in chapter 7.

It is worth consideration whether presentation should precede report or report precede presentation. If the report is presented first there is an opportunity to read it. This may, or may not, happen but the audience will have it during the presentation for reference. This can mean that objections have been identified and developed before the presentation. It can also encourage glancing through the report rather than listening to the presentation. Both of these are unwelcome possibilities.

If the report follows the presentation you can expect full attention during the presentation. Objections and clarifications can be responded to immediately. Reference can be made during the presentation to the detail available in the report while seeking agreement to the principal proposals.

The choice is yours regarding how you report your findings. The quality of the effort put into the analysis will be judged by what happens as a result. You will increase your chances of gaining acceptance of your proposals by reporting them effectively. This will help justify the investment made in carrying out the AOTN and further investment in training.

The advantages and disadvantages of the written report and the oral presentation can be summarized as follows:

Written report
Plus points:

- Can present detailed information
- Can include source documents
- Can present analytical arguments.

Minus points

- May not be read
- Does not get commitment
- Takes a lot of effort to prepare
- May be rejected summarily
- Gets a delayed response.

Presentation
Plus points

- Gets an immediate response
- Gains access to senior management
- Trainer can discuss objections
- Trainer can answer questions
- Can obtain commitment for action
- Can gain resources.

Minus points

- Limited detail
- May appear superficial
- Time pressures restrict content.

Successful face-to-face presentation of the recommendations will result in a clear commitment to action.

Implement proposals

Once the proposals have been accepted and agreed, their implementation needs to be planned in detail. This may require the redeployment of training resources and training staff. The analysis of jobs and tasks, design of training, development of materials and selection of external training all require input of resources. The workload will need to be scheduled in with existing commitments.

Implementing the developed training solution will require:

- Attention to non-training factors to support performance
- Preparing staff to learn
- Implementing the training
- Follow-up after training.

Review, modify, revise

When the proposals are being implemented they will need to be monitored. The process of implementation itself will produce new information, which can be fed back to review the issues and problems identified and the solutions proposed. As other factors develop, such as changes in the economy, technology and competition, the plans will need to be reviewed. The review may be expected to result in modifications to the plans and the revision of proposals.

Summary

AOTN is a resource intensive process: collecting and confirming information, then going back to management for agreement. This all takes up management time as well as that of trainers. There are several reasons for undertaking a regular AOTN, probably at a frequency of every two to three years, depending upon circumstances.

For the trainer the benefits are:

- A valuable step back from day-to-day work
- A review of what you are doing
- Getting you known across the organization
- Getting you face to face with senior management
- Helping you set priorities
- Helping allocate limited resources
- Justifying investment in training (and protecting training resource)
- Building training into the business
- Building credibility
- Building a network of contacts.

For the organization the benefits are:

- A different view on strengths and weaknesses
- Clarification of the role training can play

- Planning to improve performance areas:
  - building on strengths
  - reducing weaknesses
- Building training into the business
- Justifying investment in training.

Some trainers feel AOTN is too wide-ranging and that it is more of a management consultancy exercise. They argue that this is not what a trainer should be doing in analysing training needs, which should be focused on techniques such as job and task analysis. The view taken here is that trainers should concern themselves with making training part of the business. Everyone in the organization should recognize that training is contributing to the performance of the organization. To do that the trainer must have a wider view of the organization and communicate with management and staff the way in which training will be, and is, contributing to the organization. AOTN is the key to deciding where to use job and task analysis in order to identify the performance requirements of specific jobs. These techniques are resource intensive and can occupy all the training resource without improving organization performance.

This decision will form a firm foundation to deploying resources in the design and development of training. By establishing clear statements of the issues and problems to be addressed, the validation and evaluation of training interventions becomes more feasible. Building training into the business makes it an essential service rather than a nice add-on, which can be dropped when the going gets tough.

Further reading

Boydell, T.H. (1976) *The Identification of Training Needs*. London: BACIE.

Harrison, R. (1988) *Training and Development*. London: Institute of Personnel Management.

Kenney, J. (1986) *Training Interventions*. London: Institute of Personnel Management.

Kubr, M. and Prokopenko, J. (1989) *Diagnosing Management Training and Development Needs*. Geneva: International Labour Office.

Romiszowski, A.J. (1981) *Systems Approach to Education and Training*. London: Kogan Page.

Turrell, M. (1980) *Training Analysis*. London: Pitman.

Ulschak, F.L. (1983) *Human Resource Development*. Reston, Va.: Prentice-Hall.

Zemke, R. and Kramlinger, T. (1982) *Figuring Things Out*. Reading, Mass.: Addison-Wesley.

Appendix A Analysing organizational training needs

Potential sources of information on training needs include:

Organizational sources

Mission statement
Corporate objectives
Business plans
Job/management inventories
Skills inventory/versatility
Organization climate:
  Turnover
  Absenteeism
  Productivity
  Accidents
  Sickness
  Customer complaints
Organization chart
Management succession charts
Exit interviews

Corporate policies
Performance indices:
  Profitability
  Cost of labour
  Cost of materials
  Quality of materials
  Equipment utilization
  Wastage
  Downtime
  Late deliveries
System changes
Management requests for training
Work planning schedules
Quality assurance

Job sources

Job descriptions
Job specifications
Performance standards
Perform the job
Observe the work
Review literature on job:
  Other industries
  Professional journals
  Competence statements
  Academic research
  Trade associations

Ask questions about job:
  Of job holder
  Of supervisor
  Of senior management
Analyse operational problems:
  Downtime reports
  Waste
  Repairs
  Late deliveries
  Quality control

Individual analysis sources

Performance indicators:
  Productivity
  Absenteeism
  Accidents
  Sickness
  Grievances

Tests:
  Job knowledge
  Skills
  Achievement
Attitude surveys
Performance appraisal

Waste

Interviews

Late deliveries

Work diaries

Quality

Questionnaires

Downtime

Critical incidents

Repairs

Assessment centres

Customer complaints

Work samples:

Coaching

Observation

Appendix B Responses to performance problems

Do nothing?

Environmental changes

Redesign workflow
Restructure management/supervision
Change organization structure
Introduce new tools/equipment
Automate, use new technology
Redesign products/services
Change organization culture
Relocate jobs
Networking/home working/job sharing
Change recruitment and selection criteria
Reallocate workload/restructure workplace

Motivation/incentive changes

Tell staff exactly what is required and why (performance standard and role clarification)
Link remuneration to performance
Incentive schemes: provide consequences of performance
Introduce counselling, career planning, mentoring
Resolve personality clashes
Job rotation

Lack of knowledge/skills

Redesign job to remove requirement for the lack of knowledge and skills
Remove job holder:
   Terminate – dismissal, retirement, redundancy, resignation
   Move – transfer, promote, demote

Strategies providing learning events:
Reading/professional journals
Provide feedback on performance
Provide practice in performance
Provide performance aids/documentation
Secondment
Projects
Visits
Sabbaticals
Train – report training, new strategy, revised design; on-job, off-job internal, off-job external

Appendix C Priority list

Problem	Training implications	Other implications	Priority
Present quality system inadequate to meet major customer requirement – BS 5750 system demanded	• If undertaking a BS 5750 approach, needs of entire workforce are involved • Appreciation and briefing of all shop floor on system training of individuals, groups and function in use of techniques, paperwork system etc.	• Decision on use of consultants to help accreditation process • Need to communicate and gain commitment of workforce to accreditation • Inform suppliers and customers of progress • Clarify the responsibilities and roles of all functional line managers, in relation to quality control (QC) staff • Develop quality manual specific to company • Upgrading of QC equipment needed, calibration of measuring instruments • Introduction of machine capability studies	1

Problem	Training implications	Other implications	Priority
Retirements in the next two years of finance director, production manager and distribution manager	• Train and develop people as spotlighted by succession plans	• MD to recognize and implement plan • MD to help personally with the development of successors • MD to recognize high levels of stress felt by these job occupants	2
Unacceptable accident levels	• Implications for induction training • Implications for job training • Implications for supervisor training • Implications for training of safety representatives	• Possible revision of safety arrangements, priorities, machine guarding work practices • Management responsibility investigated • Accident investigation procedures amended • Safety reps appointed • Review of factory and office layout and warning signs • Use of protective equipment • First aid facilities to be reviewed • Accidents statistics to be further investigated	3

Appendix D Training plan

Job title	Need	Proposed training	Proposed action	Time-scale	Responsibility
Chief inspector	• To be able to introduce quality assurance (QA) system BS 5750	• Introducing quality system to a high-tech maufacturing environment: PERA workshop, 3 days • Open learning package 'The Quality Man'	• Work with QA consultants to draw up manual and implement system • Serve on audit team	9 months	Managing director
Setters	• To analyse individual training needs	Dependent on individual needs analysis: • Formal on-the-job instruction with production manager • Short off-the-job technology courses • Visits to machinery manufacturers • CBT package, simulation of process, fault identification • Secondment to technical department (1 month)	• Registration on standards of performance scheme (NCVQ ratified) • City and Guilds knowledge and practical tests taken	2 years	Works director

Job title	Need	Proposed training	Proposed action	Time-scale	Responsibility
Supervisors	• To improve staff management skills	• Basic supervisors' programme – 3 days; independent consultant • 'Helping People to Learn' – 3 days; college • 'Safety and the supervisor' video	• Form team with production manager to undertake recruitment of operators • Introduce induction and job training programme	18 months	Works director
Operators	• To improve technical communication skills • To interpret engineering drawings and specs accurately • To operate visual inspection and SPC quality systems	• In-company programme with language centre • In-company programme with works director	• Be fully involved in all relevant QC checks as specified in manual	12 months	Works director

Appendix E Training strategies checklist

On-job:
  No organized training
On-job planned experience:
  Delegation
  Understudying/deputizing
  Attachment
  Working parties
  Job rotation
  Performance aids
  On-line with coach and mentor
  Off-line with formal training – travelling tutors, supervisor
  Assignments
  Projects
  Quality circles
  Career development
Off-job internal training:
  Menu of general courses
  Responding to specific need
Off-job external courses:
  Open training courses
  Tailor-made training courses
  Development training
  Action learning
  Education
  Conferences
Off-job planned experience:
  Secondment
  Visits/study tour – suppliers, customers, competitors
  Voluntary work – professional bodies, charities
  Sabbaticals
Individualized training:
  Open learning
  Distance learning
  Flexible learning centre
  Technology-based training
Experiential learning
Self-development with organizational support
Self-development by private study and reading
Organization development

4
Learning to Learn

SYLVIA DOWNS

Personally I'm always ready to learn,
although I do not always like being taught.

Winston Churchill, 1952

Introduction

It is often said that changing technology and markets mean that the workforce has also to change to an adaptable, responsible and versatile group. This entails people moving away from rote learning and using physical skills to a position where developing concepts is of increasing importance. Many hierarchical layers of management are being removed as work teams develop which are, to a large extent, self-managing and capable of taking initiatives. All this is having a profound effect on many training departments as it becomes apparent that one role of trainers is to encourage and develop the characteristics in the learner which are required to match the needs of companies.

The aim of this chapter, therefore, is to encourage trainers to revise their training design and methods in line with the changing needs of industry. In concert with learning, the end product of any training, trainers need to help learners develop better learning skills to enable them to be responsive and adaptable to learning needs. This is based on the general thesis that learning consists of a number of skills which, if made overt and practised, can be improved. This thesis has been tested over eight years' research and a further three years' disseminating the findings in different industries.

Because comprehension is so important and this can best be arrived at by trying ideas out in practice, this chapter is written in a way which illustrates the various messages; such as getting trainers/learners to think about their previous experience and use this in learning material; involving trainers/learners actively by posing questions before giving information; getting trainers/learners to compare and contrast the new material with other familiar material.

This method of presentation has been successfully used by a correspondence college and writers of computer-based training packages and is employed to give trainers experience in the changes to design and methods they would have to make to help their trainees improve their ways of learning.

Learning Blockages

Before considering the development of learning skills, it is often necessary to take one step back and ask people to think about the sorts of things which prevent them learning. The majority of people suffer from bad learning experiences and these can set up blockages which seriously inhibit any learning taking place.

A large number of learners were asked about what prevented them learning and their statements were collected. The statements fell into four main categories, as seen in the learning blockage questionnaire which follows. Try filling in the questionnaire, remembering that the statements have all been collected from learners.

Learning blockage questionnaire

On the next few pages you will find a number of statements made by people about the way they learn and the things that stop them from learning effectively. Go through the statements in turn. First of all, decide whether you agree with the statement, disagree or have no opinion either way. Next decide how strongly you agree or disagree and tick the appropriate box. Only use the middle box if you understand the statement and have no opinion either way.

You will see on the right hand a column headed 'Score'. This you will use after completing the questionnaire.

Section 1

	Strongly agree	Agree	Neither agree nor disagree	Disagree	Strongly disagree	Score

1 I can't understand something unless I can do it myself.
[a] [b] [c] [d] [e] ☐

2 There's no point in practising bits of tasks, you've got to do the whole lot.
[a] [b] [c] [d] [e] ☐

3 When I have to learn something by heart I just sit and stare at it.
[a] [b] [c] [d] [e] ☐

4 When I don't understand something I try to memorize it.
[a] [b] [c] [d] [e] ☐

5 Unless someone shows me exactly what to do, I can't do it.
[a] [b] [c] [d] [e] ☐

6 The only way I can memorize something is by repeating it to myself.
[a] [b] [c] [d] [e] ☐

7 I can't learn how to do something without watching someone else do it.
[a] [b] [c] [d] [e] ☐

8 When learning, I often overlook the obvious.
[a] [b] [c] [d] [e] ☐

9 I think the best way of learning to do something is by reading about it.
[a] [b] [c] [d] [e] ☐

10 I can't keep things in my head for long.
[a] [b] [c] [d] [e] ☐

11 When I'm trying to learn something, I can't recover if I get confused early on.
[a] [b] [c] [d] [e] ☐

12 I find it difficult to follow written instructions.
[a] [b] [c] [d] [e] ☐

13 I don't need to understand things as somebody usually tells me what to do.
[a] [b] [c] [d] [e] ☐

Running total ☐

Strongly agree   Agree   Neither agree nor disagree   Disagree   Strongly disagree

Score

14 I suffer from a bad memory.   a b c d e ☐

15 I find it hard to know whether I've under-   a b c d e ☐
stood something or not.

16 The only way to learn something practical   a b c d e ☐
is by trial and error

17 I can't learn numbers and things by heart   a b c d e ☐
unless I use them a lot.

18 I find it difficult to relate new things to   a b c d e ☐
stuff I already know.

19 I don't practise something unless I've got   a b c d e ☐
all the tools I need.

20 I don't try to memorize anything; if it   a b c d e ☐
clicks, it clicks.

21 I can't see how learning one thing can help   a b c d e ☐
me learn another.

22 Unless I can see something working I have   a b c d e ☐
difficulty understanding it.

Section 1 total ☐

Section 2

Score

1 I can't concentrate on things when I'm in a   a b c d e ☐
strange place.

2 I find myself thinking about my problems   a b c d e ☐
when I ought to be learning.

Running total ☐
(to be carried over
to next page)

	Strongly agree	Agree	Neither agree nor disagree	Disagree	Strongly disagree	Score
3 My attention wanders easily after a heavy lunch.	a	b	c	d	e	
4 I'm easily distracted by people around me.	a	b	c	d	e	
5 Even with a niggling problem, I can't get it out of my mind.	a	b	c	d	e	
6 If I'm tired I can't attend to anything.	a	b	c	d	e	
7 I find myself staring out of the window rather than listening to a supervisor/trainer.	a	b	c	d	e	
8 I think about my social life rather than what I should be learning.	a	b	c	d	e	

Section 2 total ☐

Section 3

	Strongly agree	Agree	Neither agree nor disagree	Disagree	Strongly disagree	Score
1 I feel embarrassed when I'm asked a question in a group.	a	b	c	d	e	
2 I worry about keeping up with others.	a	b	c	d	e	
3 I don't want people to think I'm a swot if I do well.	a	b	c	d	e	
4 My mind goes blank when I'm asked a question.	a	b	c	d	e	
5 I feel shown up when I make mistakes in front of others.	a	b	c	d	e	

Running total ☐

Strongly agree Agree Neither agree nor disagree Disagree Strongly disagree Score

6 I'm nervous about learning to do a new job at my age.   [a] [b] [c] [d] [e] ☐

7 People might think I haven't been listening if I ask questions.   [a] [b] [c] [d] [e] ☐

8 I'm frightened about breaking expensive new equipment.   [a] [b] [c] [d] [e] ☐

9 I don't like the idea of being tested.   [a] [b] [c] [d] [e] ☐

10 I feel nervous about asking questions in a group.   [a] [b] [c] [d] [e] ☐

11 I'm nervous about using modern machines.   [a] [b] [c] [d] [e] ☐

12 I'm worried about going to strange places and meeting new people.   [a] [b] [c] [d] [e] ☐

13 I don't think I am good at learning.   [a] [b] [c] [d] [e] ☐

14 I can't learn anything to do with computers.   [a] [b] [c] [d] [e] ☐

Section 3 total ☐

Section 4

Score

1 Teachers and trainers use too much jargon.   [a] [b] [c] [d] [e] ☐

2 People won't let me make mistakes.   [a] [b] [c] [d] [e] ☐

Running total
(to be carried over
to next page) ☐

	Strongly agree	Agree	Neither agree nor disagree	Disagree	Strongly disagree	Score

3 I'm given too much information in one go when I'm learning something.   a   b   c   d   e ☐

4 People get impatient with me when I don't understand.   a   b   c   d   e ☐

5 I'm not told whether I have got something right or wrong.   a   b   c   d   e ☐

6 When I'm being taught something, people go too fast and I miss things.   a   b   c   d   e ☐

7 I get taught things I don't need to know.   a   b   c   d   e ☐

8 People who teach and train think they're better than us.   a   b   c   d   e ☐

9 People don't explain things fully enough when I'm trying to learn.   a   b   c   d   e ☐

10 I find teachers and trainers are too bossy.   a   b   c   d   e ☐

11 The order in which people teach things doesn't make sense to me.   a   b   c   d   e ☐

12 Teachers and trainers don't give me time to think about what they've said before going on to the next thing.   a   b   c   d   e ☐

13 People ignore what I already know when they teach me things.   a   b   c   d   e ☐

14 I get taught the theory but not how to use something.   a   b   c   d   e ☐

15 I find that people don't explain how one thing links to another.   a   b   c   d   e ☐

16 I think it's the teacher's job to make sure I learn.   a   b   c   d   e ☐

Section 4 total ☐

Scoring the learning blockage questionnaire

Now that you have filled in the questionnaire, go back and check that you have ticked a box for all 60 statements.

To score the questionnaire, look at the boxes you have ticked and if you have ticked an 'a' put a 2 in the score box, if 'b' put a 1 in the box. All other letters score 0. Do this for all of the statements.

When you have done this, add up the numbers in the score boxes for each of the four sections and record them below.

Score for section 1 ☐   Learning skills

Score for section 2 ☐   Distractions/concentration

Score for section 3 ☐   Worries and fears about learning

Score for section 4 ☐   Learning from others

Fill in the boxes below:
My two highest scores are for

☐

and

☐

You will have noticed that the higher the score, the more blockages occur. Look at your own answers and decide if there are any sections where you have a high mark and which particular questions are involved. Then try answering these questions:

1 What should I do or not do to avoid reinforcing or creating blockages in other people?
2 What should I do to counteract or cope with my own learning blockages?

Once you have given your answers, compare them with the following ones.

Ways that trainers can use to overcome or prevent learner blockages

1 Be clear about the aims of the training and make these clear to their learners.
2 Try to find out the learners' previous knowledge and experience so that the training can be pitched at the right level.
3 Deliberately think of ways of linking the learners' previous learning and experience with the new learning, so that they can make a contribution.
4 Make sure the learners' existing ideas are correct so they will not be confused with the new learning.
5 Allow enough success in the early stages of training to build up the learners' confidence.
6 Allow for learners who have not been involved in learning for a long time to be rusty at learning, and therefore help them to practise and build up their learning skills.
7 Let learners know clearly where they are right and wrong.
8 Enable learners to think for themselves.
9 Have the right mix between theory and practice.
10 At intervals, help learners relate what they are learning to the overall programme.
11 Check that the learners can see and hear properly.
12 Do not overload with detail at the early stages of learning.
13 Where appropriate make comparisons between new and old technology to clarify similarities and differences.
14 Do not use jargon and abbreviations until learners are familiar with them.
15 Avoid time pressures as much as possible, especially where the learner is learning new material.
16 Do not constantly repeat material. Use other methods which involve the learners questioning or identifying their learning problems.
17 Be clear about the standards of work expected at different stages of training.
18 Look on mistakes as a clue from which to work out learning problems.
19 Use visual aids which are simple and clear.
20 Where a lot of facts need to be memorized, give written material.
21 Make sure that learners master their learning before moving on to new learning.
22 Help the learners to accept that learning is not always easy and that often understanding does not take place for some time. A period of confusion is normal when new ideas are being learned. The learner must be helped to persevere through this confusion and not give up.

Ways of reducing your own learning blockages

1 Accept that you are never too old to learn.
2 Check out what you know and what you do not know.

3 Do not be afraid of admitting that you find learning difficult; everyone has problems.

4 Even if your experience of learning at school was bad, think of all the many things you have learned at home, at work or in your hobbies or leisure activities.

5 If you find it hard to concentrate, try to set yourself short learning tasks which you can achieve. In time you will find your length of concentration increases.

6 If something is hard to understanding do not be afraid to ask questions of your workmates, more experienced workers or your instructors.

7 Do not look on mistakes as bad, but use them as clues to let you know how or where you went wrong and plan how to put this right.

8 Do not expect to learn everything by trial and error; some things such as electronics cannot be learned this way.

9 Be prepared for some of your old ideas not to fit with new methods or systems.

10 Accept that for some learning, you will initially have to accept ideas without proof. This is because the proof may be beyond your present knowledge.

11 Do not try to tackle too much at once.

12 Make sure that you have really mastered what you have just learned before you go on to something new. It is important to get plenty of practice.

13 Make sure that you get someone to tell you honestly how you are doing. Use instructors, more expert workmates or examples – whatever is available or suitable.

14 Check that you can see and hear well if someone is giving a talk or demonstration.

15 Realize that you will probably have to memorize certain facts, such as names or formulas, before you can start to understand.

16 Ask for any factual information you need and write it down for later reference.

17 When you are trying to understand something, compare and contrast it with things you know. If appropriate, think of things that could go wrong, their causes and how to put them right. Think of the purpose of what you want to understand.

18 Ask questions that check your ideas, rather than just asking people to explain.

19 If you need to study for exams, get advice on study skills such as note taking, exam techniques, planning your time and abstracting information from books. All of these involve techniques which can be learned.

Before you move on to the section on developing learning skills, jot down any particular points relevant to you as a trainer or learner in helping reduce or prevent learning blockages.

Helping to Develop Learning Skills

A number of trainers, works managers and senior supervisors were each asked to think of a supervisor whom they thought was good at helping trainees learn for themselves. They were then asked to describe the behaviours which led them to their judgement of the supervisor. These behaviours were listed and the eighteen most frequent are given below. They were accepted as stated and without evaluation or alteration. They were given on separate cards to supervisors and trainees, who were asked to pick out eight or fewer statements which would, in their view, help trainees learn for themselves.

Which statements would you select from the eighteen? Compare your results with those from the research and then check through the list of some guidelines for developing the skills of learning.

Stated behaviours

1 The supervisor tries to avoid letting the trainee make mistakes.
2 If the trainee suggests there is another way to do a task, the supervisor asks him or her to try the new way out.
3 When trainees make mistakes the supervisor tells them what caused them.
4 The supervisor repeats things many times.
5 The supervisor leaves the trainee alone if the trainee is trying to work something out.
6 The supervisor gives the trainee a project to design and when it is finished the supervisor marks it right or wrong.
7 When the trainees ask a question the supervisor does not answer directly but gives them hints so they can find the answer for themselves.
8 The supervisor gives help to the trainee when the trainee is puzzling over a task.
9 The supervisor tells the trainees in great depth the skill they will have to learn.
10 The supervisor praises every step that a trainee completes even if sometimes it is not up to standard.
11 The supervisor begins to demonstrate a task and asks trainees to say how they think it ought to be done.
12 The supervisor always tells trainees what is wrong with a machine so they know how to mend it.
13 The supervisor continually helps the trainee when the trainee is trying to do something.
14 The supervisor explains in detail to avoid trainees having to ask questions.

15 The supervisor asks trainees to try things out for themselves and to ask questions when they need help.

16 The supervisor sometimes deliberately lets the trainees make mistakes so that the trainees themselves can correct them.

17 The supervisor ignores some mistakes the trainee makes if they are not considered very important.

18 When trainees make mistakes the supervisor corrects them so they can carry on with the task.

As you will see from table 4.1, both supervisors and learners chose behaviours where the learners asked questions, were left alone to work things out by themselves and were encouraged to identify and correct their own mistakes. Furthermore, both groups thought learning skills were developed by learners trying out new ways.

Few supervisors or learners chose behaviours which depicted the supervisor continually helping when the learner was doing a task, or explaining in detail to avoid questions being asked, or ignoring mistakes. Both groups also realized there was little learning skills development when the learners' work was simply marked either right or wrong.

While most of the choices of the supervisors were echoed by the learners, there were some important differences. Supervisors' choices indicated a tendency to overprotect the learners. Half of them believed that praising every step, even if it was below standard, developed learning skills.

Some guidelines for developing the skills of learning

Do	*by*
Show that all your trainees have a contribution to make	Making sure that you take notice of their views
Do not	*by*
Make things too easy	Doing the difficult parts for trainees
Do	*by*
Make them seek help when they need it	Not rushing in with help too soon.
Do not	*by*
Do it for them when they ask for help but encourage them to work it out for themselves	Giving them clues or hints
Do	*by*
Encourage trainees to identify and correct their own mistakes	Providing models and guiding them with questions

Table 4.1 Results of card-sorting

Card no.	% chosen by trainees	% chosen by supervisors	Trainees' most often chosen cards	Supervisors' most often chosen cards	Trainees' least often chosen cards	Supervisors' least often chosen cards
1	27	25				X
2	61	88	*	*		
3	68	75	*	*		
4	18	31			X	
5	64	75	*	*	X	X
6	20	25				
7	59	50	*	*		
8	56	88		*		
9	43	19				
10	23	50		*	X	
11	61	38	*			
12	52	19			X	X
13	20	6			X	X
14	11	6				X
15	75	62	*	*		
16	39	44				
17	16	6			X	X
18	43	25				X

Supervisors N = 16
Trainees N = 44

Do not	by
Make the learning too easy	Breaking it into small parts – get them to break it up for themselves

Do	by
Allow them time to work something out for themselves	Giving them pondering time – if they feel pushed for time they may become stressed

Do not	by
Give unrealistic feedback	Giving undue praise or over-critical comment

Do	by
Develop the trainees' interest in learning to do things for themselves	Discussing with them how they intend to go about learning something

Do not	by
Belittle your trainees' attempts at learning	Laughing at them or comparing them unkindly with others

Do	by
Develop the trainees' awareness of how to assess what they have done	Getting them to check their own work and assess it for quality

Do not	by
Give tasks which are too easy or too hard	Not selecting a task which is appropriate to their previous experience

Do	by
Make your trainees realize that practice is necessary for both consolidating learning and gaining skill.	Encouraging them to do things a number of times giving careful attention to any mistakes they make.

Do recognize that the way you present something to be learned will directly influence the learning skills developed by your trainees.

As you will have seen, there is a clear distinction between behaviours which, while teaching product, at the same time help learners to improve their learning skills, and behaviours which only.enable trainers to teach products.

Three Categories of the Ways of Learning in a Simple Taxonomy

During the researches, it became clear very early on that a great number of people muddled the basic differences in ways of learning needed to learn something, and that these people would be most helped by a simple taxonomy.

In the following list there are three categories according to different ways or strategies of learning you would use to learn. Try to put each item into one of the three categories and say what distinguishes them.

1 Names of plants
2 How temperatures and moisture affect growth of different plants
3 Names of bones
4 Welding two pieces of plate together
5 Purpose of quality assurance
6 Riding a bike
7 A car registration number
8 Lifting weights
9 Steering a car
10 The need for safety at work
11 Appropriate road behaviour at junctions
12 Road signs
13 Tightening wheel nuts
14 Tyre pressures for different cars and wheels
15 Good manufacturing practice
16 Number of calories in certain foods
17 Reasons for a machine breakdown
18 The address of your place of work
19 How to run a business
20 Icing a cake
21 Names of tools
22 Swimming
23 Telephone numbers
24 Sawing a piece of wood
25 Dates of battles
26 Typing
27 How a computer works
28 Hitting a target in archery
29 Reasons for using satellites in communication
30 Reasons for war.

You will probably have arrived at the memorizing–understanding–doing (MUD) taxonomy with which you may be very familiar. You will also undoubtedly have had reservations about some of the 'doing' items, because so many of them often require a degree of procedural learning and understanding. Hitting a target in archery, for example, requires some ideas of dynamics and gravitational effects. Two points should therefore be made about the MUD taxonomy. In the first place, the categories are often combined in learning and the value of the taxonomy is in distinguishing the different ways of learning involved, so that appropriate materials and methods can be used to help the learner. In learning to drive a car, for example, we can assist by providing self-testing cards for memorizing road signs; practice with feedback in such physical skills as steering and gear changing; and learning about road behaviour through videos or scenarios, during which people can think through appropriate behaviour based on their understanding of what is happening.

Secondly, the word 'doing' can often cause confusion, because we could be said to 'do' something when we memorize a fact or understand a concept. In the MUD taxonomy, however, the 'doing' category has the more restricted meaning of the exercise and practice of physical skills. When you compare your analysis of the thirty statements with the suggested categories, you may well find that you have interpreted one or more differently. This in itself is not important provided that the reasons are understood for distinguishing the two areas of facts and concepts, which are so often confused.

Facts to be memorized	*Ideas to be understood*	*Activities to be done*
1 Names of plants	2 How temperatures	4 Welding two pieces
3 Names of bones	and moisture affect	of plate together
7 A car registration	growth of different	6 Riding a bike
number	plants	8 Lifting weights
12 Road signs	5 Purpose of quality	9 Steering a car
14 Tyre pressures for	assurance	13 Tightening wheel
different cars and	10 The need for safety	nuts
wheels	at work	20 Icing a cake
16 Number of calories	11 Appropriate road	22 Swimming
in certain foods	behaviour at	24 Sawing a piece of
18 The address of your	junctions	wood
place of work	15 Good	26 Typing
21 Names of tools	manufacturing	28 Hitting a target in
23 Telephone numbers	practice	archery
25 Dates of battles	17 Reasons for a	
	machine breakdown	
	19 How to run a	
	business	
	27 How a computer	
	works	
	29 Reasons for using	
	satellites in	
	communication	
	30 Reasons for war	

While it could be said that the MUD taxonomy suffers from its own simplicity, it does distinguish three different groups of things to be learned, each of which uses different methods:

- *Facts* which need to be *memorized*
- *Concepts* which need to be *understood*
- *Physical skills* which need to be experienced by *doing*.

In the past, a great deal of education and training relied on memorizing and practising. If tasks were done by rote and no decisions were called for or allowed, then memorizing and practising were sufficient. Today's needs demand a greater understanding and use of initiative on the part of everyone, and so merely memorizing would be an inappropriate if not dangerous learning method. However, just telling people they must now understand something does not help, and what is needed is that people should be helped to improve their understanding.

The following list gives examples of how people can memorize, develop understanding and learn physical skills. These are amplified in some notes for learners in the following pages. As trainers, it is interesting and sometimes salutary to look through such notes to see how often the trainer encourages or explores ways of memorizing and doing and, for example, sets up the circumstances in learning from a demonstration which allows the learners to behave in the ways stated. When material has been memorized or practised, getting it wrong makes unlearning difficult, as with a golf swing or someone's name. When developing ideas on a topic, getting it wrong in fact increases our understanding and we learn from our mistakes. This is an important difference we must allow for when designing training materials, and this is developed later in the chapter.

Memorizing	*Understanding*	*Doing*
E.g. dates and names	E.g. safety policy	E.g. physical skills – swimming
Some ways of learning	*Some ways of learning*	*Some ways of learning*
Associating	Comparing	Practising
Self-testing	Contrasting	Watching
Using mnemonics	Experiencing	Assessing
Repeating	Questioning	Copy checking
Copy checking	Linking	
	Relating	
	Transfer checking	

Common aids to memorizing

1 Association:
   (a) Verbal: – *Group* things together, e.g. it costs the same to send an
                      airmail letter to Argentina, Canada, Kenya and South Africa.
                 – *Pair* things, e.g. knife and fork.
                 – *Link* with things you already know, e.g. Brighton is in Sussex,
                      Worthing is near Brighton, so also in Sussex.
                 – Make up *unlikely associations*, e.g. chalk and cheese.
                 – Make up a *story* linking things together.
   (b) Visual: – *Group* things together and *visualize* them.
                 – *Visualize the location*, e.g. imagine opening the pantry door
                      and seeing the things on the shelves to remember what food
                      to buy.
                 – Write a *list* and *visualize* it.
2 Repetition:
   (a) Written: *write out* a number of times, e.g. spelling mistakes.
   (b) Verbal: *repeat aloud* a number of times, e.g. poetry.
   (c) Aural: *listen* several times to a tape or record.
   (d) Visual: *read* over and over again.
3 Self-testing: used in combination with *repetition*, this is particularly helpful.
4 Part-learning: if there is a lot to be learned, break it down into parts. Learn
   each part thoroughly before going on to the next part. For older learners, it is
   helpful to revise the first part while learning the second part (*cumulative part-
   learning*). Test yourself on the first two parts before going on to the next part
   (*progressive part-learning*).
      Learning all the parts separately before testing yourself (pure part-
   learning) is *not* a good method.

Special aids

1 Rhyme rules: for example, to help to remember the number of days in each
   month, 'Thirty days hath September, / April, June and November', etc.
2 First-letter mnemonics: for example, to learn the colours of the spectrum
   (red, orange, yellow, green, blue, indigo, violet), ROYGBIV, or 'Richard of
   York Gained Battles In Vain'.
3 Number rhyme systems: first memorize associations between numbers and
   rhyming objects, e.g. one – bun, two – shoe, three – tree. Then form unusual
   associations between the things to be remembered and the rhyming objects,
   e.g. if objects to be remembered are piano, daffodil and chocolates, one could
   imagine a piano piled high with buns, a shoe used as a vase for daffodils and a
   tree with chocolates as fruit.
4 Spelling associations: where there is confusion between the spelling of
   similar sounding words with different meanings, such as stationery and

stationary, the correct spelling can be helped by associating station*e*ry with *e*nvelopes.

5 Roman Greek: this involves having a strong mental picture of a large house or palace, with a number of different rooms, passages and stairways which you can 'walk through' in your mind. You then associate each window or doorway with an idea or thing which you want to remember.

Conditions for good recall of things you have memorized

1 Errors: try to avoid making mistakes when learning it for the first time.
2 Recency: there is a tendency to remember the last thing you read.
3 Frequency: the more you test yourself the more you learn and the longer it lasts.
4 Intensity: the more you concentrate the more you learn.
5 Importance: the more important the material is to you, the more you learn. If you understand it or know why it is important, it is easier to memorize.
6 Feelings: your state of mind, or how you feel at the time of learning, affect what you learn.
7 Association: the more you can relate the material to be learned to other things the more you learn.

Learning from a demonstration

1 Watching someone:
  (a) *Watch* carefully. Notice: body movements; which hand and foot are being used; when sight, sound, smell or touch are involved; how tools and materials are held.
  (b) *Ask questions* until you know what is being done.
  (c) Try to find the *key points* in the cycle which might cause particular difficulty. If the sequence is long or fast try to break it up into parts and jot down the order of movement.
  (d) Look out for *inspection checks* and memorize them.
2 Before you try:
  (a) *Mentally* go through the sequence; use your notes.
  (b) *Get the feel* of the materials and tools you will use.
  (c) *Decisions* often need to be made. Make sure you know when to make them.
  (d) Consider whether there are any points where you need to *do two things at once*.
  (e) Remember that it is important to be aware of any *danger points* and any *safety precautions*.
3 When you start:
  (a) Try to start *as soon as possible* after watching someone or being shown.

(b) Concentrate on doing the key points *slowly* before you attempt to speed up.
(c) Don't hurry at the beginning. It is more important that you *get it right*. Once you have learned something wrongly it is often difficult to correct it.
(d) *Practise as often as you can*, especially in the beginning.
(e) Learn until the movements become *automatic*.

Understanding

First, try giving your views on the following questions:

- Why do we have trainers? What purpose do they serve?
- Compare and contrast conventional training with training for learning: how are they the same and different?
- How does training appear to management?
- What problems do you consider trainers have?

Compare your answers with the following; bearing in mind none is right or wrong, but the answers have been collected from different groups, of which those shown here are a selection.

Why do we have trainers? What purpose do they serve?
Trainers:

- Introduce new entrants to what the company is and means and how it does things
- Introduce and improve skills and knowledge
- Achieve a more knowledgeable and efficient workforce
- Provide feedback on performance
- Provide a training skill to management
- Achieve correct and consistent behaviour from everyone
- Organize information for others so it can be readily understood
- Analyse training needs
- Design relevant training programmes
- React to people as individuals according to their developmental needs
- Create more efficient cost/benefit training.

Comparison of the two approaches: how they differ

Conventional training	Training for learning
1 Skills of learning are covert	1 Skills of learning are made overt and discussed
2 Concepts are explained by trainer	2 Concepts are developed by trainees

3 Information is controlled by the trainer with stress on convergent thinking

3 Learning content is explored by both with stress on divergent thinking

4 Trainee is receptive of information (passive)

4 Trainee is seeking information (active)

5 Product is all-important

5 Product and process are important

6 Mistakes are mostly avoided

6 Mistakes are viewed as useful

7 Trainer often poses questions and gives solutions

7 Trainer poses problems, discusses trainee's solutions

8 Measures and standards are concerned with product

8 Measures and standards are concerned with product and process

9 Trainer checks and marks

9 Trainee can check and mark

10 Concerned with what is learned

10 Concerned with how and what is learned

11 Individual differences only in terms of success and failure

11 Individual differences in trainees allowed for and explored through the teaching material

Comparison of the two approaches: how they are similar

1 Trainers take overall control for the learning in terms of how, what and where.
2 Trainees are under trainers' control.
3 Product learning is important.
4 Standards and measures are important.

How does training appear to management?

- It is stuck in old-fashioned times.
- It is all right as far as it goes, but it does not go far enough.
- People get very bored and try to get out of attending courses if they possibly can.
- Some trainers talk to us and find out what we want, and this is very good.
- It can be very helpful with putting what we want into practice.
- It is just a cost.
- It ought to prove the value of what it does.
- It is useful for rewarding people who need a break.
- It can be used as a bargaining tool in industrial relations.

What problems do trainers have?

- Lack of feedback from the group
- Constant questions

- Personality clashes
- Stress
- Conflict of interest – e.g. training v. production
- Lack of confidence
- Having to present an uninteresting topic in an interesting way
- Handling awkward trainees
- People not wanting to learn – having to try to encourage them
- Sustaining interest
- Establishing a base level of knowledge
- Lack of materials
- Shortage or over-abundance of time
- Distractions (trains, cars, environment)
- Pressure of work.

What you have done is go through a set procedure for tackling a topic, designed to broaden ideas and understanding of what is involved. This set procedure we have called *keys to understanding*. A valid question is: why follow this set procedure?

Why have keys to understanding?

Many jobs in the past were competently done using procedures that could be rote learned. This meant that memorizing and practising were the major ways of learning. The changes which are occurring today mean that far more understanding is required of the implications and effects of one's actions. With increased mechanization and automation, job responsibilities are increasing and safety and quality factors demand a greater awareness and understanding of what is going on. Procedural learning still plays its part, but the need to understand is increasingly important.

Understanding is a different form of mental activity from memorizing. It involves linking, transfer and association; so that, for example, if we need to carry out the following:

- Changing a belief or attitude
- Reorganizing data
- Reviewing or assessing
- Taking a decision
- Making a plan
- Forming a hypothesis
- Solving a problem

then we also need to exercise understanding. Developing a greater degree of understanding can be helped by using certain 'keys', which are designed to increase our database by generating a large body of ideas.

We have called the approaches 'keys' because each gives entry to some understanding, although all of them may not be relevant for every occasion. Most involve ways of questioning either the person's own knowledge or experience, or that of other people. Some of the more important keys are listed later.

If you wish to ask questions based on the keys it is helpful to ask them in a particular order so that ideas are first broadly expanded before narrowing down to specific details. After clarifying what one wishes to understand by means of a purpose or definition question, comparisons and viewpoints questions begin to broaden people's ideas. Questions about problems help to develop understanding of issues which need to be tackled; however, they can limit ideas if introduced too early. Having identified problems, ways of overcoming them need to be found, and this leads to specific action planning.

The four keys which are primarily used, and which form the previous example on understanding, are:

1 *Purposes*: thinking of the purposes of what one wishes to understand. To do so, be prepared to define and describe what needs to be understood.
2 *Comparisons*: comparing and contrasting with other experiences to identify similarities and differences.
3 *Viewpoints*: imagining things from other directions, or from others' viewpoints.
4 *Problems*: thinking of all the problems associated with what you want to understand. What could go wrong?

Some reference has already been made to the problem of error and memorizing and the advantages of error in developing understanding. This is amplified in the next section.

The Role of Error

A crucial distinction between memorizing and understanding is that error should be avoided in memorizing wherever possible and, if occurring, should be corrected as soon as possible. Error in understanding, on the other hand, helps expand understanding, and from that point of view should not be avoided.

The identification of error is important in both, for without that, mistakes in memorizing will be imprinted, and in understanding, unidentified errors will not help further the understanding and may well distort reasoning.

- In memorizing, fair copies and self-testing are two aids which can avoid or quickly identify and rectify error.
- In understanding, it may sometimes be necessary for the trainer to point out an error has been made, but without spelling out what the error was, or how to deal with it. The danger of the trainer saying how to deal with error is that the responsibility for learning has been transferred back to the trainer and the learner is more likely to take the passive, subservient role which lies at the root of much bad learning experience.

This important aspect of error can be seen in a small example. If we take the statement, 'The sea is blue', we might say 'Not always'. If we say, 'The sea is as likely to be red as blue', then we have gone beyond the parameters of likelihood; in other words, into error. But we have established, in doing so, the important concept that the statement, 'The sea is blue', is seldom accurate, although the sea is far more likely to be nearer to blue-greys than to reds.

A common way of testing error is to ask (for this example), 'Under what circumstances might the sea be red?'. If the answer is 'Never', then it is a definite error. There may, however, be examples where the sea might be seen as red in colour, at which point concepts have been increased.

None of this important process in the learner would be likely if the trainer had told the learner that sea colour varied from greys to greens to greeny-blue, with some interesting variations at times like sunset and sunrise. This would most probably be accepted without surmise – in other words, the learner passively accepts what he or she is told; the antithesis of what this chapter is about.

The Training Method

So far, blockages to learning have been illustrated, the MUD taxonomy has been demonstrated and its constituent parts discussed and amplified.

Developing learning skills, however, requires a particular form of training method which is different from much conventional training, as already described in the example of the key to understanding of comparing and contrasting. A great deal of the method will undoubtedly be familiar, but there are two aspects which should be described here:

(1) *Pair working*: in one of the researches it was found that people learned naturally by discussing with others their ideas and concepts, and obtaining ideas and information in return. This cooperation in learning extends to any topic requiring understanding, such as identifying and solving problems and planning. As one respondent said, 'learning is a social activity.'

This is the basis for dividing a learning group into pairs; people working together tend to develop more concepts than working on their own. At the same time people find it less stressful, as it removes the onus from the individual, but not his or her responsibility for participation.

(2) *Ponder periods*: these are introduced after periods of learning and at the end of each training day. Learners are asked to think about what they have learned and note this down on a worksheet. This follows the Kolb learning cycle, which postulates experience – reflection – development of concepts – testing in experiments – leads to further experience and so on, as the way in which we learn conceptually.

If the ponder period, or reflection, is omitted by the trainer, then learning is often not consolidated and is submerged by subsequent learning experiences.

The following notes on a process for encouraging active learning and understanding summarize the major points of the training methods needed.

A process for encouraging active learning and understanding in a group

The method involves:

1 First, explaining both the purpose of the exercise and also that a special procedure will be used to ensure that all views are heard and recorded.
2 Listening before giving information.
3 Asking a question or questions which are neutral, do not lead and have been carefully constructed to develop understanding.
4 Pairing people to discuss each question. This generates more ideas and ensures that each individual can develop ideas and share them in a non-threatening way. The pairs use worksheets in order to clarify their ideas in writing, but these worksheets are not collected or the pairs identified.
5 Asking each pair in turn to state one of their ideas, until all ideas have been said. All ideas are written on flip charts, which is highly motivating to participants as it acknowledges the importance of their views. This record of all the ideas can be typed up without being modified and given back to the group as a whole.
6 No evaluation is made, either positively or negatively, at this time. Where,

however, the ideas are not clear then further explanation or clarification should be asked for.

7 The recording on the flip chart is done personally by the trainer or supervisor running the session. This is important to ensure that the trainer is seen to be fully committed to the process of listening to the ideas and recording them.

8 When every point has been collected, which may involve going back to each pair several times, a number of things can be done. If appropriate, the ideas can be reviewed or grouped. A handout can then be provided by the trainer, and the group can be asked to compare and contrast the two lists. The workshop leader can then discuss any new points that have arisen. On other occasions, where two questions are being addressed, it might be best to collect the answers to both before distributing handouts and entering into discussion.

9 The methods must be kept to, namely:
   (a) Pair working
   (b) Acceptance and recording of all points *without evaluation*, although clarification can take place
   (c) Systematic and disciplined collection of responses from all the pairs
   (d) No discussion of the ideas until the above requirements have been met; however, time must be allowed for discussion afterwards
   (e) Input from the group leader and any handouts always follow responses from the group
   (f) Where action would logically follow, action plans should be developed.

Initially the people involved may be suspicious if they are not used to being asked to contribute in this way. It is therefore important to emphasize that their written notes will not be collected nor their comments identified, as the typed-up flip charts represent the views expressed by the entire group. No assessment is involved, as the process is to help share views and understanding and to clarify issues so that they can be dealt with.

Exercises to relate method to objectives

Below are given three training objectives in developing skilled learners; try filling in the centre with the training behaviours you would consider necessary to move learners from the left-hand to the right-hand side:

1 *How trainers can encourage confidence and responsibility*

Some learners arrive with:	Behaviours of trainers which help:	The learners should leave with:
Bad experiences of learning		Greater self-confidence

Some learners arrive with:	Behaviours of trainers which help:	The learners should leave with:
Expectations of passivity		Sense of responsibility
Expectations of boredom and disinterest		Involvement and commitment
Fears and self-consciousness		Sense of pride in themselves

2 How trainers can promote active learning

The learners arrive with:	Behaviours of trainers which help:	The learners should leave with:
Previous knowledge		An enlarged database
Skills		Ability to transfer and apply new learning
Attitudes		
Experience		Greater autonomy

3 How trainers can encourage change

Some learners arrive with:	Behaviours of trainers which help:	The learners should leave with:
Apathy		An intention to do something
Cynicism		An understanding of why they are doing it
Disbelief		
Frustrations		A renewed belief in themselves, their management and the company

Compare your answers with those in the following examples.

1 How trainers can encourage confidence and responsibility

Some learners arrive with:	The trainer helps by:	The learners should leave with:
Bad experiences of learning	Listening without comment	Greater self-confidence
Expectations of passivity	Recording accurately what is said	Sense of responsibility

Some learners arrive with:	Behaviours of trainers which help:	The learners should leave with:
Expectations of boredom and disinterest	Phrasing questions which make people search their minds for relevant experiences	Involvement and commitment
Fears and self-consciousness		Sense of pride in themselves
	Arranging for people to work in pairs in order to exchange ideas and solve problems	
	Showing that everyone's ideas are valued by collecting information systematicaly	
	Allowing people to check their own work and identify their own misconceptions against other people's ideas	
	Not scoring, ranking, assessing or encouraging a competitive atmosphere	
	Demonstrating that he or she is sharing in learning by learning from the trainees	

2 How trainers can promote active learning

The learners arrive with:	The trainer helps by asking the learners:	The learners should leave with:
Previous knowledge		
Skills	For ideas before giving information	An enlarged database
Attitudes	To clarify their ideas by having to record them	Ability to transfer and apply new learning
Experience		Greater autonomy
	To think of what they have learned	

Some learners arrive with:	Behaviours of trainers which help:	The learners should leave with:
	To think how they might apply the learning	
	To think about purposes and problems	
	To think about things from different viewpoints	
	To compare and contrast	
	To think of ways to check their ideas	

3 How trainers can encourage change

Some learners arrive with:	The trainer helps by:	The learners should leave with:
Apathy	leading learners towards defining their own relevant and realistic actions	An intention to do something
Cynicism		An understanding of why they are doing it
Disbelief		
Frustrations	Encouraging shared group understanding, impetus and support towards carrying out the necessary actions	A renewed belief in themselves, their management and the company
	Ensuring that people have the knowledge and skills to carry out their action plans	
	Ensuring that people have the necessary authority and management support to carry out their action plans	
	Where people do not have the necessary authority, ensuring that managers take on this responsibility	

In some circumstances, you may be already behaving in such ways. In some, you may disagree with the concepts. If this occurs, ask yourself if you are teaching product or if you are trying to improve the autonomy, responsibility and learning skills of the learner while they learn product. It is a profoundly different training position which is indicated in the following summary of key points and in the section on ways of evaluating training material to assess its compatibility with active learning.

Summary of key points

1 Learning can be seen as the relationship between the processes we use in order to learn and the material or product which we intend to learn.
2 The processes, or skills of learning, can be grouped in terms of difference in the product to be learned. These differences relate to factual material, concepts and physical skills. (memorizing – understanding – doing, giving the mnemonic 'MUD').
3 Skills of learning can be identified, learned and practised; for example, memorizing strategies and ways of questioning.
4 For learning skills to be used appropriately and deliberately, they have to be made overt.
5 For learning skills to be improved, people have to take responsibility for their own learning, which involves pursuing actively the learning skills associated with a particular product.
6 The learning environment must be appropriate and encouraging. People have to be encouraged to ask questions and check themselves, while feedback should be both relevant and realistic.
7 While error should be avoided in relation to learning facts or physical skills, it is a valuable aid to understanding something.
8 There are blockages which hinder learning. It is necessary to identify those which affect us or are within us. It is equally important to identify blockages we are creating in other people, so that remedies can be applied and learning improved.
9 Everyone can learn, and everyone can be helped to improve her or his ways of learning.

Ways of evaluating training material to assess its compatibility with active learning

Criteria:	Notes and methods:
1 Concepts are developed by the learners, not always given in advance.	• Learners are given an opportunity to examine/solve problems in order to develop concepts.

Criteria:	*Notes and methods:*
	• Learners are asked to think or reflect on their experience in order to develop principles (especially when working in pairs).
	• Learners experience something before learning the theory.
2 Learners are given maximum opportunities to transfer what they have learned to new situations.	• Learners are asked where else this might apply.
	• Learners are asked to compare and contrast with other situations.
3 Learners are given maximum opportunities to seek information for themselves.	• Directed assignments
	• Fact-finding exercises
4 Material essential for memorizing is clearly marked in the text.	• A range of suitable memorizing methods is indicated.
	• Errors are minimized when material needs to be memorized.
5 Errors are used by trainers to aid understanding (may not be applicable to all aspects of a module).	• Simulated problems are used to encourage the type of errors which aid understanding.
6 Learners are given maximum opportunity to check their learning.	• Learners are asked to devise a quiz to test each other.
	• Learners are asked to assess their own work, or give feedback to others.
	• Self-testing cards
7 Learners are given maximum opportunity to review and consolidate their learning.	• There are ponder or review sessions at regular and appropriate intervals.
	• Learners are given problems to solve which require use of all the previous material in the module.
8 Modules allow for individual differences in the learners.	• A range of optional material is available for use with quicker learners.
	• Trainer checks each learner's starting point at beginning of module.
	• Trainer assesses the need for unlearning as well as new learning.

Criteria:	*Notes and methods:*
9 Jargon/technical terms are avoided until explained to the learners.	● Provide checklists of terms or abbreviations to be memorized or referred to. ● Encourage learners to ask regularly which terms they are not clear about.
10 Passive review/revision of material is avoided.	● Ask learners to teach aspects of the task in order to revise/consolidate. ● Ask learners to summarize (possibly in pairs) rather than the trainer summarizing for them.
11 Learners are made aware of what is usually expected of them at each stage of learning within the module.	● Learners are told the normal level of performance by learners at stages toward the overall objective of the module (or part). ● Trainer allows reviews/discussion of how all the learning within a module is coming together.

Summary

The researches on which this chapter is based showed that a number of people of different levels of achievement and ability could be helped to become better learners, actively involved in the process and taking responsibility for their own learning. For this to happen, the training methods have to change from imparting knowledge to facilitating learning. Obviously, some imparting of knowledge has to occur, but a great deal of this tends to be factual material. The role of a trainer is in developing understanding of the relationship between facts and their significance and not the transmission of the facts themselves. Facts are, more often than not, best transmitted by means of printed sheets, publications and so on.

Frequently, learners have shown that they are familiar with a subject. In considering safety, for example, groups were asked to say what they saw as the purpose of a safety policy, having been given background information to compare and contrast safety in their own company with safety in other organizations; identify problems arising from their increased understanding of safety; and finally, say what they could do about improving safety and overcoming the stated problems. In all cases, what input there was followed the responses from the groups and generally merely reinforced what had been said. The same approach was used with groups considering changing working practices and quality. If, therefore, people are allowed first to say what they know and develop understanding about a topic, then the trainer can identify what, if any, further input is needed and in what form.

As described earlier, the change in the role of the trainer also involves changes in the training method. Worksheets are extensively used for participants to note down their ideas stimulated by the structured series of 'keys to understanding' questions. Participants also frequently work in pairs in order to gain from each other, a process that culminates in total group responses to the questions on each worksheet. The approach has been used in large companies and has had the effect of changing relationships between management and the workforce; getting workforces to practise the initiative, adaptability and responsibility of which they are capable; and forming effective and integrated working groups.

At the same time, the approach can backfire if it is misused to try to sell ideas; if decisions have already been made which the sessions pretend to identify; or if they are used merely to transmit information. Equally, the actions which are generated by the approach fall into the categories of those the individual participants should carry out and those which should be referred to management for processing. If management seem uninterested in the actions agreed as necessary by the individuals or are not seen to process the referred actions, then the result is often increased frustrations and cynicism throughout the workforce.

Management and trainers therefore have to work in partnership to achieve the effective changes the approach can offer. Sessions require careful planning and design and management should be involved throughout. The time and effort involved are considerable and continuing, but the end result of developing and using learning skills is a more involved, participative and responsible workforce, which is one of the keys to a more effective and productive economy.

Further reading

Downs, S. (1987) Developing Learning Skills. in M. E. Cheren (ed.), *Learning Management: Emerging Directions for Learning to Learn in the Workplace*, Columbus, Ohio: ERIC National Center for Research in Vocational Education.

Downs, S. and Perry, P. (1981) *How Do I Learn?* London: FEU PR9.

Downs, S. and Perry, P. (1984) *Developing Skilled Learners: Learning to Learn in the Y.T.S.* Sheffield: Manpower Services Commission.

Downs, S. and Perry, P. (1987) *Helping Adults to Become Better Learners.* Sheffield: Manpower Services Commission.

5
Objectives and Evaluation

GILL SANDERSON

---

*If a man will begin with certainties he shall
end in doubts but if he will be content to
begin with doubts he shall end in certainties.*

Francis Bacon, 1605

Introduction

In planning a training or learning programme there are four fundamental
questions a trainer needs to pose:

- What is the purpose of the training?
- What is it that needs to be learned?
- What experiences should be provided in order to meet this need and how
  should they be organized?
- How can the total effects of the training be determined?

These are questions about needs, objectives, training design and
evaluation.

The first two questions need to be answered before the training can be
designed. If the aims and objectives do not reflect the needs then,
however well delivered, the training is unlikely to be successful. The last
question also needs to be answered in advance. Unless we plan what and
how we are going to evaluate, it is unlikely that we will be able to collect
the right data at the right time, and opportunities to improve both
ongoing and future training will be missed.

Objectives

The first essential is to re-examine why the training was thought necessary. Are the training needs clear and is training the best or only solution to the problem which is presented?

To look at an example: a national company with a high intake of graduates instigated a series of courses to counteract the low morale of this group. The graduates were doing routine tasks and had little responsibility and poor prospects of promotion. Turnover was not high because there were few alternative jobs in their field. Management was aware of these problems but hoped to alleviate them by demonstrating concern. Subsequent to the training (which was rated as highly successful by the participants), morale improved at first. But some months later it was lower than ever before, and turnover increased. The real problem was that the graduates were doing jobs more appropriate to technicians. The courses raised morale temporarily but exacerbated the situation in the longer term. The residential training had resulted in the graduates making contact with each other and establishing a network with shared frustrations, which were reinforced by the realization that others felt the same. It was eventually decided to recruit more technicians, not graduates, and to change the job description of the remaining graduates. The training solution delayed tackling the real problems.

Given that the needs have been established by a thorough analysis and that training is an appropriate solution, the next step is to translate the needs into aims and then objectives. The process of formulating aims is the opportunity for the training designer to capture the essential purpose of the training. Aims provide a starting point, a direction in which to go, however broad. Aims encapsulate the aspirations of the training and should help to shape and limit the objectives. Checking objectives against a well-stated aim can ensure that the spirit of the intent has not been lost or trivialized. The business of deciding an aim can itself be of value in clarifying for the trainer – and others – what is to be done and why.

The process of deciding whether the objectives of a training programme are realistically based on an accurate initial identification of training needs is *external validation*. Worthwhile evaluation may be more related to the purpose of training than to the achievement of specific objectives. It is quite possible for a training event to meet the objectives but fail in its overall purpose. For example, a training programme in a steelworks had the objective of enabling foremen to complete the company vacancy form accurately. At the end of training it was clear that foremen could meet this objective. However, no improvement in the completion of actual forms was noted. Eventually it was realized that the forms were completed by managers. The aim – of improving vacancy reporting – was not met, but the objectives were.

Why do we need objectives?

Objectives provide goals. They are the starting point for training design, giving a rationale for selecting methods and content. They are an aid to design, not a strait-jacket. From the learners' point of view, if they are aware of the objectives they have greater ownership of the learning process and can organize and direct their activities effectively. Empirical evidence suggests that where learners can control their own learning, making objectives available decreases learning time very significantly – by up to two-thirds.

All too often we trainers finish running an event with no real knowledge of how the participants are different as a result of training. What idea we do have is often gleaned by accident, perhaps from the content of a question that reveals that the learner does not know what we thought we had imparted. The learners also may have little idea and no confirmation of their new knowledge and skills. If learners are tested against clear objectives then we have a means of validating training and of assessing and giving feedback to learners on their performance.

Internal validation is a series of tests and measurements designed to ascertain whether a training programme has met the specified behavioural objectives. The sense of achievement gained by both learners and trainers from the experience of being assessed and receiving constructive feedback can be enormous. Unfortunately we often require learners to practise skills or display knowledge but do not give back adequate detailed assessment, either norm-referenced or criterion-referenced. What assessment we do give is often part of the course rather than an end process of achievement recognition. The knowledge that each participant is required to carry out a demonstration, conduct an appraisal, complete a questionnaire and so on itself focuses on and increases learning.

An objective communicates the goals of the programme to both the learner and the trainer. It provides a basis for evaluating and improving the learner, the trainer and the training.

What is it that needs to be learned?

When asked to formulate objectives for a training session it is not uncommon for a trainer to list the topics of the course or to tell you what he or she is going to do: for instance, 'identify the role of the supervisor', or 'provide opportunity to practise appraisal skills'. Both these responses are routes, not goals. The former tells you the contents of the course, and the latter identifies the process. The trainer is telling you his or her goals, not the learning objectives. Such statements tell us nothing about the outcomes of the course – we need to know how the learner will be different as a result of training. An objective describes the desired outcome of a training event, not the route.

Stung by these criticisms the trainer may then inform you that, by the end of the course, the learner will 'appreciate how to appraise staff', or 'understand fault-finding on the XYZ machine', or 'know how to lay out a letter'. But what exactly do these statements mean in terms of what the learners should be able to *do*? Should they be able to write an essay about appraisal or should they be able to conduct an appraisal? How well should they be able to conduct one? The issue of how to formulate useful, clear objectives was addressed by Robert Tyler in the 1940s and 1950s, by Miller in the early 1960s and by many others; but by far the greatest impact was made by Robert Mager whose book, published in 1962 and revised in 1975, tackled how to write objectives. This and successive books by Mager are short, practical and entertaining and have had an enormous influence out of all proportion to their size.

Mager-type behavioural objectives

The behaviour component

Mager was concerned with clarity and communication. Useful objectives are ones which enable all involved to be in agreement about the behaviour required of successful learners. Words commonly used in objectives such as 'know', 'understand' and 'appreciate' describe mental operations which cannot be observed, but have to be inferred from behaviour. We need to describe the activities which demonstrate understanding and appreciation, using words which are open to few interpretations.

Words open to many interpretations:	*Words open to fewer interpretations:*	
To be aware of	To solve	To operate
To know	To compare	To label
To understand	To construct	To recite
To appreciate	To write	To point to
To believe	To list	To repair
To comprehend	To select	To identify

The behavioural component of an objective describes, in clear terms, what a learner has to do to demonstrate successful learning. Mager called this the *terminal behaviour*.

The conditions component

It is not sufficient to describe the terminal behaviour of the learners. We need to state the conditions or limitations under which they perform. If a soldier has to dismantle a gun, do we want him or her to follow a particular method? Should he or she be able to dismantle a range of weapons? Does he or she need to do this with or without a manual? Under battle conditions or in the relative peace of a training room? In darkness? Prone or upright? It may be of little use assessing a soldier's ability to maintain equipment in a well-lit, quiet environment with the help of a manual if he or she has to use the skill prone, in total darkness, in the heat of battle.

In order to be clear an objective may need to specify any tools or equipment available to aid the task, or the range of problems to be solved or equipment to be mastered. If it is desired that the learners use a particular method then this should be stated, together with any special requirements about place. Examples of conditions are:

- 'Without help'
- 'Using a calculator'
- 'Given a standard toolkit'
- 'Given a list of'
- 'In darkness'
- 'Lying in the prone position'
- 'Using any model of electric typewriter'.

The criterion component

The criterion provides the standard of performance; that is, it tells us how well the learner has to do to be considered successful. The standard can be concerned with speed, quality or accuracy. Quality can be conveyed by specifying how many questions, problems or tasks have to be answered, solved or completed correctly. Where 'correctness' is not obvious, we need to specify what is meant. This can be done by referring to a manufacturer's specification or a checklist identifying the key parts or sequence of competent performance, or by providing a template and an indication of how far the learner can deviate from this. Examples of criteria are:

- 'Within five mintues'
- 'Accurate to + or − 3 cm'
- 'According to the company specifications'
- '80 per cent of the technical terms to be spelled correctly'
- 'No more than two incorrect entries per page'
- 'According to the criteria on page 3'
- 'To the nearest whole number'

There is no need to specify conditions and criteria beyond the point at which the intent is clear. Mager suggests that the test of an objective is this: 'Can another competent person select successful learners in terms of the objectives so that you, the objective writer, agree with the selections?'. If the answer is yes, then the objective is sufficiently defined.

Problems in using Mager-style objectives

Most jobs are complex: the time and effort spent in reducing skilled performance to a set of specific objectives can be enormous. One educational programme had over 10,000 objectives. A solution is to focus on using objectives only for key areas of training – where the training is of critical importance or where trainees find a skill or knowledge particularly difficult to master. This is the 80/20 rule: put 80 per cent of effort into the crucial 20 per cent of the programme. Another problem is posed by complex, open-ended jobs such as management, where it is difficult to formulate precise standards or statements of desired behaviour.

But do we always need to produce the detailed specifications of performance recommended by Mager? Educational research reported by Ivor Davies (1976) suggests that objectives are effective in promoting learning but that specific behavioural objectives are not more effective than general objectives. The essential element is the action verb.

Process skills such as selling or responding appropriately to telephone enquiries cannot be reduced to a simple statement of the activity without losing the key features of effective performance. A solution to this problem has been proposed; instead of specifying the precise behaviour of the learner, the objective of the behaviour can be described. For example, the objectives of behaviour for a sales representative informing a customer that the goods ordered are not available and that a substitution has been made are:

- Reassure the customer that everything is going according to plan and that he or she will receive a product that will do the job equally well or better.
- Convince the customer that he or she is valued and receiving special treatment.
- After completing the sale, reassure the customer that he or she has made the right decision.

This approach is called behaviour modelling and is based on eliciting the key behaviours and the sequence of behaviours shown by particularly competent employees.

A last solution to the problem of writing objectives is not to! If we have access to a 'bank' of ready-made objectives, designed and agreed by groups who represent the occupational area, then we have objectives which have authority, make comparisons possible and, if we wish, may be useful to accredit individuals and to evaluate different routes to competence.

The national standards programme

In 1986 the government launched a programme which aimed to establish national standards for all occupations in the United Kingdom by 1992. Standards are developed by lead industry bodies (LIBs) which represent tbe industry or occupational area and have the standing and authority necessary to consult, establish best practice and commission developmental work. Occupations such as management, training and clerical/administration span most employment sectors and their LIBs are drawn from industry, commerce, public service, training organizations, trade unions and the education sector.

Structure of standards
The standards are developed by functional analysis. The key functions in an occupational area are disaggregated to produce *units of competence*. The units are in turn analysed to generate *elements of competence*. Elements, together with performance criteria and range indicators, define the outcomes expected of a competent performer in the role (see figure 5.1 for the units of competence for trainers and figure 5.2 for a breakdown of one of the three elements of unit C21, showing

performance criteria and range indicators). Competence, incidentally, is much more than the ability to perform tasks. It incorporates the skills needed to manage the unpredictable, prioritize, integrate tasks and manage relationships with others. These are more fully described under the headings of task skills, task and contingency management skills and role skills.

The standards have many potential uses. They are a basis for job descriptions, recruitment and selection, accreditation. For our purposes standards provide:

● A basis for objectives
● A basis for validation and evaluation
● A measure of individual progress.

The standards programme is the basis for national vocational qualifications. As competence is about performing real work roles, work-based assessment is a central part of the model. Candidates are assessed in the workplace, carrying out their normal work roles, against the performance criteria under standardized conditions determined by an awarding body.

The standards may be translated into objectives for the training required to enable individuals to reach competence. They also provide a vehicle for identifying training needs and for evaluating training.

Levels of objectives

So far, objectives has been described as if we are concerned solely with the point in time at which training ceases; that is, the behaviour we want the learner to demonstrate at the end of training. But objectives may be set for behaviour both before and after this point.

Most skills are complex and depend on the acquisition of subordinate knowledge and skills. If the learners need to be able to change a wheel on a vehicle, they have to have safety knowledge, be able to select and use a variety of tools, check tyres for tread type and depth, interpret tyre pressure charts and so on. If they need to read charts, then numeracy and reading skills will be required. We may need to design subordinate objectives appropriate to each stage of learning. But perhaps more importantly, we need to be able to discriminate between subordinate and final objectives. A common problem in the process of deciding objectives is to be overwhelmed by their sheer numbers, or to find that they describe trivial behaviours. This is often because the designer has not realised that he or she is formulating objectives for skills and

Figure 5.1   National standards for training and development
Reproduced with the permission of the Training and Development lead body

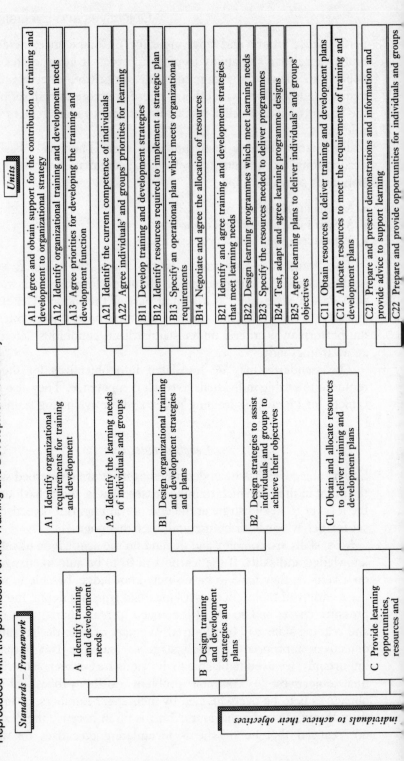

Standards – Framework

Units

A1   Identify organizational requirements for training and development

- A11   Agree and obtain support for the contribution of training and development to organizational strategy
- A12   Identify organizational training and development needs
- A13   Agree priorities for developing the training and development function

A2   Identify the learning needs of individuals and groups

- A21   Identify the current competence of individuals
- A22   Agree individuals' and groups' priorities for learning

B1   Design organizational training and development strategies and plans

- B11   Develop training and development strategies
- B12   Identify resources required to implement a strategic plan
- B13   Specify an operational plan which meets organizational requirements
- B14   Negotiate and agree the allocation of resources

B2   Design strategies to assist individuals and groups to achieve their objectives

- B21   Identify and agree training and development strategies that meet learning needs
- B22   Design learning programmes which meet learning needs
- B23   Specify the resources needed to deliver programmes
- B24   Test, adapt and agree learning programme designs
- B25   Agree learning plans to deliver individuals' and groups' objectives

C1   Obtain and allocate resources to deliver training and development plans

- C11   Obtain resources to deliver training and development plans
- C12   Allocate resources to meet the requirements of training and development plans

- C21   Prepare and present demonstrations and information and provide advice to support learning
- C22   Prepare and provide opportunities for individuals and groups

A   Identify training and development needs

B   Design training and development strategies and plans

C   Provide learning opportunities, resources and ... individuals to achieve their objectives

Develop human potential to assist organizat...

C2 Provide learning opportunities and support to enable individuals and groups to achieve their objectives

- ... to manage their own learning
- C24 Prepare and provide technology-dependent learning resources to support individual and group learning
- C25 Coordinate the preparation and delivery of learning opportunities
- C26 Assist and support the application of learning
- C27 Originate learning support materials

D Evaluate the effectiveness of training and development

D1 Evaluate the effectiveness of training and development

- D11 Plan and set up systems for evaluating the training and development function
- D12 Evaluate the training and development function
- D13 Modify systems and practices to improve training and development

D2 Evaluate individual and group achievements against objectives

- D21 Plan and set up systems to evaluate the achievement of objects
- D22 Evaluate the achievement of outcomes against learning objectives
- D23 Modify and adapt learning plans

D3 Assess achievements for public certification

- D31 Assess candidate performance
- D32 Assess candidate using diverse evidence
- D33 Coordinate the assessment process
- D34 Verify the assessment process
- D35 Identify previously acquired competence

E Support training and development advances and practice

E1 Contribute to advances in training and development

- E11 Contribute to training and development practice
- E12 Evaluate and disseminate advances in training and development

E2 Provide services to support training and development practice

- E21 Administer training facilities
- E22 Establish and maintain information systems
- E23 Establish and maintain financial systems

C212 Present information to groups of trainees ————

The element describes what people are expected to be able to do in terms of the results needed in employment.

a Information is clear and accurate and presented in a tone, manner, pace and style appropriate to the needs and capabilities of trainees.

b Visual support materials are legible, accurate and used in a manner which enhances the clarity of the information presented.

c Trainees are encouraged to ask questions, seek clarification and make comments at identified and appropriate stages in the presentation.

d Clear and accurate supplementary and summary information is provided on request and where appropriate to reinforce key learning points.

e Visual aid equipment is regularly maintained and fit for use when required.

Performance criteria are the critical indicators by which you would tell that someone is performing competently. They describe the outcomes you would expect a competent person to achieve. They are needed to assess performance evidence.

Range indicators ————

Type of information: principles/theories, factual information, analysis/evaluation

Presentation mode: one to small group with potential interaction, one to large group with limited or no interaction (e.g. conference/lecture)

Visual aid equipment/type: projection systems (overhead projectors (pre-prepared and written *in situ*), slide projectors), non-projected display systems (flip chart, white/blackboard, magnetic boards – pre-prepared and written *in situ*)

Range indicators define the range of applications the element has: i.e. the types of relationships, resources, methods, processes and locations for which achievement of the specified outcomes is required.

Figure 5.2   One of the three elements of unit C21
Reproduced with the permission of the Training and Development lead body

knowledge that need to be mastered before the terminal behaviour can be achieved. Possibly not all these subordinate objectives need to be identified.

We also need to bear in mind that the performance of a learner at the end of training will usually fall far short of that of an experienced worker. Practice and experience are needed to develop skills. It is useful to set objectives, not only for the performance at the end of training, but also in relation to on-the-job performance and for the desired change in the organization:

● Subordinate objectives – the knowledge, skills and attitudes (KSAs) desired at key stages in the training

- Immediate objectives – the KSAs desired at the end of training
- Intermediate objectives – the desired changes in the learner's work behaviour
- Ultimate objectives – the desired changes in the organization.

The elements of competence and performance criteria generated by the standards programme provide an example of intermediate objectives. The last three levels of objectives, suggested by Warr, Bird and Rackham 1970, will be referred to in the next section, where they are a key reference point for evaluation.

Evaluation

The ultimate purpose of training is to improve the efficiency or the effectiveness of the organization. Evaluation is concerned with measuring how far training has achieved these goals. Earlier in the chapter internal validation was defined as 'a series of tests and measurements designed to ascertain whether a training programme has met the specified behavioural objectives'. External validation was defined as 'the process of deciding whether the behavioural objectives of a training programme are realistically based on an accurate initial identification of training needs'.

How does evaluation fit with these constructs? Internal validation is the process of deciding what you are getting and external validation is establishing whether it is what you wanted. Evaluation embraces both of these processes plus deciding what good the training is doing and whether or not you were right to want it in the first place. It is about the total effects of training. It would be quite possible for a training event to have objectives which reflected needs and to be successful in meeting immediate objectives, but for the contribution to the organization to be negligible. Further, where training has positive benefits to the organization, it is quite conceivable that the cost of training could exceed the value of the benefits accrued to the organization. Evaluation is the process of obtaining and weighing all the evidence about the effects of training and processes such as identifying training needs or objective setting. It is the systematic collection and analysis of information necessary to make effective decisions related to the selection, adoption, design, modification and value of a training programme.

The pros and cons of evaluation

Most writers on evaluation bemoan how little is done and exhort trainers to do more. Why is it that trainers are so reluctant to undertake evaluation? Commonly expressed reasons are:

- Evaluation is unnecessary. The beneficial effects of training are obvious.
- Evaluation is threatening. It may reveal inadequacies in trainers or that training is ineffective.
- Only rigorous and scientific evaluation is worthwhile. Such approaches are difficult or impossible to implement in real-life situations.
- Trainers lack the knowledge, skills and incentives to evaluate.
- End-of-course reaction sheets are sufficient and their contents demonstrate that training is effective.
- Evaluation will use scarce resources needed for the prime task of training.
- Evaluation would involve line managers and other non-training staff. It is difficult to get their support and cooperation.

There is some truth in many of these statements, so why continue?

There is a trend in our society towards increased accountability and quality assurance; can we continue to justify the expenditure of training budgets without convincing evidence of the contribution made to the organization? Training will be evaluated by management with or without systematic evidence. Every time a training budget is set, judgements have been made about relative worth and value. The low priority given to training by many organizations suggests that trainers may convince themselves, but do not succeed in convincing management, of the value of training and development.

The Cooper and Lybrand report 'Challenge to Complacency' (1985), commissioned by the government states:

> Few employers think training sufficiently central to their business for it to be a major component in their corporate strategy; the great majority didn't see it as an issue of major importance . . . this complacency was reinforced by a widespread ignorance among top management of how their company's performance in training compared with that of their competitors . . . a high proportion of senior executives . . . had only a limited knowledge of the scale of resources devoted to training within their own company . . . training [is] rarely seen as an investment but as an overhead . . . few companies said that they saw a direct link from training activities to profitability.

Trainers need to acquire facts and figures to market and sell their activities within their own organizations. A more comprehensive set of reasons for evaluation is as follows:

- To determine whether the objectives of training were met
- To determine whether the objectives of training were the right ones
- To improve current and future programmes
- To improve trainers
- To establish the cost effectiveness or cost benefit of programmes

- To establish the contribution of the training function
- To provide marketing data
- To determine unmet training needs.

So how can we reconcile the benefits of evaluation with the drawbacks? Perhaps one issue should be about using evaluation selectively. If a training programme is a one-off, there may be little to be gained unless the programme is expensive and of long duration. If an extensive, high-cost series of events is planned there may be great benefit in attempting evaluation. The type and extent of evaluation will depend upon the purpose: if our intent is to market training to managers, it may be sufficient to collect the opinions of managers who attended previous events.

What should be evaluated?

Kirkpatrick (1976) put forward a conceptual framework suggesting four levels of criteria:

1 *Reaction:* the participants' opinion of the materials, facilities, methods, content, trainers, duration and relevance of the programme
2 *Learning:* the skills, knowledge and attitudes (KSAs) learned during the programme
3 *Behaviour:* the change in on-the-job performance which can be attributed to the programme
4 *Results:* the effect on the organization of the changes in behaviour, such as cost savings, quality improvements, increases in output.

Other theorists have suggested models which are essentially similar to Kirkpatricks's but a rather different approach was suggested by Warr, Bird and Rackham (1970). They also had four levels, the first letters of which form the acronym CIRO:

1 Context evaluation
2 Input evaluation
3 Reaction evaluation
4 Outcome evaluation

Reaction evaluation has the same meaning for both Kirkpatrick and CIRO. Outcome evaluation is subdivided into three levels, corresponding to Kirkpatrick's last three levels. Context evaluation is about obtaining and using information on the operational situation in order to decide training needs and objectives. Objectives can be set at three levels; *immediate*, which concern the KSAs desired at the end of training;

intermediate, relating to changes in job performance; and *ultimate*, which are the desired changes in the organization. Input evaluation concerns making judgements about the alternative inputs to training.

This view of evaluation is a much broader one than Kirkpatrick's and encourages us to see evaluation as a continuous process, starting with identifying training needs and closely interwoven with the training process. An adaptation of their model is shown in the following list, suggesting the key questions the evaluator needs to pose at each level of evaluation.

1 Context evaluation: what needs to be changed?
  Is a training solution appropriate?
  Are the objectives the right ones?
  Do they relate to the training needs analysis (TNA)?
  Is the TNA acceptable?
  Are the objectives clear, achievable and measurable?
  How will we measure immediate, intermediate and ultimate objectives?
2 Input evaluation: what procedures are most likely to bring about change?
  How much time is available?
  What are the relative merits of different training methods?
  What were the results of previous similar courses?
  Should you use an external training organization?
  What should be the content, and what evidence is there to support the choices made?
  Does the content reflect the objectives?
3 Reaction evaluation: what are the trainees' opinions of the training?
  Should there be an end-of-course paper and pencil review or follow-up?
  Should these be anonymous?
  Should there be evaluation of each session as well as at the end of the course?
  Should you use a rating scale or questionnaire?
  Should you convert answers to numerical score to make comparisons possible?
  What should the content of the review be?
  Should it be conducted by the trainer or a neutral observer?
  Should session reactions be fed back to the tutor to improve the ongoing event?
4 Outcome evaluation: what evidence is there that change has occurred?
  (a) Immediate:
    What changes in KSA have resulted (or have the immediate objectives been met)?
    How can we measure changes?

(b) Intermediate:

What changes are there in on-the-job performance (or have intermediate objectives been met)?

How can we be sure that these changes are the result of the training?

(c) Ultimate:

How have the changes in job performance affected the organization (or have the ultimate objectives been met)?

What overall effect on profitability or effectiveness is there?

Both frameworks view the last level of evaluation as the most difficult, the least often done and the most valuable. Reaction evaluation is the easiest, the least useful and the most frequently used method. Kirkpatrick's learning and behaviour levels and the CIRO immediate and intermediate outcome evaluation lie in between on these three judgements of difficulty, usefulness and frequency of use.

There are particular difficulties in measuring intermediate and ultimate outcomes because many other factors besides training influence job performance and organizational performance. This is particularly true of management and supervisory training, where the organizational climate, the influence of other people and an individual's personality also determine behaviour and outcomes. Warr, Bird and Rackham suggest that, in terms of the effort/reward ratio, it is sensible to focus on the easier levels of evaluation. They believe that if we have carried out proper context, input, reaction and immediate outcome evaluation, then the intermediate and ultimate outcomes are likely to be successful. This makes sense if we have limited resources of time and money. They point out that there are special cases where intermediate outcome evaluation is more practicable; for example, where the whole or a substantial part of a department is being trained. If single managers are involved, the decision on whether to carry out intermediate outcome evaluation or not should be based on the importance of the programme. Factors would include the cost, length, numbers involved, the extent to which it is intended to repeat the programme, available resources, support given by line staff and the estimated reliability and usefulness of the information that could be collected.

Warr, Bird and Rackham's book *Evaluation of Management Training*, although published in 1970, is still well worth reading. The authors are psychologists, with concern for the niceties of experimental design and academic rigour, yet the thirteen case studies that they report abound in examples of how evaluation can interact with planning and training to improve effectiveness. Their approach is a combination of practical common sense with a concern for validity and reliability. A central theme is the idea that training should be a self-correcting system. They give examples where reaction evaluation or immediate outcome evaluation were fed back to the trainer to identify and improve weaknesses in an ongoing series of courses. To take one case example from their research: two series of five knowledge-based training courses were run. A pre-test and post-test of the knowledge imparted was given to all participants. At the end of each session, participants also rated the event for enjoyment, relevance, appropriate length and information given. The trainer for one of the series was not given access to any of this information and had only his own informal feedback to rely on. The trainer for the second series of courses had access to the test results and the reaction evaluation. Figure 5.3 shows the results: the series without feedback improved by 10 per cent whereas the series with feedback improved by 70 per cent.

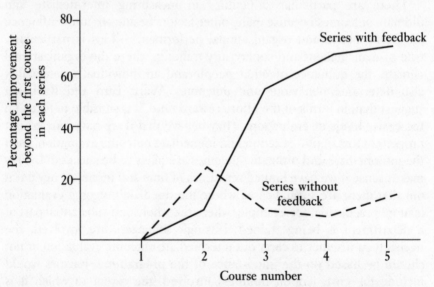

Figure 5.3   Comparison of course series with and without feedback
Taken from Warr, Bird and Rackham 1970. Reproduced with permission

Two spin-off benefits of evaluation are worth noting. In order to draw up the knowledge test the speakers were questioned, and so were forced to think more clearly about their objectives and content. This in itself resulted in improvements in both series. Further, several studies have shown that pre-testing learners itself causes an improvement in post-test scores, even when different questions are used, or no training takes place.

These points also illustrate one of the problems of evaluation.

Measurement itself causes changes in what we are measuring. As practical trainers and evaluators we should be aware of the effects of testing and ready to utilize the benefits.

One of the great problems of traditional courses, particularly where individuals are sent to external course providers, is that participants return with new knowledge, skills and ideas for change, but find no encouragement or support on their return to work. The ideas and enthusiasm generated by training are quickly dropped. They do not, therefore, change their behaviour. Devices such as action planning, work-based projects and follow-up visits are all effective ways of providing necessary support. They are also vehicles for evaluation. Following up participants to question their achievement of action plans made or targets set while in training can itself mean that the participants and their managers are more likely to implement change.

Reaction evaluation

Reaction evaluation is concerned with the feelings and opinions of the learners. Reactions are usually collected by a questionnaire or a rating scale. An example using both methods is shown in figure 5.4. Questionnaires can require respondents to chose from a range of predetermined answers or can be open-ended. The latter can elicit a vivid and individual response but are difficult to summarize and cannot readily be used to compare events. The answers to scales and fixed-choice questionnaires can be converted to a numerical score, making possible comparison between courses, tutors and methods. However, a numerical score still represents subjective judgements and should be treated with caution. The evaluator needs to ask if the questions or scales encourage an overly critical or, more usually, an overly favourable response. In the USA McCallon has established norms, or typical scores, for an evaluation scale based on the responses of 40,000 participants in a range of adult education workshops. The use of such norms can provide a useful base-line, revealing that apparently 'good' ratings may be low when compared to the norm (Davis and McCallon, 1974).

One of the problems with reaction evaluation is that participants often overuse the average or middle position and tend to give positive answers when they feel quite differently. Motives can vary from the desire not to upset a pleasant but ineffective tutor to avoidance of an inquest if they are critical. Some of these problems may be reduced or eliminated by careful design of questionnaries, by guaranteeing anonymity or by using a third party to collect responses.

EVALUATION

COURSE QUESTIONNAIRE

COURSE TITLE.. Date ....

1 What was the main value of this course to you? ....
....
....

2 Which topics did you consider the most useful? ....
....

3 Was the course: Too long? ☐   Too short? ☐   Just right? ☐
....

4 Which topics were too long? ....
   Which topics could have been expanded? ....
....

5 What did you like best about this course? ....
....

6 What would you change? ....
....

7 What topics would you add? ....
....

8 What will you change now as a result of this course? ....
....

9 Did the course meet its objectives?   High   Low
   (PLEASE TICK A BOX)

5	4	3	2	1

10 How do you evaluate course presentation and teaching?
   (PLEASE TICK A BOX)

5	4	3	2	1

11 Any other comments ....
....

THE FOLLOWING INFORMATION IS OPTIONAL AND CONFIDENTIAL:
NAME ....

Figure 5.4   Reaction evaluation form

The areas covered by evaluation will depend on the purpose, but they could include:

- Pre-course briefing or joining instructions
- Objectives
- Content

- Methods
- Resources
- Facilities/accommodation
- Duration
- Relevance to job/intended changes
- Tutor
- General comments.

Opinions can be collected directly from participants at the end of an event or at the end of each session. The latter enables the trainer to identify weaknesses in a course, to compare different training methods and to modify an ongoing course rather than be aware of problem areas after the event. Alternatively, reaction evaluation can be undertaken after the participant has returned to work and has had time to digest the training and see it in perspective. This has the drawback that the response rate is likely to diminish and it is more time-consuming and expensive to collect. Memories may have faded.

If participants have to report to their managers on their opinion of the training and their intended actions as a result of that training, it may be more likely that they will implement changes. However, we have now introduced the possible bias and prejudice of the managers to complicate matters. If they were responsible for sending an individual on an event, they may consciously or unconsciously influence the participant to tell them it was a worthwhile experience, especially if it was costly!

Other indicators of reaction include requests for further training, the return of participants for further help and their recommendation to others to attend events. An important question for those who rely on reaction evaluation concerns the relationship between opinions and actual change in job behaviour. Research findings vary. Some studies find a clear relationship, others have found none.

A last point concerns the danger of trainers disregarding information once it has been collected and the importance of involving all concerned parties. To illustrate this with a cautionary case study: in the early 1980s the MSC (later TEED) established accredited training centres, which were given a budget to provide 'free' training to a range of organizations engaged in delivering the YTS and, later, ET. The manager of one such ATC evaluated training solely via reaction evaluation. Participants attending events completed a rating scale about the ambience, contents, methods and perceived relevance of the training. This was administered by the tutor at the end of each course, as postal questionnaires had a low response rate.

The feedback was positive, some was outstanding, and the few negative responses were sometimes ignored, sometimes acted upon. Although aware of the tendency for such responses to be more bland and positive than people's real feelings, the manager interpreted the feedback as evidence that the centre was satisfying customer wants, if not perhaps their needs. Unsolicited praise reinforced the manager's beliefs.

However, TEED received rather different messages. Several ET and YT schemes had ceased to use the ATC and the reasons they gave included course cancellations, repetitive content and courses not related to needs. They also had criticisms of individual tutors. Some staff had left their organizations after gaining national awards as a result of attending courses. Other organizations had not been able or willing to spare staff for training and had to justify this state of affairs to TEED. The message that managers gave to TEED was a critical and negative one. TEED were also conducting, in effect, a reaction evaluation, albeit of a much more ad hoc nature than that carried out by the ATC.

The outcome was that the ATC had its contract withdrawn. It was replaced by another, and to date there are just as many critical comments circulating. The new centre is just as happy as the old one with the positive news that it is getting from reaction evaluation – its contract is currently under review.

The moral of this tale? You find what you want or what you expect to find. The reaction evaluation excluded members of the population of potential users and only included those who used the ATC and were presumably relatively content. The evaluation did not examine the feedback given by participants to their managers and did not involve at any stage the managers or TEED, which funded the ATC. The process was owned by the ATC and feedback sheets were filed, with little systematic attempt to use the information on them. The process had become mechanical and unthinking.

This tale is not a criticism of reaction evaluation in general. It is not saying that outcome evaluation would have been better (although it might have been). The suggestion is that lip-service to evaluation is more dangerous than none at all. Evaluation, like training, is a living process where we continually question what we do, involve all concerned parties, cross-check information and attempt to improve.

Immediate outcome evaluation

Here we are concerned with measuring the changes in KSAs that are the result of training. If we have validated the objectives – that is, we are confident that they represent the needs – then immediate outcome evaluation is a matter of measuring how far the objectives have been met. This is a relatively straightforward business if the objectives are Mager-style ones with clear statements of behaviour, standards and conditions. But life is seldom that simple.

Where individuals might reasonably be expected to have pre-existing KSAs, we should try to measure these prior to the start of training, so that we can isolate the effects of the programme. It is generally easier and more usual to pre-test attitude and knowledge rather than skill. The same test can be used at the end of training, or similar items substituted, but in either case learners are likely to improve their score because of exposure to the pre-test as well as because of training. In an ideal world, the use of a control group, who experienced the pre-test and post-test but who were not given training, would enable us to measure the effect of training. Alternatively, use of a control group could allow us to dispense with a pre-test, as comparison of the post-test scores of the trained group and the control group would provide a measure of the effects of the programme. Such rigorous experimental designs are seldom possible in the real situation.

If cost and time considerations prevent use of pre-test and control groups, it is still worthwhile to measure the achievement of objectives. If we want to measure skill development, then we need to use a performance test of some sort. If we are concerned with verbal, social or analytical skills, such as those required of a manager, then we can observe learners in role plays, mock interviews, group exercises, in-tray exercises and business games. Most of these are essentially simulations which attempt to model real situations such as staff appraisal interviews. In general, the more like the real situation these are, the more likely it is that successful performance in the simulation will predict transfer of these skills to the real situation. It is important that observers are trained, that there are clear and appropriate criteria for performance and that learners are aware of the criteria and have clear instructions giving the 'rules of the game'.

If a manual or perceptual skill is being measured then we will need to use a simulation, or observe the learner using the skill on a model or in the real situation. Again, it is important that observers are trained and use checklists which identify the key skills, have clear standards and elicit related underpinning knowledge and understanding.

If we want to ensure that our conclusions are valid then it is important that the content of our test reflects the content of the course and the objectives. If it tests ideas, skills and facts not represented in the course, or excludes KSAs for which training or objectives were provided, then our measure of success is contaminated or deficient.

The recommended books by Jack Phillips (1983) and Warr, Bird and Rackham (1970) give guidance on the construction of questionnaires and rating scales and on the use of observers for evaluating performance.

Intermediate outcome evaluation

Intermediate outcomes are the changes in job performance which result from training. But, as mentioned earlier, there are problems in isolating the effects of training from other causes of change. A salesman sells seventy-five kitchens in a year. After attending a training course, he sells a hundred over the next year. Can we attribute this improvement to the training? Not necessarily. It may be that the product has been improved or a major advertising campaign launched; the economic climate may have changed; he may have been given a better territory, perhaps because of his course performance; his manager may have introduced better incentives or support systems; the salesman may have improved simply because he has gained in experience or maturity.

If we want to be confident that the improvement is due to training then we need to compare the performance of a trained group of sales staff with another group who have not had training. The two groups need to be matched in terms of previous performance, territory, experience and so on, so that differences between them are due to the training.

In practice this is not as easy as it sounds. It is tempting for managers to want to offer training to those whom they think have potential, or to want the poorest performers to have help. It may also be difficult to involve sufficient sales staff so that we can be confident of the significance of the differences in performance between the control and the trained group.

Direct measures

The measure of performance for our salesmen was the number of sales. Other objective measures that could be used in other jobs are output, scrap rates, number of customer transactions or forms processed and so on. Such information can often be obtained from performance records kept by the organization, and most such data can easily be converted into cash values.

For many jobs, however, such data is not possible or appropriate, and we may have to use indirect or subjective methods of judging performance.

Indirect measures

If we can assign a numerical value to subjective judgements of performance they can also be translated into cash terms. It must, however, be remembered that the reliability and validity of the original judgement is suspect unless we have evidence to the contrary.

The performance of individuals in a group can be measured by asking a judge, usually a manager or supervisor, to rate individuals on two dimensions, motivation and skill. The judge is asked to identify the best and worst performer and place them on the grid shown in figure 5.5, where 2 is the best they have known and 0 is the worst they have known. The process is repeated with the second best and second worst and so on. The use of descriptors for each possible score on the grid can improve the consistency between and within supervisors' judgement, providing 'behavioural anchors' (Jackson 1989). In a typical work group, the largest number of individuals will be somewhere in the middle with smaller numbers at the extremes.

The score for an individual is calculated by adding the motivation and skill score and dividing by two. This calculation gives the *performance rating*. The information thus obtained can be presented on a graph, providing a picture of the distribution and average performance of the

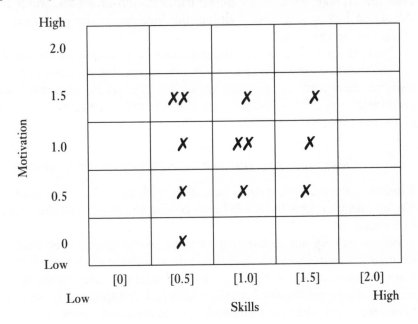

Figure 5.5   Performance grid

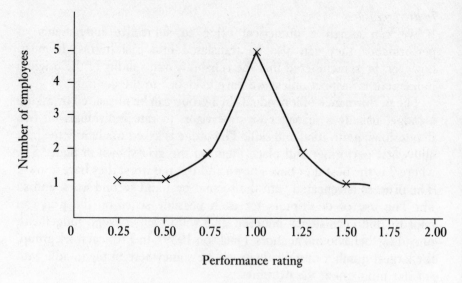

Figure 5.6   Performance distribution graph

group (see figure 5.6). Training should reduce the spread of scores and raise the average score. If the performance ratings of a work group are calculated before and after training, the increase in the performance rating can be calculated.

Other indirect data on performance can be collected by interview, questionnaire, observation or even attitude survey. Job performance can also be measured by assessment against the units, elements and performance of NVQs and by evaluating the implementation of action plans and projects.

Ultimate outcome evaluation: costing the effects of training

Ultimate outcome evaluation is concerned with the effect of training on the organization. Our focus will be on costing and predicting the effects of training.

Before making any investment in plant or machinery, it is usual to estimate the costs involved, to compare these with the likely savings to be made or financial benefits to be gained and finally to calculate the actual cost and the actual financial gains (or losses). Correspondingly, we need to be able to calculate the estimated and actual costs of an investment in training, the estimated and actual benefits and the time it will take to recoup the investment.

- *Cost effectiveness analysis* is the examination of training costs in monetary terms as compared to the benefits of training also in monetary terms.
- *Cost benefit analysis* is the examination of training costs in monetary terms compared to the benefits expressed in non-financial terms. The latter could be expressed in terms of morale, improved attitudes, health and safety indices and so on.

Methods of costing training are beyond the scope of this chapter, but selected methods of costing the benefits, including human resource value, DIF analysis and payback time are outlined.

Human resource value
The performance rating described earlier can be converted to a cash value by multiplying it by the personnel cost. The personnel cost is the total cost to the organization of employing an individual. This calculation yields the human resource value, or HRV.

The increase in HRV due to training can be calculated by remeasuring the performance rating after training, calculating the new HRV and deducting the original value. For example:

Personnel cost =	£20,000 per annum
Performance rating before training =	0.75
HRV = Personnel cost × Performance rating =	£15,000
Performance rating after training =	1.25
New HRV =	£25,000
Increase in HRV =	£10,000

The HRV thus provides a measure of the relative value of an individual which enables us to make comparisons of worth. It also enables us to decide which individuals or groups would benefit most from training.

DIF analysis (Cascio and Ramos, 1986)
A simple technique such as performance rating gives an overall measure and fails to take into account that most jobs involve multiple activities. Moreover, each activity within a job differs in its criticality, difficulty and frequency. Multiplying these three factors together gives a relative weighting of the activities in a job.

Clearly, if an activity is difficult, frequent and important it will have a higher weighting than an infrequent, easy and unimportant activity. It is likely that training will be worthwhile, especially if the job holder has a low performance rating. If we know the performance rating of an individual for each activity and the personnel cost, then we can calculate the value of an individual's performance for each activity.

Each job activity is assessed in terms of frequency or the percentage of time devoted to it. The importance and level of difficulty are assessed on a simple scale, in our example 0 to 4. As these are crude and subjective ratings, it is suggested that the scale should have few divisions.

To take an example: the direct personnel cost of an individual is £20,000. The DIF for her four main job activities is shown below, together with her performance rating. The performance value is the relative weighting multiplied by the personnel value.

Job activity	A	B	C	D	
Frequency (F)	50	20	20	10	
Difficulty (D)	1	2	3	4	
Importance (I)	2	1	3	4	
D × I × F	100	40	180	160	= 480
Relative weight [(D × I × F) ÷ (Sum of D × I × F)]	0.21	0.08	0.38	0.33	= 100
Personnel cost per activity (Relative weight × Personnel cost)	£4,200	£1,600	£7,600	£6,600	= £20,000
Performance rating	1.00	2.00	0.75	0.5	
Performance value	£4,200	£3,200	£5,700	£3,300	= £16,400
Performance rating after training in areas C and D			1.25	1.00	
New performance value	£4,200	£3,200	£9,500	£6,600	= £23,500
Increase in performance value					= £7,100

In the example, area C has a high personnel cost as, although it occupies only 20 per cent of total time, it has the highest relative weight. Training is worthwhile, as the performance rating is low. Similarly, activity D has a high relative weight and low performance rating. Training resulted in an increase in performance value of £7,100.

DIF analysis can be used to evaluate individual performance; to decide which parts of an individual's job should be given priority training by indicating likely gains; and to evaluate the effectiveness of training programmes.

Payback time
If we know the total cost of training and the savings or proceeds, then we can calculate the time it will take to recoup an investment.

$$\text{Payback time} = \frac{\text{total investment}}{\text{Annual savings or proceeds}}$$

Payback time can be used to forecast whether a programme is likely to be worthwhile before the investment is made. If staff leave before the cost of training is recouped, then the investment is not worthwhile.

For example, if the savings or profit in increased production is estimated at £30,000 per annum and the total cost of the training is £45,000 then the payback time is eighteen months. If the average stay of a production worker is over eighteen months then the investment is worthwhile. If the average length of stay is under eighteen months then the investment is unlikely to pay off.

A caution

The danger of converting assessments of performance, difficulty and importance into figures is that they look objective and scientific. But they are in fact subjective, crude measures, with inbuilt assumptions. For example, we have assumed that someone with a performance rating of 2 is worth two people rated at 1. Moreover, it would be inappropriate to assume that the organization had actually saved a thousand pounds by increasing an individual's HRV by this amount: rather the techniques outlined provide a rationale for chosing where and when to invest in training and give a means of comparing different investments. The calculations involved are relative, not absolute.

Summary

Training is about changing people. The process of setting objectives defines what changes we intend to produce, and facilitates assessment of those changes. Determining whether or not training has been effective and worthwhile can be difficult and daunting, but a number of frameworks have been developed to assist in the formulation of evaluation strategies.

The main purposes of evaluation are to:

- Improve the training
- Justify the investment made.

In some cases, these are straightforward exercises – especially if objectives have been determined in advance and adequate measurements taken – but in others, less direct and more subjective approaches are needed. Various techniques of evaluation help to address these problems. The development of national standards will provide a comprehensive set of objectives and assessment criteria which should make the process of evaluation more meaningful and relevant to the job of the trainer.

Further reading

Cascio, W.F. and Ramos, R.A. (1986) Development and Application of a New Method for Assessing Job Performance in Behavioural/Economic Terms. *Journal of Applied Psychology*, 71, 20–8.

Davies, I.K. (1976) *Objectives in Curriculum Design*. Maidenhead: McGraw-Hill.

Davis, L.N. and McCallon, E. (1974) *Planning, Conducting and Evaluating Workshops*. Austin, Texas: Learning Concepts.

Jackson, Terence (1989) *Evaluation: Relating Training to Business Performance*. London: Kogan Page.

Kirkpatrick, D.L. (1976) Evaluation of Training. In R.L. Craig and L.R. Bittel (eds), *Training and Development Handbook*, New York: ASTD/McGraw-Hill.

Mager, Robert (1975) *Preparing Instructional Objectives*. Belmont, California: Fearn.

Phillips, J.J. (1983) *Handbook of Training Evaluation and Measurement*. Houston: Gulf Publishing Co.

TDLB (1991) *National Standards for Training and Development*. Sheffield: Department of Employment.

Warr, P., Bird, M., and Rackham, N. (1970) *Evaluation of Management Training*. Aldershot: Gower.

6
Learning and Training Design

JOHN ROSCOE

A little learning is a dangerous thing.

Alexander Pope, 1711

Introduction

The starting point for any design of training should be that a need has been identified. Before a design is begun, consideration should be given to whether other solutions may be superior. If another approach can resolve the identified need more quickly, cheaply or effectively it should be used. The alternatives to formal training considered in chapter 3 should be reconsidered by the training designer and discussed with the person who requested the design of training.

When the need for training has been established and agreed, then further analysis is usually required to provide the detailed and specific information which will form the basis of the design. The design may be for very specific training to attend to the performance of an individual or a small group, or for much larger and more general needs. Job analysis and task analysis may be appropriate to collect information about the desired job performance.

The design of a training intervention is a complex activity with many variables and prerequisites. Often the designer can lose sight of all those variables and the underlying assumptions about what is fixed and what can be changed. Many designers start off with a ready-built model in their heads and just fill in the blanks with specific content. This can lead to a weak design which will not be effective. The approach developed here allows the design variables to be managed and can be used for any application.

The Learning Unit Model

A useful way to approach design is by way of the learning unit model. By considering each learning outcome as a separate learning unit, it is possible to design any size of training activity, whether it is large, medium or small. What is within the learning unit and how learning units can be assembled into a complete training activity will be developed in this chapter.

Our starting point is that a need has been identified for training, alternatives to training have been discounted, resources have been committed for training and further job and task analysis has been undertaken where required. All of the above are prerequisites to designing training. Now let us turn to the learning unit model (see figure 6.1).

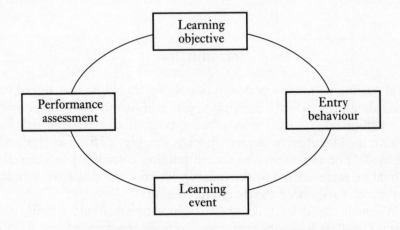

Figure 6.1   The learning unit model

The learning unit model has four stages and can be considered as a sequence very like a systematic approach to training. Each stage can be considered to have implications for all of the other stages. This reinforces the point that training design is a process where all the variables interact dynamically. Every decision made will have implications for following decisions and may require preceding decisions to be modified.

The first stage is the *learning objective*. As described in chapter 5, an objective is a clear statement of the performance to be achieved, under what conditions and to what standards. The identified need and the analysis provide a basis for preparing an objective. A decision will need to be made on whether the learning objective is to match job performance, under job conditions and to job standards. Very often it is acceptable to set an objective which is different from the performance required on the job by an experienced worker. If a learning objective is set below the job performance level, agreement should be obtained with the line management. This will ensure that the performance gap after training is recognized (see figure 6.2).

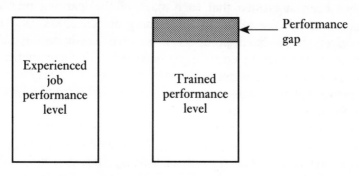

Figure 6.2   Performance gap

Very often the analysis enables a series of objectives, often called enabling objectives, to be identified. Each of these can be addressed by a separate learning unit with a specific learning objective. The learning objective describes the desired performance at the end of the learning event.

The second stage of the learning unit model is *entry behaviour*. This is a slightly clumsy term for a very useful idea. Entry behaviour is concerned with what those who are to be trained already know and can do; it is also concerned with how they learned it (see figure 6.3).

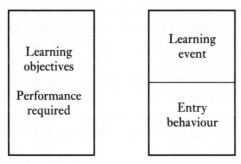

Figure 6.3   Entry behaviour

All designers of training use the idea of entry behaviour, whether consciously or unconsciously. Where the training will begin is decided by the designer. Decisions about methods of training to be used will be made on the basis that the learner will be able to learn from them. Focusing on the entry behaviour of those to be trained can provide a lot of useful information for designing training. Without it the design process proceeds on the basis of assumptions which may prove accurate but may equally well be inaccurate.

It has been suggested that each stage of the learning unit model interacts with all the others. The learning objective, you may argue, must surely be a fixed point as it is what needs to be learned. Information provided by considering entry behaviour may indicate that the proposed objective is not achievable. Then it will be necessary to go back to the objective, reconsider it and get approval from those who own the problem for any modification.

The third stage of the learning unit model is the *learning event*. This is where the learners do their learning. In designing a learning event, decisions are made about the sort of learning strategies to be adopted and the details of what happens within that event. The learning event needs to be tailored to the first two stages of the model, the learning objectives and the learners.

The learning event does not have to be an off-the-job course with a group of learners for a fixed period. There are many strategies which can be adopted to help people learn, and it is up to the designer to choose one appropriate to the objectives and the learners in the organizational context. Possible training strategies have been introduced in chapter 3, appendix E, and will be considered later. If the learning event is predetermined in any way, such as by methods to be used or duration, then it may force revision of the entry behaviour and learning objective.

The fourth stage of the model is *performance assessment*. This is where measurement takes place of whether the learning objective has been achieved. Performance assessment is about how the successful achievement of the learning objective will be measured and assessed. It is concerned with appropriate techniques to measure the performance described in the learning objective. It is also necessary to identify who will make the assessment, whether the conditions for the assessment will be those in the objective and what are the consequences of not achieving the learning objective.

To summarize, the learning unit is about providing a learning event which will build on the learner's existing knowledge and skill. It will achieve a defined learning objective and confirm that the objective has been achieved (see figure 6.4). The illustration does not imply that the learner has very limited entry behaviour. The entry behaviour shown is that relevant to the task. The learning event is specifically designed to develop the additional knowledge and skills relevant to desired performance.

Figure 6.4   The learning event

The learning unit model, as developed so far, has looked at a single learner. As soon as we consider a group of learners we will be faced with a range of entry behaviour. This will have implications for the learning event:

● Can everyone have the same performance assessment?
● Will different approaches be necessary?
● Can everyone achieve the objective?

The learning unit is about providing a learning event which will help specific individuals to achieve desired performance and demonstrate that they have achieved it.

Ways People Learn

In designing the learning event, it is helpful to have some model of how people learn. A simple model, which can be checked out from your own experience, puts up four ways that people can learn. These are:

● Trial and error
● Being told
● Imitation
● Thinking.

This model can be quite helpful when designing a learning event. It allows you to consider the learning outcome desired, the objective, against the means you are proposing to use, the learning event.

Trial and error

Everyone uses trial and error as a basis for learning. We try to do something, we succeed and then we do it that way again. We continue to use the way that succeeded until it fails. When the approach fails, we try another which our experience suggests may succeed. If that fails, we try another. We keep trying different approaches until we succeed or give up trying through frustration, tiredness or indifference.

Trial and error has a number of weaknesses, but is a very powerful way of learning. When there is no prescriptive way of performing, then trial and error will be an essential part of achieving the desired performance. If we can recognize that trial and error is essential then it can be built into the learning event. If it cannot be built into the learning event, then the objective must be changed.

The primary weakness of trial and error as an approach to learning is that it relies on the learner recognizing that an error has occurred. Many tasks provide immediate feedback on success. You want to open a bottle, you try with a bottle opener and it does not work. In this case you clearly knew the objective and that it had not been achieved. From this you can go on to try again. For trial and error learning to work effectively, immediate feedback of results is desirable. In many industrial and commercial tasks immediate feedback of results is not available. The performance attempt is made but feedback is received perhaps never, perhaps days or weeks later. This is not a very good basis for learning, particularly if the feedback just says 'Right' or 'Wrong' rather than why it was wrong and to what extent.

Errors made on machinery and equipment may injure the operator or others, damage the equipment or waste materials. In some cases, this may rule out trial and error as an acceptable way of learning. What it may mean is that we must simulate the real situation so that trial and error learning can take place without the consequences of errors occurring. Training simulators for aircraft and nuclear power stations are examples where learning events can be created to allow trial and error learning without incurring the penalties of errors. These simulations make extensive provision for feedback to learners on the nature of their errors to support learning.

Being told

As an approach to learning, this is often the one first considered by the lay person and the trainer alike. Someone needs to learn, then provide another person who can explain the required performance. Being told can take many forms. It can be 'sitting by Nellie', a lecture to a group of learners, a video tape, an audio tape, a handout, a book, even a performance aid. The essence of 'being told' is that what is required can be communicated to the learner.

As an approach, being told is fine if the learning objective is about knowledge. We can gain knowledge from being told, although what we are told, how much, how quickly and at what level needs to be matched to what we already know and can do – our entry behaviour. If the learning objective requires us to be able to do something, then being told will require supplementing with at least trial and error at some stage.

Imitation

This is a very powerful way of learning. It plays a part in most learning situations. We observe how someone else handles a situation and we copy what we saw them do. Imitation is useful for many manual and social tasks that we learn to cope with. As children we observe adults walking, talking, greeting one another, swimming, using the telephone, driving a car and so on.

For imitation to work effectively as a way of learning requires the performance to be observable. It also requires a recognition of what cues are being used to select the appropriate response. When meeting new people how do we decide whether to kiss, on lips or cheeks, shake hands, nod, smile, say hello? Somebody who observes you greet your mother could make a big mistake if they used the same response when meeting their tax inspector – or maybe not!

Imitation as a way of learning relies on having the required underpinning knowledge and skills, which will support performance. Without the requisite entry behaviour for a learning event which uses imitation, the event could go disastrously wrong. The required knowledge may be provided by being told and the performance practised by trial and error.

Some learning objectives will not be appropriate for the imitation approach. For some tasks and outcomes there is nothing to observe. Learning objectives which require mental processes do not lend themselves to imitation, which leads us into considering the fourth way of learning.

Thinking

Thinking is an approach to learning which underpins all the other methods. It can also be considered as an independent one. If we know the desired learning objective, we can often learn through thinking about how we would achieve it. This idea would seem to be supported by research results which show that learning increases significantly for those who have a clear learning objective to work to before the learning event, when compared to those starting a learning event blind.

When using trial and error as a way of learning we expect thinking to support the performance before, during and after each trial. Using being told as a way of learning the expectation is that thinking will be stimulated to integrate the new knowledge into existing experience. Imitation as a way of learning requires thinking to link what is observed to the cues which stimulate the responses.

Variables in Designing a Learning Unit

Having introduced the design of training and described the learning unit model and the four ways of learning, let us review the range of decisions to be made in training design. The starting point is often considered to be the objective of the training. While this is generally true, the learning unit model suggests that we may also start from entry behaviour, the learning event or performance assessment. Wherever we start the process, all the decisions are linked.

The justification for starting to design training is that there is a training need for which the organization is prepared to invest resources. The nature of this need will form the basis of all the decisions in training design. Therefore a clear grasp of the need is essential to the designer.

Constraints

When the need is clearly defined and the resources available to meet the need are assigned, whether formally or informally, a boundary for the design task can be determined. This can be called the constraints within which the design will be undertaken. It is worth specifying the constraints because often they are self-imposed. Listing them can help distinguish between externally imposed and self-imposed constraints. The list can also be useful to check back with the client on the constraints (see figure 6.5). When a particular constraint makes it difficult or impossible to achieve the learning objective, it can be confirmed with those who own the need to see whether the constraint can be relaxed or the learning objective changed.

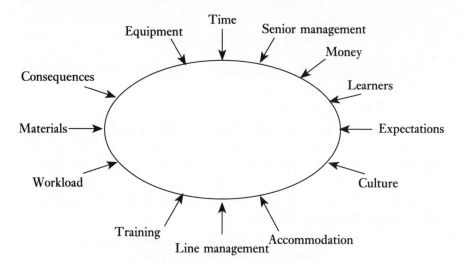

Figure 6.5   Constraints in the design

The constraints which bound a design are all the things which limit what and how training will run. A list of those things which will constrain the design includes:

- The learning objective:
  Must job performance be achieved?
  Can conditions be relaxed?
- Those to be trained:
  Their entry behaviour
  The numbers
  When available for training
  How many at one time
  For how long they can be released
- Acceptable training strategies
- Acceptable training methods
- Available training resources:
  Trainers
  Residential accommodation

Training accommodation
Training aids
Technical support
Equipment, e.g. computers
Training software, e.g. videos, films, vu-foils
- How much money can be spent in:
Preparing
Running
- Duration of the learning event
- Time to develop the design and training materials
- Performance assessment:
Will individual assessment be required?
What methods are acceptable?
Who will have access to results?

All of the above are potential constraints. The actual constraints you face will be those imposed by your organization and yourself. The flexibility of those constraints will determine the freedom of choice in the various elements of the design. In looking at the constraints we have developed a list of the design variables. Decisions must be made about these during the design process.

Designing a Learning Unit

So the starting point is the need and the nature of the training need. Before undertaking the detailed analysis of the performance it must be established that training is the most appropriate solution. The analysis of required performance allows the development of the learning objective(s). Having developed these – the required outcome of the training – the analysis will allow enabling objectives to be identified. Each enabling objective can be seen as the learning objective for a specific learning unit.

Next must be considered the entry behaviour of the learners:

- What are their existing experience and competence?
- What are their motivation and expectations?
- How do they like to learn and how do they learn best?
- What are their existing learning skills?
- How many of them are there?

These and additional questions which can be generated need to be asked and answered. They are important variables in the design.

Using the learning unit model, and having started from the learning objective and considered entry behaviour, the next stage is the learning event. The learning event is the opportunity to learn which we are creating in the design process. Firstly we need to recognize that there is a range of training strategies which may be adopted.

Any strategy which provides a suitable learning event can be appropriate. Some strategies will be more acceptable than others within a particular organizational context and for particular learners. Selection of a particular strategy will be determined by the constraints operating, learning preferences, client expectations and the designer's judgement.

Within the learning event, using the adopted strategy, the variables which will need to be considered include:

- Content
- Sequence
- Place
- Trainers
- Time
- Methods.

Decisions about these variables will need to be made within the constraints identified as bounding the design.

The last stage of a learning unit is performance assessment. Unfortunately its position tends to encourage the designer of training to leave it until last – sometimes to leave it out altogether. If design were a neat linear sequence, it might be appropriate to leave it until last. In practice it needs to be considered before the learning event is designed in detail. Only then will room be made in the time available for training for the use of performance assessment measures.

The designer must be very clear what the requirements of the performance assessment are. Some measures may be required to provide formative feedback – that is, to support trial and error learning. Some measures will be to check that the learning objectives have been achieved – summative assessment. There are other reasons you may have for building in assessment measures to the design, which we will consider later.

Having been around the learning unit model, there are some other variables which will need to be considered. These include:

- Costing of the design, development and delivery
- Budgeting for the activity
- Scheduling resources
- Marketing of the learning unit to clients and learners
- Accreditation of the learning outcomes
- Record keeping and administrative support

All of the above constitute additional variables with which the training designer must come to terms.

A training programme, which leads to the achievement of the required job performance, can be seen as a series of learning units. Each learning unit is an independent entity but the units are structured so that learning from earlier units is supported and used. In this way the learners will gain reinforcement and practice on their learning. The exit behaviour of one learning unit becomes the entry behaviour for the next. Where formal off-job courses are involved, the exit behaviour from the off-job training becomes the entry behaviour for a learning unit based on the job.

Design should not be seen as a simple linear process. There can be no rigid sequence for undertaking design. You should recognize that the variables interact and a decision made during the process may cause the revision of earlier decisions as well as shaping subsequent ones. Often many of them go unconsidered when the designer approaches the task with a preferred design solution. This is likely to result in less effective training in absolute terms, but may reflect the organizational constraints within which the design is developed.

Learning objective

We have now considered all the variables of training design within the context of a learning unit. The learning objective has been discussed earlier in this chapter and is developed in detail in chapter 5. A well-expressed objective will have a clearly identified and observable performance, with specific standards to be achieved under stated conditions. The learning objective, in the context of the identified training need, is a good starting point for design.

Entry behaviour

The training should start from where the learners already are in terms of knowledge and skill. If this is ignored there will be time wasted on training for competences already possessed; alternatively time will be wasted because the learners lack prerequisite knowledge and skills to benefit from the learning event (see figure 6.6).

There are two aspects to existing knowledge and skills, one job-related and the other concerned with learning skills. Job-related skills and knowledge include mastery of tools and equipment, knowledge of facts, concepts, principles and procedures, and the ability to perform

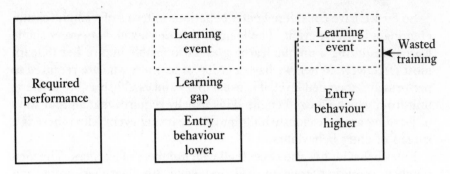

Figure 6.6   Differences in entry behaviour

tasks on the job. These will have been developed through a combination of education, formal training and experience. The existing entry behaviour in terms of job performance may be in direct conflict with the learning objective. Someone who has learned to perform a task incorrectly will have to unlearn the behaviours. This can be very difficult and requires more time than someone learning a task for the first time can be expected to need. For design purposes it is important to recognize whether any unlearning will be required by learners.

The second aspect of entry behaviour is concerned with learning skills. Underpinning all learning is the motivation of the individual. Those who do not wish to learn, or do not recognize the need to learn, can be expected not to succeed. The motivated learner will have preferred ways of learning and different experiences of various learning events and training methods. Preferred ways of learning can be considered from the viewpoint of learning styles and the work of Kolb and Honey and Mumford, and also within the 'four ways of learning' model. Some people prefer trial and error learning, others being told. Some learners will have substantial experience of being told through formal education and training. Others may have used imitation and trial and error extensively. Those using trial and error as their usual way of learning may find being told unhelpful, frustrating and demotivating. Information on the learners' ability to learn from various learning events can be used to make decisions about the learning event being designed.

Wrongly assuming the entry behaviour in terms of the existing competences can completely invalidate the learning event. For example, a learning event relying on written material will be totally inappropriate for those unable to read. Another example may be building the learning event around the use of a computer when the learner is not familiar with computers, keyboards, disks etc.

So far we have considered entry behaviour in terms of a single learner entering a learning event. The logic of this view extends to every single learner requiring a unique learning event to enable him or her to learn most effectively. When we have a group of learners who are required to perform at a specified level, it is usual to try and establish a core learning unit from which all can benefit. This usually requires that all four ways of learning are consciously built into the learning event when there is a spread of entry behaviours.

Entry behaviour is also concerned with numbers of learners. The total number requiring training will influence the learning event and performance assessment. In addition to numbers, such factors as availability for training, location of workplace, and how quickly they are to be trained need to be identified. This information will influence the nature of the learning event.

Having considered the need for information about entry behaviour, we must consider how to collect it. The range of methods of collecting such information is, as outlined in chapters 1 and 3, essentially from records, from observation and from questioning. Observation can be extended into testing if a specific entry behaviour is essential to a learning event. The test can establish whether or not the required behaviours are possessed.

Entry behaviour investigation is an opportunity for 'analysis paralysis'. It is possible to continue seeking information about the learners and never get to the point of designing and implementing the learning event. The other extreme is to not bother at all about entry behaviour. A pragmatic approach allows the use of easily available information to judge whether further investigation can be justified. The purpose in considering entry behaviour is to improve the quality of the learning event and ensure achievement of the objective.

Entry behaviour requirements may be specified as a prerequisite to a learning event and it may be left to learners to decide whether they meet the requirement. Alternatively, preselection by trainers may be used to decide whether a particular learner can benefit from a learning unit. This type of process can be used to identify remedial training needs. It can also be used to redesign the learning event to suit a particular individual or group of learners.

Assessment of entry behaviour may show that some learners do not need the learning event, as they can already demonstrate the required performance. Learners who can demonstrate required performance may still be trained for reasons such as team building and accreditation of competence.

Performance assessment

We will now consider performance assessment. Although it follows the learning event in the model, decisions about assessment need to be incorporated into the learning event. Unless the performance assessment measures are clearly identified, there is a a danger of them being squeezed out of the learning unit by the constraints bounding it.

The purpose of performance assessment should be clearly thought through. At the most obvious level we wish to establish whether the learning objective has been achieved by each learner. There are other issues with which the performance assessment measures may be concerned, such as:

- Helping the learner to change performance through feedback
- Rewarding the learner by verifying learning
- Certification of competence(s)
- Identifying needs for remedial training
- Providing feedback on trainer performance
- Providing information to revise the learning unit
- Showing value for money
- Comparing cost effectiveness
- Marketing the learning unit.

The users of the results also need to be considered. This will help in selecting the performance assessment measures to be used and when and how they will be used. The results of the performance assessment measures may be for all, or any, of the following people:

- Learner
- Training designer
- Trainer/instructor
- Training manager
- Line manager
- Personnel staff
- Senior management
- Potential future learners
- Accrediting bodies – verifiers and moderators.

Unless we are clear what is or are the purpose(s) of the assessment, and whom the results are for, sound decisions on selecting appropriate measures cannot be taken. In selecting performance assessment measures, attention must also be paid to whether a measure is valid and reliable for a particular learning objective. The range of performance assessment techniques is described in chapter 5.

Having identified potential assessment measures, the following questions arise:

- Are the skills to develop and use the measures available, or can they be bought in?
- Is there time and opportunity to develop and test the measures?
- Will there be sufficient time in the learning unit for the measures to be used as intended?
- Will the measures be acceptable to the learner(s), trainers and management?

See figure 6.7.

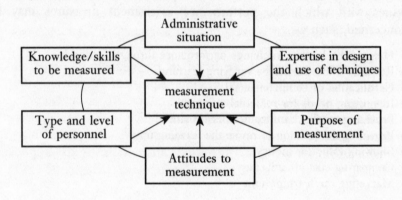

Figure 6.7   Choosing performance assessment measures

Performance assessment in the learning unit is largely about internal validation – whether the learning objective(s) have been achieved. Another issue to consider is external validation. This is the extent to which the learning unit transfers to job performance and allows sustained improvements in job results.

Designing the learning event

We have described a lot of areas to be considered before arriving at the point where many trainers start in designing training. The learning event will reflect the adoption of a particular training strategy. This may be selected as appropriate by the training designer, forced by the constraints of resources and facilities or sometimes imposed by management or learner expectations.

For a given strategy, a series of decisions needs to be made, developed from the learning objective, the entry behaviour and performance assessment measures. This involves deciding, in the context of the constraints operating and resources available:

- Content
- Sequence
- Methods
- Media
- Trainer
- Place
- Time

These need to be fitted together to support the empirical principles of learning which have proved helpful in training. These are outlined in appendix A. Particular aspects of adult learning and learning blockages are developed further in chapter 8.

Seven variables have been listed in the context of designing the learning event. As with design of other aspects of the learning unit, no strict sequence applies; the variables are interactive. As a general rule, a selected method will strongly affect the choice of trainers, appropriate training media, accommodation requirements and time required. Constraints imposed by entry behaviour, time available, accommodation and trainers may all work back in influencing the selected training method.

Content
The following points should be considered when deciding the content. It:

- Must cover the objectives
- Must link to entry behaviour
- Should help transfer to job/another learning unit.

Another way to determine content is by focusing on the objective. The designer can often identify lots of possible content which is related to the objective – more than can be included in the learning event. This content can then be assessed against the criteria of what *must* be learned to achieve the objective, what *should* be included if possible and what *could* be included, but is not really needed to achieve the objective. See figure 6.8.

Sequence
There are a number of approaches to sequencing the content of a learning unit and a series of learning units. The most straightforward is

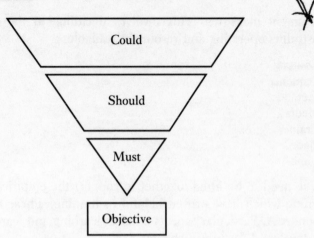

Figure 6.8   Deciding content

to base it on the analysis done and apply the 'logical sequence' derived from that. This may not be the best sequence for learning, as it may be perceived as a series of unconnected activities by the learner. The sequence needs to build upon the entry behaviour of the learners.

Subsidiary skills should be practised, as far as possible, throughout the learning event. Feedback should closely follow practice, with further opportunities to practise in order to allow application of the feedback. As learners learn at different rates the learning event should allow for such variations.

There are general rules of thumb which can help decisions about sequencing content:

- To help the learner to learn as quickly and effectively as possible:
  Start from existing knowledge, skill, and attitude.
  Minimize interference with previous learning.
  Offer more than one practice to develop skills and use feedback.
  Give spaced practice to allow development of performance standards.
  Feedback should follow closely upon practice.
  Follow advice with practice (link knowledge and skill).
  Explanation/advice is absorbed more effectively in the mornings.
  Small group/individual activity maintains effort in the afternoon.
  Practise subsidiary skills throughout the learning event (consolidation).
- For adults it is preferable to put the whole learning in context, then introduce the parts.
- Continuity of subject matter is superior to a series of unconnected activities (move away from school model of 40-minute periods of French, maths, etc.).

- Use links between learning – as learners learn at different rates allow individual learners to use/progress through the learning event at their own pace.
- Sequence can generally be summarized as:

Known   → Unknown
Concrete   → Abstract
General   → Particular
Observation → Reasoning/Theory
Simple   → Complex
Overview   → Detail

- Sequence follows from content and learners. It should not be imposed independently.

Training methods

Selection of training methods for a learning event is shaped by the objectives, entry behaviour, trainers, accommodation, time and resources. The major influences are objective and entry behaviour. The methods selected must enable the performance in the learning objective to be developed. If knowledge is to be acquired, then methods such as reading, lecture/lesson and computer-based training may be appropriate. Where skills are to be developed in the learning event, other methods are usually needed.

Different training methods will require resources in terms of trainers, accommodation, technical support, material and other factors. These need to be identified and considered as part of the design process. The decisions will be made within the constraints operating on the design.

In the learning event, there will need to be:

- Explanation
- Advice
- Demonstration
- Practice
- Feedback.

Participative methods generally take more time and are more demanding in trainer skills and accommodation requirements. However, there is no replacement for such methods if skills are to be developed in the learning event. If the constraints operating make it difficult to build in participative methods, then either the objective has to be changed or some way found to relax the constraints. This may involve the selection of a new strategy for the design.

For learning events to be used with more than one learner, the training methods selected should allow all four ways of learning to be used. It is therefore important not to let the learning objective take overwhelming precedence in deciding the training methods to use. In designing the learning event, we are interested in the characteristics of the methods rather than the detailed material which will need to be produced to implement them.

A range of face-to-face training methods is considered in chapter 7 and non-face-to-face ones in chapter 8. A list of training methods is shown in appendix B.

Media

There are many training media which can be used to support different training methods. The basis for selecting any medium must be the help and support it provides for learning. Media should assist learning in the context of the learning methods selected for the learning event. The use of training media should always support the learning event rather than determine the shape and nature of the learning unit.

Another factor which influences the use of specific training media is the facility of the trainer with the hardware and software. The designers of training are also limited to selecting media with which they are familiar, at least to the extent of recognizing applications.

The other determinants of selecting training media are availability and cost. Media which are readily available may be selected in preference to more appropriate, but less available, ones. If new hardware and software need to be procured then a budget and time must be available. Specially produced film and video is expensive and time-consuming to create.

A final consideration may be the extent to which the selected media support the performance of the trainer. Some trainers may need support because they are less experienced or have limited expertise in a particular area. The provision of media resources may give structure and direction to the learning event to help the trainer. This may be very desirable when the constraints force the use of trainers who need support.

There is often confusion between training methods and training media. Film and video are sometimes presented as methods when they can be used to support training methods like the demonstration, lecture and case study. They can also be used to support coaching, when used in an active mode to record individual performance and then replay it to the learner. A list of training media is given in appendix C.

The way specific media are used can turn them into a training method. Computer-based training uses a computer to present information, obtain individual learner responses and provide personal feedback. Interactive video has similar features, which are more sophisticated both technologically and in the production of software. They can only be justified where commercial software is available or in large organizations where many staff have the same need. What makes both computer-based training and interactive video methods is the very structured way the media are used to help learning.

The detailed preparation of learning materials to support the learning event can be left until the draft design has been finalized. Those responsible for developing the training resources to support a learning unit need facility with developing the media software. This often requires other equipment to be available for producing software. The trainers managing or facilitating the learning unit need to be competent in managing or using the media. All these considerations will influence the selection of training media.

Trainers

Answers to a series of questions help when considering the trainer in the learning event:

- What trainers are available for the learning unit?
- What skills and expertise do the trainers possess in the subject area of the learning objective?
- What role is the trainer expected to play in the learning unit?
- What skills does the trainer possess in implementing the learning event and the performance assessment measures?
- How credible is the trainer with the learners?
- How many trainers are needed for the methods/learners?

The questions above illustrate the interactive nature of the design process. If the trainer skills are not available then revisions of the design in terms of learning objectives, entry behaviour, the learning event and performance assessment will need to be considered.

If trainers are not available internally there are two major implications: whether the culture of the organization will accept external trainers, and whether external trainers are available and can be afforded. Many organizations operate from the belief that training interventions should be resourced internally. The benefits of using external trainers are their availability at the organization's convenience, and their expertise and credibility in specific topics. The costs incurred will generally be less than having an internal trainer in post full-time, and it releases trainers to undertake other activities.

Place

The location for the learning event must cope with the numbers of learners using the methods and media planned. The location must fit the expectations and status of the learners if optimum learning conditions are to be achieved.

For individualized learning the place must allow freedom to concentrate without workplace interruptions. The individual learners also need access to help and support. This should be readily available to maintain motivation and avoid feelings of isolation.

For group learning the training room must be large enough to accommodate the group to be trained. It must also allow the use of the proposed methods and media. This encompasses the physical arrangement of the furniture, allowing discussion between participants where appropriate and enabling small-group work to take place. Some media require power supplies, room blackout, the accommodation and security of specialist equipment and technical support. The selection decision for the place must consider all of these in the context of total overall costing and the training accommodation available.

Residential accommodation may be considered when learners have had to travel from different locations. It may also be preferred when the learners need to be away from day-to-day work pressures. In addition to the costs and quality of the training accommodation, thought needs to be given to learner expectations, comfort, travel and recreation arrangements. A remote residential location may be ideal for an intensive five-day training activity working an extended day. It would be inappropriate for a one-day 10.00 a.m.–4.00 p.m. seminar, where a convenient local venue is preferable.

Time

The time required for a learning event is easy in principle; it is the time required to achieve the learning objective. This simple answer becomes more complex when a group of learners is involved and the learning event requires the learners to work together with a trainer.

For an individual the learning should continue until performance assessment demonstrates the learning objective has been achieved. The learning event should be structured to allow everyone as long as he or she needs, with regular opportunities to review progress. Time for group learning events must be decided initially by judgement based upon consideration of the training gap and the methods being used in the learning event.

Rules of thumb suggest that input of knowledge should be limited to a maximum of around an hour at a time. Where skill objectives are to be achieved the time for practice should exceed the time for knowledge input by a factor of two or three. Practice, or application of knowledge, should follow the input immediately. Review of practice and feedback should follow as soon as possible after the practice sessions. Learners will also benefit from a period of reflection on their learning and further opportunities to practise.

The timing of sessions during the day will influence the learning too. Input of knowledge or theory is generally best done in the mornings, when attention is usually at its highest. Later in the day is a time more appropriate for practice, feedback and review.

Decisions about timing may be forced on the designer by the constraints operating on the learning unit. If the learning unit is to be run on a regular basis, then there is opportunity to review and revise the timings. The trainer implementing the learning event can also make tactical decisions on the use of time within the learning unit. See figure 6.9.

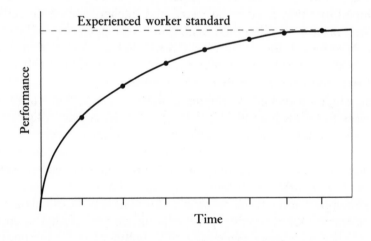

Figure 6.9   Time to learn

A general rule about the use of time in the learning event is that if more time is available then increase practice. If less time is available than desired then reduce practice. When time is inadequate for the proposed learning event then the selected methods and the learning objectives need to be reviewed. Without sufficient time to practise, the required level of proficiency will not be achieved.

In most training designs there is an acceptable duration of training for a particular need with a specific group. This becomes a constraint within which the designer needs to work. For a given time constraint some methods to achieve the objective cannot be used. This may mean that the objectives cannot be achieved. When this situation arises the trainer must go back to the client to negotiate either more time or revised learning objectives.

Development and Implementation

The design process described here results in an outline of the learning unit which will require further detailed development. Training materials including detailed lesson plans, handouts, exercises and visual aids will need to be obtained or produced. This is often done by involving the trainers who will implement the learning unit in producing the materials they will use. It can include purchasing materials from commercial sources and getting internal and external people to prepare required materials. The performance assessment measures will need to be developed too: they need to be tested and implementation procedures prepared prior to running the learning unit. Arrangements will need to be made to book trainers, learners and training accommodation so that all are available together. Support equipment and materials will also be necessary, and need organizing and administering.

The whole process of development and implementation will require resources to be made available. A budget for the activity will often be required. It will be sensible to separate the development costs from the implementation expenditure. Development costs will be incurred to complete the design and produce and procure materials; implementation costs will be incurred each time the learning unit is run.

Every organization tends to have a different way of calculating the costs it incurs. Rather than suggest what might be included in costing training, it will be more productive to establish what the organization recognizes as training costs. Depending on who controls the training budget, training will either be a free service to operational staff or chargeable. If there is a centralized training budget most costs will be borne by the training department, although usually not learners' salary costs. Additional expenditure for a specific training intervention will come from reducing planned activity or gaining supplementary budgets. Where training budgets are allocated to line management, the training department will need to charge for its services. Again, what is chargeable will vary from organization to organization. A judgement will need to be made on how to present the cost of the training to line management. It can be shown as a cost per trained person or a cost per learning unit. This will be decided on the basis of what is likely to be most acceptable to line management in releasing the money.

Summary

Training design is often approached as a simple task of filling in the blanks on a daily timetable. If it is done that way, a whole series of assumptions underpins the decisions being made. It is likely that the inexperienced designer will make better decisions if those assumptions are examined. The approach adopted in this chapter allows many of the variables in design to be identified and examined before getting to a timetable.

The design of training is a complex process with the variables being highly interconnected. Therefore it requires continuous reassessment of previous decisions when a new decision is made. All the design variables are limited by the constraints which are applied, both by the organization and client, and by the designer. The learning unit model and the four ways of learning can be helpful in undertaking design. They help structure the task and provide a focus for design decisions.

The amount of effort put into perfecting the design before it is implemented can vary. If there is a long-term need and many people to be trained it may be acceptable to pilot the training and then revise it. When an important need for a small group of learners is being met, greater attention to getting it right first time may justify higher development resources.

The design produced can be judged by looking at the objectives in relation to the entry behaviour, performance assessment measures and learning event. There should be obvious links between the performance required and the methods used. The content and structure should reflect the objectives. There should be sufficient time to use the methods and the assessment measures, so that a judgement can be made on whether a training design looks right.

The real test of any design is whether the learners actually achieve the learning objective through the learning event. Only then can a judgement be made upon the success of the design. The results achieved will be due not solely to the design but also to how it was implemented, the motivation of the learners, the performance of the trainer and all of the other factors which influence the outcomes of training activities. The success of training will be judged more by changes in job performance than by whether the learning objective was achieved.

The process of designing training sets out to anticipate and plan for the factors which determine learning. The better the plan the more likely the expectation of success. A well-designed and implemented training intervention, with demonstrated results and impact, does more for the credibility of training than anything else. Success builds upon success and clients come back when they feel they have achieved the results they wanted.

Further reading

Davies, I.K. (1971) *The Management of Learning*. New York: McGraw-Hill.
Harrison, R. (1988) *Training and Development*. London: Institute of Personnel Management.
Honey, P. and Mumford, A. (1986) *Manual of Learning Styles*. Maidenhead: Peter Honey.
Huczynski, A. (1983) *Encyclopaedia of Management Development Methods*. Aldershot: Gower.
Kenney, J. and Reid, M. (1986) *Training Interventions*. London: Institute of Personnel Management.
Kolb, D. (1985) *Learning Styles Inventory*. Boston: McBer Company.
Mager, R. and Beach, K.M. (1990) *Developing Vocational Instruction*. London: Kogan Page.
Nadler, L. (1982) *Designing Training Programs*. Reading, Mass.: Addison-Wesley.
Romiszowski, A.J. (1981) *Systems Approach to Education and Training*. London: Kogan Page.
Romiszowski, A. J. (1982) *Designing Instructional Systems*. London: Kogan Page.
Sauer, S.F. and Holland, R.E. (1981) *Planning In-House Training*. San Diego: Learning Concepts.

Appendix A Learning principles checklist

1 Encourage motivation by:
   (a) Attending to work-related problems
   (b) Giving responsibility to the learner
   (c) Providing a clear performance target
   (d) Providing variety, interest and impact to the learner

(e) Providing a supportive environment

(f) Putting the learning into context

(g) Allowing the learner to succeed.

2 *Allow participation* by:

(a) Getting the learning actively involved in the learning event

(b) Using the learner's existing knowledge, skill and experience.

3 *Provide practice* by:

(a) Helping each learner to develop skilled performance

(b) Developing individual mastery of the task

(c) Supporting theories and explanations

(d) Helping consolidation of learning.

4 *Provide feedback* that is:

(a) Personal to each learner

(b) Specific to individual aspects of performance

(c) Given as soon as possible after the learner's performance

(d) Reinforcing to performance by confirming learner achievement.

5 *Be flexible* in order to:

(a) Match the pace of training to suit the individual

(b) Change the time to suit the learner

(c) Let the learner try again

(d) Allow for different learning styles, through:

Variety of learning resources

Variety of media

Counselling for learner difficulties.

6 *Help transfer* by:

(a) Using a working environment

(b) Using work situations

(c) Using learner-generated material

(d) Dealing with learner-identified issues

(e) Helping learners to develop action plans

(f) Seeking line management support.

Appendix B Training methods list

Solo learning

Assignments
Programmed learning
Project – individual
Action maze
Computer-based training
Interactive video
Simulation

One-to-one training

Guided practice
Coaching
Counselling
Mentoring
Demonstration
Simulation
Guided reading
Tutorial

Group learning

Role playing
Micro-teaching
Lecture
Lesson
Discussion
Project – group
In-tray exercise
Exercises – skills
Exercises – group
Case study – paper-based
Case study – incident
Simulation
Business games
Discovery learning
Action learning sets
Brainstorming
Field trips
Open forum

Appendix C Training media list

Chalk board
White board
Magnetic board
Flannel board
Flip chart
Overhead projector
35mm projector

Vudata/teletext
Broadcast/satellite/cable television

Video disk
Compact disk (various formats)
Microfiche
Film (16mm)
Film strip
Film loop
Tape/slide
Audio tape (pre-recorded)
Video tape (pre-recorded)

Video tape (record and replay)
Telephone
Telephone conferencing
Teleconferencing
Facsimile transmission (fax)
Computer screen and disk storage
Electronic mail

Handout
Workbook
Books
Posters

7
Tutor-delivered Training

STEVE TRUELOVE

---

*If it rained knowledge, I would hold out my
hand, but I would not give myself the
trouble to go in quest of it.*

Samuel Johnson, 1778

Introduction

This chapter attempts to give useful guidance for someone who is new
to the direct delivery role of the trainer. Although the title may imply
that the trainer 'delivers' training in the way that a parcel may be
delivered to an addressee, effective learning cannot be achieved in the
same passive way. For effective learning to take place, the trainer must
ensure that sound learning principles are followed.

Training is a term which has many interpretations. The prime
objective of any training activity is to ensure that learning takes place in
an effective way. This will not always involve the traditional role of the
trainer as teacher, but rather that of a facilitator to assist the learner to
make progress for him or herself. Notwithstanding the amazing
developments that have taken place in recent years with alternative
modes of delivery, there is still a great demand for classroom-based,
tutor-delivered training. People do, however, demand and expect
training to be lively and stimulating. They will not put up with dreary,
dull and irrelevant training, and nor should they. While parts of this
chapter encourage you to do certain things, and not do others, it is for
you to assess and select the techniques and style you employ. There is
no 'right way' to train.

When considering styles of delivery, it may be useful to think of the balance between the contribution of the tutor and that of the learners (see figure 7.1). A good trainer will adjust his or her style according to the needs of the situation. Sometimes it is useful to vary the amount of involvement from time to time to be sure that different learning styles are catered for and to have a varied texture to the event.

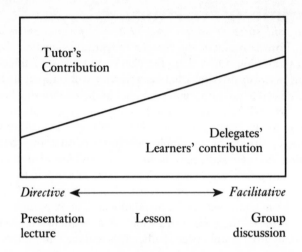

Figure 7.1   The balance between tutor's and learners' contributions

Skill in delivering training is, of course, only one component of a successful training event. The other component is technical expertise in relation to the subject matter. To an extent, a high degree of competence in one of these components can compensate for weakness in the other, but it is desirable to have strength in both. While the art of delivering training comes easily and naturally to some people, most of us need to work hard to develop competence. It is also important to realize that a wide variety of personality types can be found among successful trainers. Contrary to popular belief, the ability to talk loudly and incessantly does not mean automatic success as a trainer. Good listening skills and a genuine desire to help others to learn are probably more important. And we can all learn.

Motivating Learners

Motivation plays an important part in the learning process. People learn best when they want to learn. Obviously, the trainer cannot completely control the motivation of the learner. This is influenced by very many factors in the life of each individual, and by his or her own personality. However, because motivation is so important in the learning process, trainers should be aware of some of the factors over which they have control. The following are some key elements in the motivation of learners.

(1) *People will strive to achieve goals that they perceive as worthwhile and attainable.* For many adults, the very act of learning something of interest is sufficient motivation. Offer them the chance to learn something which will help them perform their jobs better, and they will jump at it. Sometimes, though, we need to put effort into pointing out the relationship between what they will learn and their jobs – it is not always as obvious to them as it is to us.

Learning for its own sake is not always enough. A qualification, be it a prestigious certificate or a humble operator's permit, may be important. Recognition that new skills have been learned and knowledge acquired can be imparted by public acts of acknowledgement: a picture in the newsletter, a bulletin on the noticeboard or a word of encouragement from someone higher in the organization can be inspirational. The important thing is, it is what *the learners* think is worthwhile that matters. If you offer an inappropriate goal, it will reduce rather than enhance motivation.

For optimum motivation, and subsequent feelings of accomplishment, the goal should be attainable with effort. If no effort is called for, then the value of the goal is reduced. On the other hand, if the learner believes that he or she is incapable of reaching the goal, or that the effort required is out of proportion to its value, then motivation will diminish.

(2) *Regular, informative feedback that is easy to interpret and provides evidence of progress sustains motivation.* Wherever possible, the learning situation should provide the feedback on the trainee's performance directly to him or her without the need for the trainer's involvement. This is easiest in situations such as the learning of keyboard skills on a computer, where the equipment can very easily measure and report progress.

In many training contexts this is not possible. Feedback must be given in an appropriate, encouraging manner by the trainer or by other trainees. Sometimes techniques such as video recording may allow the trainees to give themselves feedback in a way that is not normally available to them.

(3) *Adults very much want to be involved in the learning process.* Always work out ways to involve people as much as possible. Adults are not blank sheets of paper who need to have knowledge painted on them by someone with all the answers. Rather, they come to the training situation with a wealth of experience and existing skills. They relate new learning to what they already know. If they are allowed to have a say in the design and content of their learning, then their commitment will be higher than if it is imposed on them.

Adults learn best in an informal atmosphere. Learning and fun are compatible. If your trainees go away saying, 'It was hard work, but we enjoyed it and learned a lot', then you have probably got the balance right.

(4) Finally, although it is the trainer's job to make everything for the learners as conducive to learning as possible, you cannot learn for them. If they are determined not to put any effort into learning, they probably will not.

Presentation

Delivering a presentation is as much a skill as other methods of communication, such as letter writing or interviewing. There are points of techniques to be learned and practised, and all of us must evolve ways of presenting which suit our particular personalities. There is no single 'right way' to deliver a presentation, and any one person can employ a range of styles according to the particular combination of subject matter, audience and other circumstances that he or she may encounter on different occasions.

Confidence

For many people, lack of confidence is the biggest obstacle to delivering an effective presentation. This leads to nervousness and anxiety, and hence to a stilted and awkward performance. Thus the individual becomes convinced that he or she is 'no good at giving presentations', and avoids doing them. This leads to a negative cycle which inhibits learning improvement (see figure 7.2). It is therefore necessary to break this cycle to increase confidence.

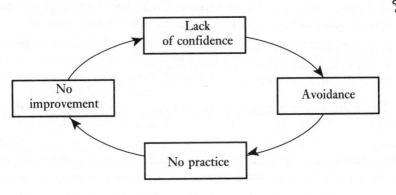

Figure 7.2   A negative cycle

Lack of confidence is caused by:

- Fear of looking foolish
- Fear of the audience's reaction
- Fear of drying up
- Lack of experience.

Confidence can be increased by:

- Preparing thoroughly so that you really know the subject matter
- Rehearsing so that it does not feel as if you are delivering your presentation for the first time
- Assessing your audience and anticipating their reactions
- Experience.

Preparing

Before you can begin to prepare a presentation, it is necessary to ask yourself a series of questions:

- What is the purpose of the presentation?
- Who is the audience?
- What are the circumstances?

The purpose

There are three categories into which the purpose of most presentations falls:

1 To communicate information
2 To make a proposition
3 To inspire and motivate.

In a training context, the presentation may serve all three of these purposes simultaneously. For example, the trainer may want to:

1 Outline an appraisal scheme
2 Persuade the audience to support the concept
3 Generate enthusiasm for the introduction of the scheme.

The commonest purpose of the trainer's presentation is to impart knowledge. When this is the case, it is usually simple to generate a concise overall objective statement such as: 'By the end of the presentation, the members of the audience will be able to list the four main stages in the selection and purchase of a new photocopier.' If more than one purpose is being served, then obviously more than one objective statement must be generated.

The audience

The members of the audience will influence the presentation in several ways. Before beginning to prepare, it is necessary to consider the following questions:

• Who will be present?
• How many will be present?
• What is the extent of their existing knowledge?
• What will be of interest to them?
• What attitudes, preconceptions or expectations will they bring with them?

The presentation needs to be pitched as accurately as possible for the audience. Explaining things at too elementary a level will leave the audience bored and frustrated; assuming they know more than they actually do can result in them losing the thread and failing to absorb the message. Either way, the audience will become irritated and will resent your lack of consideration for them.

However, it is not always possible to gain accurate information about the audience. When it is, the audience may be found to be very mixed in terms of existing expertise, age, education and so on. In this case, consider whether it is possible to reorganize the presentation to overcome these problems. It may be possible to provide background information for those that need it in advance. Otherwise, acknowledge your problem to the audience. Explain that some of them may find some aspects rather elementary, and ask for their forbearance. Plan to use their knowledge to support your presentation if possible.

The circumstances

Other factors which have to be taken into account at this stage are the general and specific circumstances in which you will be operating. They include:

• The venue
• Equipment
• The time available
• The context.

You may have a choice of venue, or you may have none. The size of the room, the furniture, position of power points, and other practical considerations all need to be known. If they are not ideal, can a better venue be found, or must you make do come what may?

You may have access to the full range of modern audio-visual equipment, or none at all. You must know what is available, and select the appropriate aids for your purpose.

Ideally, you should have as much time as you need to put across your message, and no more. In practice, you may be allocated a very specific time slot and have to make the best use of it. We often underestimate the time needed to put across a complex message, so if time is limited, the message may have to be simplified.

The context in which a presentation is delivered is important. Is it at the start of the day with a group who are new to each other, or is it the fourth item in a crowded agenda? Are you being judged against others making similar presentations, or will they only see yours? Are you bringing good news which will be eagerly anticipated, or bad news which will provoke hostility?

Only when all these questions have been addressed can the presenter move on to the detailed preparation, the planning, of the presentation.

Planning

There are various methods people use to plan a presentation. One popular way is to jot down key words or phrases to cover all the points that might be included in the presentation. At all times, the objective of the presentation should be kept in mind. At this stage, do not worry about sequence or timing.

A good presentation, like a good story, has a beginning, a middle and an end. That is:

- Introduction
- Development
- Conclusion.

Paradoxically, the introduction is best prepared after the other material. This is because the introduction will outline the content of the development section, and so this must be prepared first. To do this, the points already noted down must be grouped under appropriate main headings. Three or four major sections should evolve, and as you work a theme will probably suggest itself. Some of the points will fit best into the introduction or conclusion sections. Others may not fit well anywhere. Perhaps the section headings need to be revised, or maybe the points should be dropped from the presentation altogether. Do not expect to be able to arrive at a satisfactory plan in one go. If you get stuck or confused, leave it. Do something else for a while and let your mind clear. Often, when you return to the problem, things will fall into place more readily.

Once you have decided upon the content, the next stage is to work out a logical sequence and timings. The sequence will depend upon the nature of the content. Sometimes it will be obvious (for example, historical development); sometimes less so. It may not even be important. Try different ideas until it feels right. Timing can be achieved either by speaking aloud what you intend to say, and noting the time taken, or by making the material fit the time you decide. Your broad outline may look like this:

Time available:	20 minutes	
Introduction	2 minutes	(10%)
Development:		
Historical background:	4 minutes	(20%)
Recent developments:	5 minutes	(25%)
Case examples:	6 minutes	(30%)
Conclusion:	3 minutes	(15%)

Then prepare your notes. Try not to write a speech; rather write down key words or phrases to remind you of what you wish to say. Note down the points at which you might use a visual aid. Some people like to use cards as prompts; others are happier using a flat sheet of paper. Try different approaches until you settle on one which you are happy with.

Your notes may look something like this:

```
Start:   Welcome
         Introduction – Self
                      – Topic (equal opportunity policy)
                      – Reason for presentation
                                           2 minutes
OHP1:    'The law'
         Key points – Sex Discrimination Act
                    – Equal Pay Act
                    – Race Relations Act
                                           5 minutes
OHP2:    'Why do we need a policy?'
         Key points – Codes of practice
                    – Consistency
                    – Moral arguments
                                           6 minutes
```

and so on.

Rehearsal and practice

A rehearsal is an important element in the preparation of a presentation. If possible, use the actual venue where your presentation will be delivered. One of the key purposes of the rehearsal is to check the timing. Find out if your time estimates are near the mark, or way off. Your timings need not be absolutely precise; remember that an audience slows you down.

Even if you do not rehearse standing in front of an empty room, practise what you are going to say by using your notes as triggers. This can be done at home, and you can ask friends or relatives to give their reactions. Rehearse key points. If you are going to move around, practise this too, so that your movement looks purposeful and authoritative, instead of random and pointless. If you are using visual aids, practise their use as well. Knowing how to switch the projector on before you appear in front of the audience may sound obvious, but you will probably be able to remember an occasion when the presenter had to call for assistance!

Well before the day, decide what you are going to wear. Wear clothes that make you feel both comfortable and confident. Make sure that your chosen outfit is clean and presentable. Some people can be very put off by an unconventional appearance, so it is usually best to err on the conservative side.

Visual aids

Of the many aids available, by far the commonest currently used are: whiteboards, flip charts, overhead projectors, video tapes and 35 mm transparencies. Whichever aids are used, it is important that you are thoroughly familiar with them and their characteristics. Do not use too many aids – your presentation will look disjointed and confused.

Whiteboards:

- Check that the pens are the right kind. The wrong ones will not wipe off!
- Check that you have spare pens. The ink can run dry.

Flip charts:

- Have plenty of paper available.
- Check the pens.
- Check the stand, particularly how the paper is fixed on.
- Check that whatever you have written or will write can be seen from the back of the room.

Overhead projectors:

- Check that a spare lamp is readily available.
- Check the socket position.
- Check that the screen is clear of direct sunlight.
- Check focus and visibility.

Video tapes:

- Check how the machine is operated.
- Check that the TV/monitor is correctly tuned in. Check colour and contrast as well as the sound volume.
- Check you have the right tape.

35 mm transparencies:

- Check that you have a suitable platform for the projector.
- Check whether there is a remote control lead.
- Mark all your transparencies so that you get them the right way round and in the right order.
- Rehearse with your projectionist if you have one.

Self-review

The following checklist can be used after the delivery of a training event for your own self-assessment and review. Not all the questions may be relevant, but these and others will help you to focus on areas for improvement.

1 Was my material appropriate for the group?
2 Did the main points come out?
3 Was there too much or too little material?
4 Did I secure the attention and interest of the group?
5 Did I use my communication aids as well as possible?
6 Did I encourage participation?
7 Did I say 'Er' or 'Mm' or 'OK' (or whatever) excessively?
8 Was I heard and understood? How do I know?
9 Did I use the time well?
10 Did I achieve my objectives?

Role Playing

Role playing is one of the oldest techniques devised to assist learning by direct experience in a simulated setting. Role playing is often very helpful in working on problems in a way that produces graphic illustrations of effective or ineffective behaviour that the participants have generated for themselves. They have not simply observed someone else act out a situation, as they do when they watch a dramatized training video, but they have had to put effort, and perhaps emotion, into the process.

Role play ought to be an opportunity to practise behaviours in a risk-free, safe setting. This is not automatically the case, and people can get upset if a role play gets out of hand. Participants can get carried away with the situation, or use it to score points in an aggressive manner. For some people, the role-play method can be quite abhorrent, while others really relish the chance to demonstrate their dramatic skills.

Starting role playing

In a role play, the trainer provides a clear definition of the situation in as much detail as is necessary. Often a very brief description will suffice, but some role-play briefs can be quite lengthy. Individuals are selected or volunteer to be characters to play the various roles in acting out the situations. They may be briefed publicly or privately. The brief may be verbal or written, or a mixture. Time to prepare may be allowed. The drama may take place with or without part of the group as an audience. Some people find role playing in front of a large audience extremely stressful and it often best to leave this to volunteers.

Role plays can be left open-ended, or subject to strict time limits. Sometimes they are interrupted for discussion after interesting points have emerged. They may or may not be recorded. In any event, the process must be analysed and discussed on completion so that learning points are fully absorbed.

Uses of role play

1 To illustrate clearly a feature of some specific behaviour in a lively and direct way. This can include features of non-verbal behaviour that cannot be clearly illustrated otherwise.
2 To increase the involvement of the group. Effort is required from them and a well-performed role play leads to a feeling of accomplishment.
3 To provide a common experience for the group to discuss.
4 To practise specific behavioural skills, such as interviewing, chairing a meeting or greeting customers.
5 To help people understand a situation from the viewpoint of others. Having to play the part of someone who has the opposite role to that usually

performed in real life often produces a significant increase in empathy and understanding. For example, a manager who plays the role of a union representative defending a colleague from dismissal may achieve far more insight in this way than from simply discussing the situation.

6 To give insight into their own behaviours and the effect this has on others.

7 To make possible experimentation in a no-risk setting. Participants can try out tactics that are new to them, or employ alternative behaviours to evaluate their effectiveness.

Points to watch

1 It is usually best to keep written descriptions as brief as possible. Very long, detailed scenarios are difficult for people to memorize and items which have been inserted for background can end up dominating the discussion.

2 Sometimes it is better for the trainer to choose participants, sometimes to call for volunteers. You should aim to avoid anyone trying to perform a role play which is beyond him or her. The participant may feel humiliated or inadequate, or may 'rubbish' the exercise, with reactions like, 'It's not real', 'The brief was unclear' or 'I would never do that'.

3 Avoid boss–subordinate pairings unless you have a good reason for them.

4 Watching too many role plays one after the other can become boring for audiences.

5 Beware the over-exuberant character who turns your description of a slightly disgruntled customer into a caricature of Attila the Hun on a bad night.

6 People find it hard to play characters that are of a different age group or of the opposite gender. It is often possible to write roles which allow the participants to project themselves into the situation. Rather than 'You are a 56-year-old transport manager named Norman who wants to tell Mandy, the 19-year-old typist, to cut down on private telephone calls', try 'You are a manager who has decided to tell a subordinate to cut down on private telephone calls.'

7 It is the trainer's responsibility to protect participants from role plays which get out of hand.

8 It is sometimes possible to create role plays on the spot from incidents described by course members. For instance, members of the group may be asked to describe situations which they have found difficult to handle. One or two of these may then be acted out to determine the best way to resolve the problems described.

9 Debrief. Ensure that the mistakes made by the role character are seen as such, not as those of the person playing that character. Role plays often stimulate conflict. If the debriefing does not allow the participants to discard their roles, then you may have created tensions and animosities between course members.

10 Review what happened. Make sure that anyone who has been designated as an observer is allowed to report what she or he has observed. In leading the discussion:
  (a) Determine what happened.
  (b) Identify what went well.
  (c) Explore the way in which the situation developed and the reasons the role players behaved as they did.
  (d) Discuss how the situation might be better handled, or how real situations differ.
11 When the situation is appropriate, allow a second go to get it right.

Group Discussion

A group discussion is a method that may be used by a trainer to create a learning situation where attitudes and opinions are sought and examined. There are three key features about the process:

1 The participative environment encourages the sharing of experiences and the introduction and development of ideas.
2 The fact that all the participants are actively involved in thinking, listening and speaking leads to better learning and fuller understanding.
3 Adults like to learn in this way.

These effects do not, however, occur automatically.

Consider what would happen if you had a group of 16-year-old school leavers and said to them: 'Discuss among yourselves the differences between the approaches to learning propounded by Skinner and Kolb'. You are unlikely to get much of a discussion. Even if a topic is chosen that everyone knows about, it may be difficult for the participants to get started if they are not given some help. Accordingly, before initiating a group discussion, the trainer has to prepare.

Preparation

Topic
The first item in the process of preparing for a group discussion is the selection of the topic. Not all topics are best taught by group discussion. Indeed, the process itself may introduce no new facts to the group. What does occur, however, is the sharing of information held by the various group members (which may include the trainer). The process is valuable in the exchange of views and ideas, in problem solving and in the clarification of attitudes and understanding. You may, for example,

choose to examine the ways in which a disciplinary situation might be handled by means of a group discussion. Because people will bring a range of different experiences with them, an interesting and lively discussion is likely from which group members will learn and some attitudes may be altered.

Purposes
The group discussion process may have various purposes, such as:

● To disseminate knowledge about a subject
● To solve problems and make decisions
● To develop interpersonal skills
● To influence attitudes
● To enliven a training event
● To develop relationships within the group.

This list is not exhaustive. Sometimes it is appropriate to have more clearly defined objectives, sometimes not.

Environment
People should be sitting down fairly close to each other, ideally in a circle. If the group is too big, then some will not participate, so splitting into smaller groups may be appropriate. It may also be useful to provide flip charts or other aids to assist the group. For some topics, absolute privacy will be essential.

Getting started
There are various ways in which the initial discussion may be stimulated. With some groups and some topics, it may work simply to say, 'Now have a group discussion about X.' However, normally group discussions are more successful if they follow some other sort of input, such as:

1 Introductory talk or presentation
2 Film or video
3 Case study or written handout
4 Exercise or game.

For example, if you wanted to explore the topic of self-development you might try one of these approaches:

1 A talk about the psychology of self-development
2 A video about self-development
3 A short case study highlighting self-development
4 Ask who feels that they have contributed to their own career progression through self-development.

Films and videos, as well as imparting information, often serve as a vehicle to examine particular approaches and attitudes. For example, you might follow up a film with the question, 'Do you think that the way the problem was resolved in the film would work where you are employed?'.

How to achieve the objectives

Once you have got the discussion started, how will you make sure that your objectives will be achieved? What will you do if the participants are unable to see the points you had in mind? What if there is an adverse reaction to the topic, or someone gets upset?

The first time you try to create a group discussion of a topic, you will have little idea how long it will last and what degree of interest it will stimulate. It may also generate friction between the participants, or lead to some participants being frozen out. You must, as far as possible, prepare for all these eventualities. This may involve having back-up case study or presentation material, and you should think through how to handle any difficult situations which may arise.

Control

The degree of control will vary according to the objectives of the trainer and the nature of the group. The skill of a trainer is in selecting the most appropriate style of control as much as it is in exercising that control. The style may vary during the course of a discussion, with the trainer judging when it is right to intervene, and when it is right to withdraw. The following three styles, therefore, may be considered as a range of options which merge into each other rather than as discrete entities.

Close control

The discussion leader controls the discussion by asking questions which are replied to by group members directing the response to the leader. The leader may even decide who will contribute at which point by naming who will respond, and may suppress uninvited contributions. The leader will evaluate all contributions, and pass judgement in terms of 'That's right', or 'That's wrong'. The success of the discussion will be judged by him or her in terms of whether or not the group has reflected the leader's attitudes back to him or her.

This style is often employed where there is a specific problem to be discussed in a limited time. The degree of control, while high, is often not perceived as unwelcome by the group. Indeed, group participants may be impressed by the authority which is displayed. They feel they have participated, but are aware of the high proportion of the leader's contribution, and may value this.

The success of this style will depend to a large extent on the group's willingness to accept it, and the level of expertise of the leader compared to the group. The style will lead to conflict or non-participation if the group resents the leader's approach. In particular, a group which has been used to less control may react very negatively if this approach is adopted by a new course tutor.

Medium control

Here the trainer initiates the discussion, but permits and encourages the group to talk to each other directly, rather than through the chair. Some of the control mechanisms normally used are suppressed, and the trainer leaves it to the group to evaluate contributions. He or she intervenes from time to time to expand on points which have arisen, and to point the discussion in the required direction. This may be by encouraging certain individuals to expand their contributions, or by stating, 'I think we're moving too far ahead', or making some other such comment to restrict digression.

To encourage the group further to participate without undue deference, the leader may sit among the group to reduce the emphasis on the leader role, and may keep silent for quite long periods. If the discussion goes well, the leader does not interfere. This may sound easy; but not joining in a lively and interesting group discussion is a skill which requires some practice, particularly from people who are used to adopting a more active role.

Low control

The leader may withdraw from the discussion completely, or may sit at the back of the room and observe – participating only when invited, or when things are obviously going wrong. A group that is not used to this style often finds it uncomfortable to begin with. It tends to work better when the group has been divided into smaller groups to discuss something. They then do not expect to be led.

The leader is invited to contribute facts or to give procedural advice. If the group asks for his or her opinion of the matter under discussion then he or she will avoid giving it. Instead, the leader will turn the question back to the group, or may state a number of different opinions to give the group something to work on.

The facilitator role

The text above uses the term 'leader'. However, it will be seen that in a medium-control or low-control situation, the trainer is actively avoiding leading the group for much of the time. The trainer may then be viewed as a facilitator who is there to help the group reach its objectives – and these may have been determined by the group, not the trainer.

In order to function in a facilitating role, the trainer must be perceived as a trustworthy person who understands what is happening, and can be relied upon to prevent conflict or personal antagonism getting out of hand. In particular the facilitator may perform the following functions:

- Encouraging contributions, particularly from the less self-confident, and ensuring the more verbose do not completely take over
- Controlling conflict by stepping in if necessary to divert the discussion to a less contentious issue, or by pointing out areas of agreement; or by analysing what has caused the conflict so that the participants can take a more objective, and therefore less emotional, view
- Summarizing from time to time, and perhaps posing a question or making a suggestion to take the discussion forward
- Assisting 'weaker' participants by rephrasing their arguments for them so that these do not get lost just because they are not forcefully put across. This may also be done by testing understanding of their contribution by questioning
- Ensuring individuals receive positive feedback from the group, perhaps by acknowledging contributions that the group ignores, or by seeking positive contributions from others if a negative evaluation is given
- Providing feedback to the group as a whole as to its performance
- Providing the information and resources for the group to function effectively
- Staying quiet when all is well; permitting silences, and allowing time for people to think
- Ensuring that the discussion is brought to a close when the topic is exhausted
- Ensuring that the whole group attains common goals, and derives its greatest satisfaction from having done this together.

These skills take practice to acquire, and inexperienced trainers should not assume that they will be able to hand whatever arises in a group discussion. Group discussions are a powerful technique both in learning and attitude development, and trainers should be aware of the options they have, and the sensitivities involved.

Games, Simulations and Exercises

There is a lot of confusion between concepts such as 'game' and 'exercise' when used in a training context. For the sake of clarity, therefore, let us first distinguish between three types of activity by looking at some key characteristics.

Games:

- Are competitive
- Involve scoring or racing to produce winners
- Have 'rules'
- Have participants who are 'players'.

Simulations:

- Attempt to represent reality
- Have participants adopting roles in an in-depth way so that they become really involved in the process
- Are not carefully guided, but require the participants to behave as they would do in real life.

Exercises:

- Do not have roles
- Maintain objectivity
- May be individual or group
- Are often about analysing situations that have been described rather than experienced.

Games

Games are introduced into training events for a number of reasons. One of the main benefits of using games is that they are (usually) fun. Giving people a task to accomplish in competition with others very quickly produces a buzz of excitement and energy that participants find invigorating. The purpose of the game will often be to provide an opportunity to look at teamwork, leadership, organization or planning. The value of the game is in the lessons that can be drawn from the processes that took place during the activity, so that participants gain insight into the principles under consideration, or into their own behaviour.

There are some dangers with the use of games:

- Some people reject them as childish, and either do not participate at all or do so without commitment.
- Some people get so involved with the game that they may get upset about losing, or believe that having won they have nothing to learn.
- The lessons to be learned from the way in which the game went may be difficult to translate into a 'back at work' model.
- Some games have tricks built into them that can cause resentment.
- Some games are so widely used that there is a chance that participants will have experienced them before.
- Some trainers use the games without ensuring that the appropriate learning takes place.

Simulations

Although simulations may involve the adoption of roles, they are not role plays as such, in that role plays may usually be thought of as dramatic in their nature. Characters in role plays are often given attitudes to display, and there is usually an audience. Simulations always involve decision making about doing something or not doing something. Although roles may be assigned, it is usually the problem that is central to the simulation rather than the characters tackling the problem. Simulations involve trial and error, and errors provide a basis for learning.

The commonest usage of simulations is in the area of business or finance training. Some simulations go on for several days, with individuals adopting the roles of production planner, finance director and so on. Many computer-based simulations are available, but the use of computers is not a prerequisite of the use of simulations. Simulations may be extremely specific and created for clearly defined situations, or may be much more general in their scope.

The dangers of using simulations are:

- If they are not very carefully constructed, the feeling of realism will not develop and learning will therefore feel shallow.
- All possible decisions need to be anticipated in advance, otherwise groups will feel that they have been denied the chance to practise their skills in the way they wanted.
- If computers are used, remember they can (and do) go wrong.
- Some simulations go on too long, with participants feeling that the value of the learning is not in proportion to the time spent.
- Simulations can be rejected as not relevant – 'We don't make cars, therefore these principles don't apply to us.'

Exercises

In an exercise, participants remain themselves. They analyse and discuss situations which may be given to them in a variety of ways. Exercises can be cooperative, and may be open-ended. They may be brief, or fairly extensive. Types of exercise include:

- Case study
- Problem solving
- Task completion
- Review of participants' experiences
- Brainstorming.

As before, any exercise should be used with specific purposes in mind. During a long training course, as many different kinds of exercises as possible should be used to help maintain interest.

Case study exercises come in many different forms. They can be real cases which look at the financial situation of a particular company, the way a hospital is organized or the conduct of an industrial dispute. More often, they are fictional examples written with a particular purpose in mind. Participants may be asked to study the case example, and then explain it with reference to principles already learned. Or they may be asked to propose a solution to a problem. Usually, case studies are discussed in small groups followed by a plenary (full group) session.

Problem-solving exercises are often used to illustrate the necessity of teamwork or sharing of information, or, indeed, to look at the process of problem solving itself.

Task-completion exercises will often be used in general management or team-building courses as a vehicle for looking at leadership or the process of task accomplishment. They need not be competitive, but often small groups work in parallel so that everyone is involved and differences in approach can be studied.

Reviews of participants' experience can be extremely effective if not used too often. This type of exercise may start: 'Think of the worst training event that you ever attended. Why was it so bad?' and so on.

Brainstorming approaches can be useful to get ideas out very fast for a tutor-led discussion. For example: 'In groups of three or four, list at least twenty types of insurance policy.'

Whatever type of exercise is used, timing is often crucial – too little time, and some of the value is lost; too much, and the course begins to drag. Be prepared to modify timings with experience.

Lesson

The term 'lesson' conjures up images of school children fervently copying down from the blackboard, and may therefore produce a negative reaction. It need not, however, be like that. What distinguishes a lesson from a presentation is the amount of interaction that occurs between the trainer and the group.

Although a lesson may include elements of presentation, such as visual aids, the trainer may seek interaction with the group at frequent intervals. The key to an interesting and stimulating lesson is the use of questioning techniques. In some respects, a good lesson is very like a group discussion, except with higher than normal control. Instead of telling the group your definition of organization (or whatever), you ask them. You encourage questioning and challenging, and you get members of the group to provide examples from their experiences rather than giving them examples from your own experience. In this way, the lesson moves from being a one-way 'talk and chalk' experience to being a truly participative event in which the trainees contribute to the subject matter covered. Very importantly, trainees are allowed to display their existing knowledge if they choose. They do not have to sit passively without the opportunity of sharing what they know.

Adopting this style of delivery not only produces a good response from the audience, it is also easier. Once you realize you do not have to know more about every aspect of the topic than everyone else in the room, then you can relax a little. Acknowledge the greater experience or expertise of some of the group and you will win their respect and support. Ignore it, and they will resent you.

As far as possible, all contributions should be encouraged. This can be difficult if a trainee makes inappropriate contributions, but he or she can at least be thanked for trying. Nobody should feel that by speaking up he or she is risking ridicule or hostility from the trainer. Quiet trainees may need to be encouraged to make a contribution by asking them by name if they have something to say. It is often better to allow people to stay quiet during the early part of a course. They may contribute more fully once they are more relaxed, and have seen that speaking up is risk-free.

Another time when it may be appropriate to name someone to respond is if you see that someone is becoming distracted. Hearing one's own name quickly refocuses attention! Having said that, do not get too sensitive about the fact that not everybody will hang on to your every word throughout your lesson. Some people have difficulty concentrating on anything for very long. Others will already know what you are telling them, or they may have other things on their minds. After all, if you attend a course, do you concentrate from start to finish?

Should you find that people regularly become bored and inattentive, take this as an indication that you are doing something wrong. You are probably talking too much and preventing them from participating as they would wish. A common fault is the trainer who arrives with a set of fifty or sixty transparencies and works through them slowly and inexorably.

Getting Started

There are many ways to start a training event, and it is possible to find publications which give detailed instructions for some of them. The start of a course is important. Learners need to be relaxed in order to participate in a natural and spontaneous way. Just as importantly, the trainer needs to relax and get to know the learners.

Some of the techniques that it is possible to find under the general heading of 'icebreakers' may create more anxiety in learners rather than reduce it, and others may be rejected as patronizing or childish by some. The two most commonly used methods of getting started are self-introduction and mutual introduction.

Self-introduction

Learners are asked to tell the group about themselves. The trainer may specify what is required, such as: name, job, organization/department, years' service, and a statement of what the learner wants to get out of this course. This technique is fine in small groups, or if the learners already know each other well. In larger groups, those whose turn to report will come near the end may experience considerable anxiety about having to talk to the group about themselves. They may sit there in paralysed silence as they hear that everyone else in the room is more knowledgeable, more senior and more confident than they are. If they are prone to blushing or stumbling over their words, this is a very good way to make sure they do so. For these reasons, this technique is sometimes called 'creeping death'.

Mutual introduction

Form the learners into pairs or threes and ask them to find out about the other person or people. What they have to find out may be specified, or left up to them. It is important that they all know that they will be reporting back to the whole group about the person they are talking to so that they will make notes. Set a time limit and try to stick to it. While this technique can take ten to fifteen minutes longer than self-introduction, it is considerably more effective as a warm-up activity. If some of the learners already know each other, ask them to pick someone they do not know very well to talk to. You will probably find that even people who have worked for the same company for many years do not know much about each other, and welcome the opportunity to chat.

Getting Ideas Out and Shared

Apart from structured activities, there are many opportunities for stimulating participation in a less organized way. Using a variety of simple techniques can help.

Brainstorming

This is a long-established technique based on the principle of allowing all participants to put forward whatever ideas they have about a topic without any initial filtering of these ideas. The trainer first poses a question, and then records on the board all the ideas put forward. The trainer can stop the process when enough ideas have been generated, or when the participants are running out of ideas.

Whereas true brainstorming forbids initial filtering of suggestions, it is sometimes necessary in training to reject (kindly) some ideas if their recording would confuse others. You are also supposed to record the ideas in the words of the person putting them forward – but for practical reasons it may be necessary to shorten some contributions. For example, you might abbreviate 'People who have bought something from you which they aren't happy about and who were not satisfied with the way you dealt with them' to 'Dissatisfied clients'. It is best to check that your abbreviated version represents the idea the contributor had in mind, and that you have not missed the point.

For a fuller description of the brainstorming technique, see chapter 1.

Buzz groups

Form the large group into small units of two, three or four people with a remit to come up with ideas, examples or whatever else you want. This can be done without breaking the group up physically, and buzz groups may exist for just a minute or two. For example, you might say: 'Form together into twos or threes and see if you can come up with a reasonable definition of learning.'

Syndicate groups

These are similar to buzz groups, but may need to be organized more carefully and may require separate rooms to work in. They are given a discussion topic and are required to form a group consensus, reporting back after a given time limit.

Some trainers are uncomfortable about letting syndicate groups work for too long on their own and like to monitor them carefully. Usually this is not necessary. If they know where you are they will ask you if they have a problem. Do not be too rigid with your time limit. If they are having an enjoyable and worthwhile discussion, allow it to run over if they want it to – providing it does not unduly disrupt your overall plans. Groups differ in how much they talk and in how strictly they adhere to time limits. Some competitive groups see the time specified as a target to be beaten!

You need to decide how you want the syndicate group to report back to you. It may be better to deal with each group in turn, or let all groups contribute in an unstructured way. You may want them to present back using the flip chart or board. Do they choose their representative, or will you select for them?

Summary

This chapter has attempted to give useful guidance with regard to a range of delivery techniques. Direct trainers must experiment with techniques, and evolve their own styles and methodologies. Like most work-related areas which involve people, the delivery of training is an interactive one. What works well one time falls flat the next, or vice versa.

Above all, trainers have to be true to themselves in the way they conduct training. There is no such thing as the 'perfect trainer', but trainers who are consistently well received have five things in common:

1 They prepare thoroughly.
2 They care about the learners.
3 They are flexible.
4 They are prepared to let their own personalities come through to the learners.
5 They enjoy training.

Helping others to learn is one of the most important activities in the world of work. It can also be enjoyable, rewarding and immensely satisfying.

Further reading

Forbess-Greene, S. (1983) *The Encyclopedia of Icebreakers*. San Diego: Applied Skills Press.
Gibbs, G. (1988) *Learning by Doing*. London: Further Education Unit.
Goad, T.W. (1982) *Delivering Effective Training*. San Diego: University Associates.
Jones, K. (1989) *A Sourcebook of Management Simulations*. London: Kogan Page.
Rae, L. (1984) *The Skills of Human Relations Training*. Aldershot: Gower.
Schindler-Rainman, E. and Cole, J. (1988) *Taking your Meetings Out of the Doldrums*. San Diego: University Associates.
Stevens, M. (1987) *Improving Presentation Skills*. London: Kogan Page.
Stuart, C. (1988) *Effective Speaking*. London: Pan Books.

8
Open and Distance Learning

JIM STEWART AND ROSEMARY WINTER

> *'What is the use of a book,' thought Alice,*
> *'without pictures or conversations?'*

> Lewis Carroll

Introduction

Many organizations in recent years have turned to alternative methods of training which do not rely on direct face-to-face contact between trainees and trainers or instructors. A common term used to describe these methods is 'open and distance learning'. This chapter will examine the application and use of key methods and techniques within open and distance learning, and will also look at some of the critical issues for organizations and trainers using the methods. Some illustrative case studies and materials will be included to highlight the main points. Before describing the key methods, however, we will first comment on the development of open and distance learning in relation to more traditional methods and offer some definitions of the term 'open and distance learning'.

Open and Distance Learning Defined

The term 'open and distance learning' can be said to be something of a compromise, since the concepts of 'open' and 'distance' are in fact separate and not necessarily related to each other. What we mean by this is that a particular training activity or method can be 'open' without being 'distance' and vice versa. As we shall describe later, though, the expansion in the use of alternative methods over the last ten years has required the adoption of a fairly simple and generic term, such as open and distance learning, to provide a short-hand way of collectively defining the methods. From a training perspective, however, it is important to understand the differences between open and distance since each has different implications for trainers, organizations and learners. The following definitions will clarify the differences.

Distance learning means that the learner:

- Is not continuously and immediately supervised by a trainer or tutor
- Does benefit from the services of a training/tutorial organization
- Utilizes materials in a variety of media provided by the training/tutorial organization.

It is clear from the above that the concept of distance refers to a separation in space and time of learners and trainers, although the latter, as with traditional methods, do provide the learning opportunities. This can be contrasted with the following definition of open learning.

Open learning aims to offer/provide flexibility and autonomy to learners to decide:

- What is learned
- How it is learned
- When it is learned
- Where it is learned
- At what pace learning occurs.

The critical feature of open learning, then, is the degree of autonomy given to learners in the training activity. Such autonomy may or may not be present in distance learning. Separation of trainer and learner may or may not be present in open learning. Therefore 'open' and 'distance' are separate concepts. The separateness of the two concepts is usefully illustrated in figure 8.1.

The figure also makes the point that neither concept is an absolute. Both are continuums on which any particular method or training activity can be placed in comparison with any other. For example, a traditional training course run centrally by a training department is neither very open nor very distant. It would be placed in the bottom left quadrant of figure 8.1. By contrast, an Open University course is both more open – giving learners more autonomy in deciding when and where and what pace – and more distant, given the geographic separation of learners and training organization. Such a course would be placed in the top right quadrant of the figure.

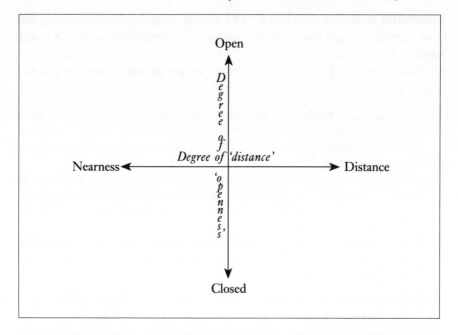

Figure 8.1   Open and distance as separate concepts

It will be clear from this discussion of the definitions that distance learning can be and often is a form of open learning. The expansion in the use of alternative training methods has tended to focus on distance learning. For these two reasons the term 'open learning' is now in common use to encompass open and distance learning methods. We will adopt that term in the rest of this chapter, but with the proviso that while distance learning is predominant in training practice it is often not very open according to the definition given above.

The Rise of Open Learning

While it is the case that open learning has expanded in recent years it is important to understand that the method is not new. Correspondence colleges have long been established as providers of education and training. Courses have normally though not exclusively been related to academic and vocational qualifications. The Open University was established in the late 1960s and offered its first courses in 1970. Even prior to that, industrial training utilized the principles of open learning in the 1950s and 1960s through programmed learning for which special machines were also developed. The history of open learning can in fact be traced as far back as the origins of organized education and training.

There are three main reasons for the recent growth in the use of open learning:

1 The concern highlighted in the 1980s to make education and training more responsive to the needs of industry and individuals in order to improve national economic performance. Open learning is seen as a means of bringing this about.
2 Arising from this, the fact that open learning has been actively promoted by central government and its agencies. The Open Tech programme, which ran from 1982 to 1987, and the establishment of the Open College in 1988 are two examples of this in practice.
3 The continuing development of information technology and its application for training purposes. Such developments provide a drive for continuing and growing use of open learning.

Although many more organizations and individuals now utilize open learning methods than, say, ten years ago, the growth has not been as great as expected or predicted when attention was first focused on the methods in the early 1980s. This is because the experience of the 1980s has provided many lessons on what makes for effective use of open learning and the relative advantages/disadvantages when compared to more traditional methods. The major lesson, as we shall see later, is that open learning is not necessarily more effective or cost efficient than formal training programmes. Before examining those arguments, though, we shall describe the major methods utilized in open learning and the lessons learned on their use.

Text-based Methods

Despite the impact of technological developments, the majority of open learning programmes still rely to some extent on text-based methods. Indeed, many in-house produced programmes to meet organization-specific needs are solely based on written materials.

Producing the materials

There are some general guidelines to be aware of in producing text-based materials, and these can usefully be considered under four key headings.

Presentation

It is important to produce as high quality as possible in terms of presentation in text-based materials. This means using good-quality paper and print-quality reproduction rather than straightforward photocopying. It also means having attractive and durable packaging materials. The use of colour in printed materials and packaging is also considered to be desirable. As well as quality of print, size is also important. Print should be large enough to be read comfortably. All of these factors affect the appearance of the materials and their acceptability to learners. This in turn will have an effect on their use and enjoyment by users. Presentation, though, is primarily concerned with the initial reaction of learners, and the higher the quality the more positive learners will feel about the materials.

Layout

Layout is in some ways similar to presentation, but it refers to how the content of the text is presented as opposed to the materials as a package. A primary consideration in layout is the use of white space. This refers to how densely the text is printed on the page. Generally the rule is to be generous with white space, and certainly text-based open learning materials need a density much less than that of this book. Spacious white borders on both sides and above and below the text are necessary, with low-density text. The use of 'boxing' for key points, learner activities, illustrative examples etc. is also a useful practice. Headings and sub-headings are important. As well as being used generously to break up the text, any one level of heading – chapter title, main heading within chapters, main sub-heading and so on – also needs to be consistent in the way it is written in order to show the reader the structure of the text; for example, using full or initial capitals and underlining. A final aspect of layout is the use of graphics and photographs. These are to be encouraged not only to illustrate the text but also to provide light relief to the eye of the learner. Anyone familiar with Open University materials will know the usefulness of pictorial content. Figure 8.2 illustrates some of these points.

Ease of use

This third guideline encompasses a number of points which are designed to make written materials 'user-friendly'. The first considera-tion is to organize the content into a logical structure. It then needs to be broken into manageable chunks and presented as a series of discrete

Defining Motivation

A useful starting point in defining motivation is to look in a dictionary. The Pocket Oxford Dictionary gives the following definition.

'What impels a person to action, e.g. fear, ambition or love.'

You will no doubt recognize in this definition the generally accepted meaning of the word. It focuses on the question Why. Why did X do so and so? Why did Y do something different? In other words what was their MOTIVE? So motivation is about explaining peoples' actions. But the word MOTIVE, the root word of motivation, also has another related though slightly different meaning. Again, the dictionary definition.

'Productive of motivation or action, especially MOTIVE POWER, mechanical or other form of energy.'

The definition suggests that motivation not only explains the reasons for a person's actions but also provides the source of energy to sustain those actions. It is obvious that people differ in the amount of energy or effort they devote to the same actions or activity. Also, a particular individual will devote differing amounts of effort to different activities. Think of some examples from your own experience. No doubt one at least of your friends spends great effort on DIY or sport or other leisure activities. Others do not and perhaps put most of their energy into work or a voluntary group or educating themselves. In all cases though they have both a source of energy for the activity and a reason for applying that energy in a particular activity. They are MOTIVATED. So, we can perhaps define motivation as follows:

'The power which drives actions and behaviour.'

Take A Moment To Think About What Is Driving Your Action In Studying This Package. Record Your Conclusions Below.

Figure 8.2   Layout in text-based open learning materials

modules or units. Both of these factors are based on sound training principles which apply equally to traditional, classroom-based courses. In open learning terms the size of a manageable chunk is much less than for trainer-delivered courses. Opinions vary on what is an optimum size, but as a general guideline learners using text-based materials should not be required to read for longer than 15 minutes without some form of activity, and should not be expected to devote more than 1 hour to a study session without a break. Modules or units therefore ideally fit into a 1-hour study session.

Learners should be provided with a study guide as part of the materials. This guide should explain what will be required of learners and provide advice on how to get the best use out of the materials. An example of a study guide is given in the appendix to this chapter.

There are two final points under this heading. First, the total package and each module or unit needs to be provided with clear learning objectives: open learners need these to point the direction of their learning and to assess their progress. Again, this is good training practice. Secondly, the use of a signposting system to guide learners through the materials is essential. Such systems are usually based on a series of clear symbols. An example of a signposting system is given in the appendix.

Interactiveness

The final guideline, interactiveness, is often the factor which is used to distinguish open learning packages from other text-based materials, such as procedural manuals or this book. The level of interactiveness can be used as a measure of the degree of openness in a set of materials.

The first key consideration in this guideline is the use of language. Open learning materials are usually written in simple and direct language. The use of jargon is avoided and all technical terms introduced with a clear explanation. In simple terms, the writing style should be closer to that adopted in the *Daily Mirror* than, say, *The Times* or the *Guardian*. Another feature of writing style is to write in the first person. This makes the writing more direct and produces a feeling of a conversation in the learner.

A second factor in interactiveness is the use of learner activities and exercises. These should be generously and regularly included in a text-based package. They can either focus on the content of the text, or they can be used to encourage and support application of learning by focusing on the learners' organization and/or job. Both kinds of activity need to be included.

A third factor is the use of self-assessment questions (SAQs) to enable learners to assess their progress. Ideally a set of SAQs should be included at the end of each module or unit. Model answers need to be provided, with an explanation of why they are chosen. Cross-referencing to the content is also useful so that learners can refer back to the text if they need to check their understanding. A set of SAQs and model answers from a package on motivation and leadership is given in figure 8.3 as an example.

The final critical feature of interactiveness is the provision of tutorial services. This can mean tutor-assessed assignments and/or tutorial guidance and advice. Each can be provided by post, telephone or face-to-face meetings. Although tutorial services are not essential, they are considered to increase the degree of interactiveness significantly.

SELF-ASSESSMENT QUESTIONS
MOTIVATION

1 Give three examples of needs associated with each of the two drives given below

TO SURVIVE

TO REPRODUCE

2 Tick whether each of the following is true or false

	TRUE	FALSE
a) The hierarchy of needs has six levels		
b) The first level of need concerns safety		
c) Sex is a social need		
d) Respect is associated with esteem		
e) The highest order of need is self-actualization		
f) The family provides security needs		

**MOTIVATION
MODEL ANSWERS**

Check your answers with my ideas below. Refer back to the page
numbers given if there are any points you are not sure of.

1 Your examples should have included items
   from the following list.

		PAGE No.

TO SURVIVE: Sustenance, e.g. food/water   16
               Warmth
               Shelter
               Avoid pain

TO REPRODUCE: Social Contact
               Companionship
               Affection
               Sexual activity

Do not be concerned if you use different words. So
long as they have similar meanings, you obviously
understand the relationships.

2 a) Is **FALSE** The hierarchy has five levels.   18
   b) Is **FALSE** The first level is physiological.   19
   c) Is **FALSE** We obviously need limited social
                  contact to meet our need for sex.
                  However, that is the ACTION that   18–19
                  we take but the need itself is
                  PYSIOLOGICAL.
   d) Is **TRUE** Respect from others is a key   19
                  part of meeting our need for self-
                  esteem.
   e) Is **TRUE** Self-actualization sits on top of   18–19
                  the pyramid and is generally
                  considered to be the highest
                  order need.
   f) Is **FALSE** Although perhaps debatably, the   18–19
                  family is generally seen as a
                  means of meeting social needs.
                  Security is associated with safety
                  needs which are more to do with
                  order, rules, laws etc. However,
                  some writers do argue that the
                  family is an expression of 'Safety
                  in Numbers'.

Figure 8.3   Self-assessment questions and model answers

Problems with text-based methods

There are of course problems in preparing and using text-based materials. The first is actually writing the text. Writing open learning materials is a definite skill which needs to be developed. The critical question is whether to use subject matter experts to write the materials or to use specialist writers. Some organizations adopt a strategy of training subject matter experts in writing skills; others utilize specialist writers who either learn the subject themselves or work with those who know the subject.

A specific aspect of writing open learning materials is constructing effective SAQs. This is a specialist skill which neither subject matter experts nor specialist writers necessarily possess. Trainers themselves may also lack the skill, and many text-based packages suffer from poor use of SAQs. Given that SAQs are an essential feature of interactiveness, it is important in producing or using text-based materials to ensure a high standard in their use.

Perhaps, though, the major problem of text-based materials is learner motivation. Many of the points given in the guidelines above are intended to overcome motivational problems; for example, presentation and interactiveness. However, it is difficult to provide variety and stimulation in text-based materials, and many learners find them boring to use. The problem of motivation is one reason why technology-based materials, such as videos and audio tapes, are usually included in open learning packages. The use of these materials is examined in the next section.

Technology-based Methods

Technology-based methods have a number of advantages over text-based material because they can add extra interest and provide further motivation for the trainee. This is simply based on the different ways other media present information:

- Audio tapes use sound.
- Video tapes use pictures and sound.
- Computer-based training uses text and graphics.
- Interactive video uses pictures, sound, text and graphics.

In this section audio and video tapes will be dealt with first, because they are the simplest, but do not allow interactions between the trainee and the training material. Computer-based training and interactive video provide a certain degree of interaction. This allows trainees to control the training they receive according to their own ability. The section will be concluded with a brief look at the emerging technologies.

Audio tapes

Audio tapes use technology (cassette players) which was developed primarily for the home entertainment market. They have proved particularly useful in language training. They can be used to record the trainees' responses (as in Linguaphone or mini-language-laboratory kits), which allows the trainee to compare their own responses to those of the tutor.

Audio tapes offer a number of advantages:

- They provide a good alternative to textual information, especially since studies (Bayard-White and Hoffos 1988) have shown that we remember twice as much of what we hear as what we read.
- They provide a more interesting form of information when speakers' skills, such as intonation, are used.
- They are a mass media technology and therefore are:
  cheap
  accessible (most people have a cassette player)
  portable (for example, they can be used in the car while travelling)
  easy to produce
  easy to use, not requiring any specialist knowledge.

However, there are several disadvantages and limits to their usefulness:

- They are only really appropriate for use with sound or information related to sound.
- They have a lower retention level than all but text methods of training delivery, because the information is only presented in one form.
- They cannot interact with the trainee, and the training they give will not respond to the trainees' ability as indicated by their responses.
- Their cheapness and ease of production means that anyone can produce this type of training material, which can therefore be of variable quality.

Hence, audio tapes tend to be used with other forms of training delivery like text.

Video

Video tapes also use technology which has been developed primarily for the home entertainment market. They provide both pictures and sound.

Video tapes offer a number of advantages:

- They can be particularly useful when training needs to show dynamic images or real activities and experiences.
- They can provide an entertaining and more memorable method of learning, as in the case of videos produced using professional actors and comedians.
- Like audio tapes they are a mass media technology and therefore are:
  cheap to buy (though less cheap to produce)
  easily accessible, using equipment which is readily available
  easy to use, not requiring any specialist knowledge
  easier to produce than the more technologically complex methods of open learning.

However, there is still a key disadvantage of videos:

- As with audios, they cannot interact with the trainee, and the training they give will not respond to the trainees' ability as indicated by their responses.

Hence, like audio tapes, they are often integrated with other training delivery methods such as text and tutors. For example, they are used with some Open University material as a source of motivation and to provide a form of tutorial support and encouragement.

Computer-based training (CBT)/computer assisted learning (CAL)

As the name suggests, this form of training delivery is based on the computer, and as such it has developed alongside the PC. Primarily it is text-based and includes graphics which can simulate movement, one of the best examples being the flight simulator. As one would expect it is particularly suitable for providing training in computer software.

Computer-based training offers a number of advantages:

- It is a convenient method of training for those with easy access to a PC.
- It can present information in a variety of forms and hence increase retention levels.
- It can provide a good method of simulating complex and dangerous situations without risk.
- The biggest advantage over video tapes and audio tapes is that the CBT package can interact with the trainees, respond to their inputs and correct their responses.

However, there are disadvantages of CBT:

- It needs a computer.
- Trainees often have to read considerable amounts of text from the screen, which can cause more eye strain than reading similar text in books.

- Unlike audio tapes and modern video tapes there are problems of compatibility between the different computers, such as IBM, BBC and Apple Macintosh.
- It is not easy to produce in terms of time, money and skills.
- Though the graphical capabilities are always being improved it cannot include real life images.
- The use of sound is limited and often not used.

And there are limitations to the interactive capabilities:

- They are not infinitely flexible. The computer's responses are limited by the programmer's ability, and the computers ability to recognize key words in typed text.
- The trainees often have to choose from a list of options, none of which may correctly reflect their views.
- The interfaces between the trainee and the computer are limited and can interfere in the process of learning; for example, a keyboard, mouse or joystick.

Interactive video (IV)

IV combines the advantages of computer-based training with video pictures and sound, producing a unique blend of audio, visual and textural databases which can be received simultaneously from one screen. The combination of these provides a dynamic method of training which, while being easy to use, can hold the interest of and motivate the trainee.

Unlike all the other technologies described in this chapter, IV is predominantly a training delivery method (65 per cent of all applications). This is because IV has not been adopted in the area of home entertainment or the workplace and therefore prices remain high. Since IV is a relatively recent and unfamiliar technology it will be dealt with in greater depth.

Basic components of an IV workstation
A typical IV delivery station will employ the components shown in figure 8.4 and described below. These can be bought separately or as a complete kit.

- *Video disk player.* This is usually a laser video disk (from which the name LaserVision or Laserdisc are sometimes used for this form of technology). It is the source of the still and moving pictures, or video sequences, and the two audio tracks. The laser video players have two main types of video signals:

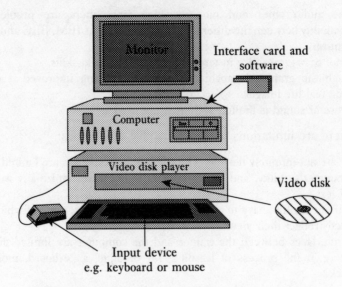

Figure 8.4   Component parts of an IV workstation

PAL, the British format, and NTSC, the American format. Most disk players are either PAL or NTSC, though dual-system players are available.

- *Computer power and software.* The computing power can come from an onboard microprocessor or an external computer such as an IBM PS/2. Generally the computer program and video run in tandem. The computer manages the video and audio material recorded on the disk and also supplies computer-generated text and graphics, which may be mixed with the video signals or displayed separately. The software runs the system, controlling the changes, fades etc. between the various pictures.
- *Monitor.* This is where the computer graphics and text and the video pictures are displayed. It must have a 'SCART' connector for carrying RGB (red, green, blue) picture signal, audio signals and control, and synchronized signals (which neither consumer-quality televisions nor many basic computer monitors carry).
- *Input device.* This is the user's means of communicating with the system and the program. This can be a keyboard, touch screen, mouse, joystick, trackerball, light pen etc.
- *Interface or overlay cards.* A special interface or overlay device, usually in the form of an extra board or card for the computer, is needed to combine (analogue) video material with (digital) computer text and graphics.

Interactive video software/courses
There are three main types of computer software or courses which can be used on an IV workstation:

- *Generic.* Generic programs are those which are for purchase or hire diectly, off the shelf. There is a wide range of generic packages available, covering most possible training topics. On average they cost upwards of £800 per disk or £2,000 per course.
- *Bespoke.* Bespoke courseware are programs which are commissioned to meet one organization's specific training needs. These are a more expensive way of obtaining training, costing upwards of £150,000, though the overall cost can be reduced if the program addresses a common topic and can be marketed.
- *Tailored.* This uses a software 'authoring package' to tailor packages to suit the specific need or to develop an in-house, cheaper version of bespoke courseware. This offers great flexibility at a relatively low cost, but there are problems of producing material to the high standard that we now expect from video and TV programmes.

Advantages and benefits of IV

A number of benefits of IV have been widely stated:

- It offers increased retention due to the range of formats in which information is presented.
- It leads to a shorter training time. It is generally accepted that compared to traditional classroom training IV can cut the required training time by up to a factor of four. This is partly because the trainee controls the speed at which the training proceeds and is not ruled by a need to allow the slowest class member to keep up.
- It has a lower cost per student, because a large number of people can be trained using IV over a limitless period of time, and because it can reduce the training time.
- It can provide effective, risk-free training, allowing trainees to explore situations without endangering themselves or their relationships with other people.

Disadvantages of IV

Despite these benefits, there are problems with IV.

- It needs an IV workstation on which to run. These can cost between £2,500 and £5,000 plus.
- It is expensive, in terms of time and money, to update or revise, and therefore is not suitable for use with material which may require amending.
- The jargon and complex technology can frighten many potential users.
- Many of the disadvantages of CBT are also relevant, such as compatibility, flexibility and interface problems. There are problems of compatibility because, as with computers, the market has yet to settle on a standard workstation and standard courseware delivery requirements. Hence no one combination of equipment (or delivery system) can play all the IV programs

available. The main areas of incompatibility are the PAL and NTSC laser disk formats, and the range of interface boards and control software.

Case study: Courtaulds' Coventry training centre
In May 1988 Courtaulds opened a training centre on its Coventry site, providing a service for its individual businesses in Coventry. It concentrates on open learning packages, both as a basic training in job-related skills in company time and for individual access out of work hours. Initially training was provided by a combination of computer programs, video and audio tapes, and text. As the centre grew and developed, more areas of training requirements were identified, some of which it was felt could be best satisfied using IV. An initial outlay of approximately £20,000 bought a range of generic courseware, primarily general communication skills, and two workstations.

A number of benefits of this introduction of IV have been identified:

- Though the IV involved a relatively high set-up cost, the courses are expected to average out at about £12 per trainee per course, compared to about £150 for similar tutor-led courses. This is based on the present usage of the IV courseware in the training centre and assuming a 5-year life span for the hardware and software.
- The level of retention of students completing the course is entirely satisfactory. Studies have shown that 74 per cent of both bosses and trainees believed that a lot or some of the course content had been applied to the trainees' work.
- The most important benefit has been its flexibility. Training has been completed at a time to suit the trainees, often fitting in with shift patterns. It has also been able to provide on-the-spot training when a need has been identified which requires immediate attention.

The inclusion of some of the IV modules as a forerunner to tutor-led courses on interviewing skills has also brought a number of advantages:

- The total length of the training courses has been reduced by up to a day.
- Less of the tutors' time has been spent covering the theory, allowing more opportunity for the trainees to practise interviewing skills.
- The courses have been able to proceed at a faster rate and to a higher level.

So the addition of IV courses to Courtaulds' Coventry training centre has proved to be a beneficial decision.

Emerging technologies

In the current multimedia market, newer digital technologies, many based on the compact disk (CD), are proliferating, but real training applications are somewhat thin on the ground and LaserVision (IV) or analogue video still predominates. This is partly because the digital video techniques have a long way to go before they can compete in terms of the quality and quantity of images, especially motion video.

The most crucial aspect of the CD technology is that it is based on common standards and likely to be more widely applicable, especially in the home and entertainment markets, which will bring costs down.

The major developments are described below (and see Chatterton and Wright 1989, Wilson 1989):

- *CD-DA (compact disk-digital audio).* Known to most as the 'compact disk', this to date has been the most successful of the CD technologies. However, it is primarily limited to home entertainment. It is only occasionally used to extend the audio capabilities of an interactive system.
- *CD-V (compact disk-video).* Containing a combination of analogue video and digital sound, this has little application in the training market and is being used for home entertainment, music videos and juke-box systems.
- *CD-I (compact disk-interactive).* This provides a flexible combination of pictures, text and audio which can be self-contained, not needing an external computer. It was initially predicted to be a major challenge for the IV LaserVision technology. However, it has been slower to develop than expected, partly because of time spent developing full-screen motion picture. It is also aimed primarily at the consumer market, though software is expected to include educational material and reference works as well as games.
- *CD-ROM (compact disk-read only memory).* This is a method of storing large volumes of digital data including text, digitized graphics and databases. It is most suitable for application where large quantities of data which do not need regular updates has to be distributed over a number of sites. An interesting application has been a service manual for the Boeing 757.
- *CD-ROM XA (CD-ROM extended architecture).* This adds encoding standards for audio, graphics and still pictures to the basic CD-ROM format. Its most likely applications seem to be for use in conjunction with LaserVision to add large databases or still-frame audio.
- *DVI (digital video interactive).* Similar to CD-I, this is an all-digital medium which allows a flexible mix of multimedia information. The key to it is the methods it uses to compress video, audio and graphical information for storage and then restore it for viewing. The efficiency compression techniques are based on storing the difference between two frames, rather than the whole frame. This is the most likely of the new technologies to move into training, perhaps in the real-time simulation area where LaserVision has the most difficulty in meeting users' demands.

Implications for Organizations

Our description of open learning thus far has indicated some of the issues that need to be addressed by organizations using the methods. It should be clear that open learning is not necessarily an easy option. A number of critical issues are worthy of closer examination.

Learner support

It is too often assumed by organizations that learners using open learning can be left to their own devices. Most of the research evidence based on the experience of the last fifteen years demonstrates that this is not the case for the vast majority of individuals. It may be true of some people but these are likely to be a small minority.

Two kinds of tutorial support are likely to be needed. The first is technical support to provide help with the subject matter and content. The second is counselling and motivational support to help learners through difficult periods and to provide reassurance. Contact and interaction with colleague learners as well as tutorial staff has been found to be beneficial for both these elements and to increase the effectiveness of open learning.

If the open learning programmes or materials are provided by an external organization such as the Open University, then tutorial services may be provided as part of the total package. If not, then the organization needs to provide tutorial support. This does not imply that this is done exclusively through training staff; subject matter experts in the organization, such as engineers or accountants, can be utilized, leaving trainers to provide counselling services. In all cases, however, organizations need to provide support to learners in applying what they learn in their jobs. This form of support is normally the role of the learners' line manager and colleagues in their department or section. Arrangements for this need to be in place and managed if open learning is to be successful.

A final aspect of support is time and facilities. Again, organizations sometimes assume that open learning means that learners study in their own time and at home. This can be true where individuals are highly motivated and initiate programmes themselves. However, if the organization initiates and implements a compulsory open learning programme it is unlikely to succeed on the basis of staff using their own time.

Similarly, facilities such as rooms and equipment – for example, video players and computers – need to be provided.

Motivation of learners

As we have seen, learner motivation is a critical issue in open learning. Many organizations have experienced high drop-out rates and low take-up in their programmes. The learner support services discussed above can be significant in maintaining motivation. There are in addition two further considerations under this heading. First, the way open learning programmes are introduced and implemented is critical. Explanations of what and why and how are necessary to create initial interest and motivation of learners. Many individuals will be experiencing open learning for the first time and may in fact be returning to formal learning of any form after an absence of many years. Both factors mean that there is likely to be a need for confidence building. Related to this is the issue of study skills. Using open learning materials effectively does require different learning skills. All of these reasons point to a need for some form of formal launch of an open learning programme. This usually involves a one-day or two-day off-the-job event which learners attend and where these issues can be addressed.

Another significant factor in learner motivation is the existence or otherwise of some individual reward. There is of course the intrinsic reward of learning and development, but this is often not enough. The opportunity to acquire a qualification or credit towards one has been found to be a significant motivational factor. Formal recognition in the job, such as progression to a higher grade and/or increased responsibilities, also leads to increased motivation, reflected in higher take-up and lower drop-out rates.

A final factor under this heading is the issue of sharing of materials. Some organizations utilize open learning on the basis of multi-use; that is, the same package is used by a number of individuals. This is often significant in arguments supporting the cost effectiveness of open learning. It is possible and generally acceptable to adopt this approach with technology-based materials such as CBT or IV. However, the same is not true of text-based materials, whether they are stand-alone or part of multimedia packages. Used materials are demotivating for learners, and the only effective practice is for each learner to be provided with a personal copy of text-based materials.

Managing programmes

What we have said so far should have made it clear that managing an open learning programme in an organization is no easy task. There are, however, even more significant considerations.

Monitoring and control are of critical importance. This means setting up systems that can record and track the progress of learners as they move through the programme. It also involves having policies and procedures for ensuring that real needs are identified and met through open learning and, as part of this, that appropriate individuals are entered on the programme(s). Methods of validation and evaluation also need to be designed and applied.

All of this demands comprehensive and sophisticated administrative systems if open learning programmes are to be effectively managed. It can be argued with some justification that open learning programmes require greater time and effort to manage than more traditional methods.

Resource implications

This last point illustrates that open learning can often be more resource-intensive than trainer-delivered programmes. All of the things we have described so far in this section cost time and money. The resources required for learner support and for managing programmes will normally prove quite expensive.

There is, though, another and perhaps even more significant resource consideration. This is that open learning materials in whatever form are generally quite expensive. There are literally thousands of commercially available programmes and packages, but they are not cheap to buy. This is because of the high development costs of open learning materials and the need for high quality in presentation. Many of the commercial packages currently available have in fact benefited from subsidized development through the government interventions mentioned at the start of the chapter. As these come to the end of their life and are replaced by newly developed materials, the cost is likely to be significantly higher. The experience of the Open College confirms the point of cost. When established, it was intended to become self-financing within three years and to do so through offering its programmes to individuals. In fact the government subsidy continued long after the planned three years and, because of cost, most of the

Open College income is generated by selling its services to organizations rather than individuals.

All of these factors are true of materials developed in-house. A useful piece of advice for trainers inexperienced in developing open learning materials is to estimate the time and cost of development – and then multiply both by a factor of five. Technology-based materials, whether bought from external providers or developed in-house, usually require a significant investment in equipment. CBT materials can, though, be an exception, if existing hardware can be utilized.

In summary, it is the case that open learning is not an easy or cheap option for organizations. This probably helps to explain why the use of open learning has not met the optimistic forecasts of the early/middle 1980s.

Implications for Trainers

It is clear that open learning provides many new possibilities for training professionals in organizations. Specialist roles are being defined and developed. These include the following:

- Open learning authors, both text and CBT
- Designers of materials and schemes
- Managers of open learning programmes and open learning centres
- Open learning tutors.

These last two roles can also be required of generalist trainers in organizations. Any trainer can also be expected to be able to provide advice and guidance on the use of open learning. This advice is likely to centre on answering the three key points considered in the rest of this section.

Open learning v. traditional methods

The first question will probably be whether or not open learning is likely to be appropriate to meet a particular need in a specific set of circumstances. The list below gives some general guidelines on this. Cases when the method can be considered as a worthwhile possibility include those where:

- The organization is not satisfied with existing provision.
- Small numbers are to be trained.
- Large numbers are to be trained, especially in a short time.

- There is a wide geographic spread of those to be trained.
- Training is for critical staff who are difficult to release for traditional courses.

Any of these circumstances, singly or in combination, can suggest good reasons for considering open learning. They may also provide the conditions necessary to ensure that open learning will be more cost effective than traditional courses. However, as we have seen, open learning needs to be well managed and the following factors need to be present or created if it is to be effective:

- Involvement of the organization through managers, trainers and colleagues
- Access to tutorial support, both technical and counselling
- Opportunity for interaction with other learners
- Quality in materials in terms of presentation and design
- Confidence and learning skills in learners
- Provision of reward and extrinsic motivation.

Assessing materials/programmes

Assuming a decision is made to utilize open learning, then the question that arises is which materials or programmes should be chosen. As indicated earlier, there is a wide range of choice from commercial providers on all subjects and topics. As a starting point, the descriptions of good open learning materials provided in this chapter can be used as relevant criteria in assessing options. Other ideas on methods and criteria of assessing materials and programmes are listed below.

- Run a pilot and apply existing evaluation procedures.
- Run a pilot and assess against existing traditional courses.
- Establish how free-standing the materials/schemes are and what additional input or support is required.
- As part of the above, establish costs of optional extras, such as tutor support.
- Establish the reputation of the providers.
- Ask for names of and talk to current and/or previous users.
- Assess the extent to which the material is general or industry-specific.
- Assess the cost against other providers and investigate discounts for bulk purchases.

Producing materials in-house

It will always be the case that producing materials in-house will be an option. Often, it may be the only alternative to traditional methods if commercial material in the subject is not available. The warning on time and cost given earlier is, though, critical in considering this option. In deciding whether to produce materials in-house the following issues need to be considered:

- Is there a clearly identified need which can be met by open learning?
- Have available materials been thoroughly investigated and assessed?
- Does the organization have the necessary expertise and skill?
- What is the estimated cost and can it be justified?
- How long will it take and will the need still exist when it is completed?
- What media will be used and does the organization have the necessary equipment?

In summary, training practitioners will be expected to be the source of expertise in organizations on open learning and need to be able to provide effective advice and guidance.

The Future of Open Learning

We close this chapter with some speculative comments on the future of open learning, based on an assessment of its relative strengths and weaknesses compared with more traditional methods.

While there has been a significant growth in its use over the last ten years or so, open learning has not become the major force in education and training expected and predicted by many commentators. There are probably a number of reasons for this. The first is the relatively high development costs of open learning when compared with traditional methods. It is certainly much quicker and cheaper to design and prepare a course-based programme of learning on a given subject than an open learning programme which delivers equivalent learning. This is true irrespective of the chosen media. These costs have to be justified and repaid. It is possible to do so in terms of delivery, where open learning can be cheaper than traditional courses. Savings on travel, accommodation and subsistence costs, as well as some contribution of the learners' own time, can mean that open learning is cheaper to operate than traditional methods. This may not be the case, though, if the unit cost of materials and equipment is high. On balance, and depending on circumstances, the cost arguments tend not to be decisive.

The other part of the equation is effectiveness, which suggests a second reason for open learning having a limited role in education and training. Opinions and the results of research vary, but a widely held view is that open learning is only really effective for knowledge-based learning. Attempts are, of course, made to address skill development and attitude formation through open learning. This is especially the case with technology-based materials such as interactive video. Even these methods, though, are likely to be less effective than course-based training. Social skills development and attitude formation in particular require the group interaction and immediacy of analysis and feedback inherent in course-based programmes. Therefore open learning can rarely provide a total solution. There is even some evidence to suggest that knowledge learning can be more effective through traditional methods in terms of long-term retention and understanding.

Open learning, then, can be less effective than traditional methods for some forms of training need. There is in addition a third reason for the limited contribution of open learning, one which is related to our definitions given at the start of the chapter. In line with these, open learning systems can be defined as those which remove or overcome barriers to learning. Administrative barriers include the following:

- Requirement to attend a specific place
- Requirement to attend at specific times
- Requirement to attend over a stated period
- Requirement for a minimum group size.

As well as administrative barriers, educational constraints also prevent access to learning. An indicative list is given below:

- Learners have to accept the sequence of teaching offered.
- Learners have to accept a teaching strategy suited to the trainer.
- Objectives and content are determined by the trainer or others without input from learners.
- Learners have to meet minimum entry requirements.

All of the above factors can be true of education or training-based vocational programmes. Many of the barriers exist for sound and justifiable reasons, but in any case there is a wealth of history, tradition and vested interest to be dealt with before the barriers can be overcome. True open learning, therefore, is unlikely to exist for the foreseeable future, whatever its advantages. Indeed, it is probably true to say that a very large majority of what is currently termed open learning has as many barriers to access as most traditional, course-based training. This is because many of the barriers to access are not there for the sake of it but for sound reasons to do with cost effectiveness and learning principles.

Summary

For the reasons stated above, it is probable that open learning will continue to make a limited though valuable contribution to education and training. The future of open learning is likely to include the following elements:

- An increasing use of technology-based media
- A growing focus on learner support and involvement
- A growing integration of open learning with more traditional methods as part of organization-based and managed programmes
- Increased use of collaborative projects between employers and specialist open learning providers.

In summary, open learning is unlikely ever to supplant more traditional methods of training. It has, though, become and will remain a realistic and important option in terms of meeting organization and individual training needs. As such, it is a form of learning that all training practitioners need to understand and to be willing to use as part of their professional practice.

Acknowledgements

The authors have drawn on information given in a number of papers presented at conferences, and in particular:

Annamalai, R. (1988) *Evaluation: The Key to Future Development*. A paper presented at the Interactive '88 Conference.
Bell, M. (1989) *Productivity with IV – An Independent View*. A paper presented at the Interactive '89 Conference.

Further reading

Bayard-White, C. and Hoffos, S. (1988) *Interactive Video – Introduction and Handbook*. London: NIVC.
Chatterton, P. and Wright, T. (1989) Emerging Technologies. In S. Hoffos (ed.), *Interactive Video Yearbook 1990*, London: NIVC.
Doulton, A. (1990) Getting Across the Benefits. *Televisual Training*. (Quarterly review. Buxton: Buxton Press).
Wilson, R. (1989) A Commercial Perspective. In S. Hoffos (ed.), *Interactive Video Yearbook 1990*, London: NIVC.
Winter, R.G. (1991) Justifying the Benefits of IV. *Training and Development*, 9, no. 3.

Appendix: Example of a study guide

MOTIVATION AND LEADERSHIP

SECTION 1
INTRODUCTION AND STUDY GUIDE

 Welcome to this distance learning package on motivation and leadership. I have produced it to enable you to increase your knowledge and understanding of these key topics without having to attend a formal course. If you are already in a management position, I hope also to increase your confidence and effectiveness in dealing with your staff.

Whatever your reason for studying the package you will find it helpful to work through this introduction. I have provided it to help you get the most benefit from the package by:

- introducing you to the idea of distance learning
- explaining what is contained in the package
- explaining what is expected of you
- giving you some advice and tips on self-study.

The What And Why of Distance Learning

Before reading any further jot down in the box below what you understand by the term 'distance learning'.

Distance Learning Means:

Your notes may have contained ideas similar to the following list.

Distance Learning:

takes place away from traditional teaching situations such as training centre or college

allows you to study where and when you choose

allows you to study at your own pace

provides you with help and support through the learning materials themselves using techniques such as:

- practical activities and exercises
- self-assessment questions to help you check your progress
- in some cases, use a variety of presentation media such as audio and video cassettes
- access to tutor support if required.

We can define a distance learning package as a set of materials which are designed to be used by students working on their own without most of the normal support which is normally available in conventional classroom learning situations.

Distance learning needs to provide that kind of support through other means such as the list given above. But why use distance learning? I have listed some of the advantages and disadvantages in the box over the page. See if you can add your own ideas to mine. There is not an exhaustive list that I am aware of so I have not provided a 'model answer'. Your attempt to extend my list will help you clarify your understanding of distance learning.

Distance Learning

Advantages	Disadvantages
No fixed time or place of study Reaches more people	No immediate access to expert on subject
Individuals control own pace of learning	No immediate access to other learners
Provides permanent reference material	May have no formal assessment.

What Is In This Package

This package is purely text. There are no audio or video cassettes. However, that does not mean you will be simply reading. I have not produced a textbook. I have produced a learning package which incorporates the best features of distance learning.

The knowledge you need to acquire forms the main part of the content. This examines both motivation and leadership from the point of view of a first line manager. Each is treated in a separate section of the package. I have presented my ideas in easy to read language and well laid out print to help you learn and to ENJOY learning. Other features to help you learn include:

• breaking the knowledge content down into manageable 'chunks'
• providing learning objectives to let you know what you are expected to learn
• giving activities and exercises to involve you in applying your learning
• setting self-assessment questions to help you assess your progress
• providing answers and discussions to self-assessment questions to help you identify what material you may need to re-study.

Practical exercises and activities are particularly important. You really need to do these if you are going to turn your new knowledge into a useful skill. Self-assessment questions are equally important as they are an essential part of the learning process. You may of course choose to treat the package as a textbook and simply read the content. I hope you won't make that choice since you will not really benefit from the package.

I have also provided a series of symbols or 'signposts' to guide you through the package. You have already seen some of them. They tell you what you should be doing at any point in the package e.g. reading, doing an exercise, answering a question. The full list of symbols is given below.

• Means you should carry on READING until you see one of the other symbols.

• Means we suggest you have done enough for one session and should take a BREAK. *An important symbol!*

• Means a KEY POINT which you should pay particular attention to.

 • Means you should carry out the ACTIVITY given in the text before carrying on reading.

 • Means an EXERCISE for you to carry out in your work to apply what you have learnt.

 • Means a set of SELF-ASSESSMENT QUESTIONS which you should complete and check before moving on.

 • Means a TUTOR ASSESSED and marked assignment.

You will see that last symbol only once in this package. I have provided a final assignment for you at the very end of the package. It is an optional assignment and therefore you do not have to complete it. If you do, then you can send it to me at Wolverhampton Business School for assessment. You will receive it back with a tutor assessment and feedback and will also be awarded a Certificate of Completion by the Business School to record your achievement in working through the package.

You might by now be thinking 'How long is all this going to take me?' I would like to be able to tell you, but remember distance learning allows you to study at your own pace. And everyone's pace is different! My guess is that most people will take between 20 and 30 hours to complete the package. But that is only a guess so don't worry if you take much less or much more.

I want you to gain genuine benefit from the package so take whatever time it takes you to complete it. You will also benefit more if you consciously try to apply your learning in your job. This will increase your skill and hopefully your job effectiveness. You can begin the process now by completing the activity below.

Read the contents page of the package. Identify and list 3 items you expect to learn which will be of direct help in your job. Then describe how this will help improve your effectiveness.

Item in Package
1.
2.
3.

Expected Learning
1.

2.

3.

Effect on Job Performance
1.

2.

3.

You can return to this activity and review it when you have completed the package. The result can be used to produce an action plan for putting the whole of your learning into practice.

I suggest you now have a break!

Some Advice on Successful Study

Most people are relatively inexperienced when it comes to using distance learning. I will assume you fall into that category. If not, treat the following paragraphs as a chance to review your previous experience. I am going to provide you with advice on three aspects of self-study.

• Seeking and using support
• Planning your time
• General study skills

Let's begin with SEEKING SUPPORT. You are not part of a formal group or class of learners, but that does not mean you need to be alone. You work for an organization and therefore have colleagues and a boss. Do they know you are working through the package? If not, tell them. Especially your boss. Your boss and colleagues can be a source of moral support and reassurance which will be helpful if you hit a difficulty. They may also be studying a distance learning package, and so would be grateful for your help too. They can also provide a sounding board for new ideas you may have as a result of your learning. I am sure they will be glad to help.

Boss and colleagues may also be a source of expertise. Perhaps they have studied motivation and leadership themselves. If so, they will be familiar with the content of the package and be of great help if you have a difficulty with the subject matter.

A central personnel or training department will also be a useful source of support. If you have one in your organization contact them. They should be able to put you in touch with someone in your organization who is familiar with the subject matter. They may also have other materials; e.g. books, articles, videos etc.; which you can use to supplement your learning.

Seeking support will be important. You may find you need a little or a lot as you work through the package. Not having it when you need it could be critical, and having it when you don't will enhance your learning. Arrange your support contacts before your start studying. Don't leave it until you need help.

PLANNING YOUR TIME from the outset is also important. The package will not take a large amount of time but you still need to plan when and where you are going to study. Organize a timetable to complete the package using the suggestions below as a framework.

- Decide on a realistic time period to complete the whole package; e.g. 1 week, 2 weeks, 1 month.
- Allocate a number of study periods to different days within this time period. Effective concentration can last for only a short time so we suggest between 1 and 2 hours for each study period including a refreshment break.
- Allow time in each study period to review your learning, say 10 minutes each period. Use this time to think about and note down the main learning points.
- Plan and allocate which parts of the package you will work through in each study period. Be flexible since you cannot always accurately predict how long individual units will take you but always try to end a study period at a logical point in the package.
- Remember to build in time for the practical activities and exercises. Allow time also for talking over your learning with your boss/colleagues/subject matter adviser.
- Try to stick to your timetable, the discipline will be helpful. However, be flexible when you need to be and plan yourself regular breaks from work and study.

Effective STUDY SKILLS will help you get the most out of your study periods. I have already said that distance learning is not the same as reading a text book. However, the following hints on reading skill and note taking will be helpful.

Your own physical state; e.g. tired or full of energy; and your physical surroundings; at a desk or in an armchair; will influence both your understanding and future memory of what you read. To understand and retain requires concentration. Concentration requires energy. Only study at times when you feel awake and alert and in a place free from distractions.

Reading speed is also important. Some units or paragraphs, especially when complex concepts are introduced for the first time, should be read more slowly than usual. This helps understanding and memory. You may also find that re-reading certain passages will be helpful.

Taking notes while reading also helps understanding and memory. They can also be used in reviewing your learning in preparation for applying in your job. Here are a few general hints to help you with note taking.

- Never copy verbatim what you read.
- Pick only the key points for noting down.
- Use your own words – re-interpret those of the text.

• Try to relate your learning to your existing knowledge and experience. Use your notes for this purpose.

The pages of the package provide a lot of space for notes if you wish to use it. Notes in the margin can often form a useful basis for summary notes you make at the end of each unit or section.

And Good Luck

I hope you now feel confident about tackling the package. Before you begin, ensure you have completed the activities suggested in this introduction. I have set out below those you need to do to prepare yourself for studying. Be sure to do them all. Enjoy your learning.

Before going any further, make sure you have:

familiarized yourself with the symbols used in the package

completed the job application exercise

identified and spoken with your support contacts

prepared a planned timetable

reviewed your general study skills.

9
Administration of Training

STEVE TRUELOVE

---

*Never do to-day what you can put off till
tomorrow.*

Punch, 1849

Introduction

For some people employed within the training function, administration
is the major part of their jobs. For others, it is something somebody else
does and to be avoided at all costs. The style and approach organizations
take with regard to administration is so varied that it would be pointless
trying to lay down 'best practice', because there is no such thing.

In particular, the size and structure of the organization will have a
profound influence on the way training is administered. Many training
officers in larger organizations will have little or no discretion with
regard to the records they keep or the reports they submit. In contrast,
there will be newly appointed training officers in small organizations
who have to establish policies and procedures from scratch and for
whom little or no help is forthcoming from within the organization.
However, advice and guidance are usually easily obtainable. Most
people in the training function are quite happy to share their knowledge
and experience with others. Establish a network of contacts, possibly
through your Institute of Training and Development (ITD) branch, and
do not be afraid to ask for help. It will usually be given freely and
willingly.

Policies

Every organization has policies with regard to the training and development function. Not all, however, have got these in a written form, and some of those which have do not widely publish them – even within the organization.

A statement of policy is a general statement by senior management on how it wishes certain situations to be dealt with. The value of having a set-down policy statement is that it helps to maintain a consistency of approach throughout the organization and ensures that the senior management's philosophy is put into effect. If no formal policy document is available for middle and junior managers to refer to, then either decisions will be made on the basis of guesswork and personal preference, or there will need to be constant reference to the appropriate authority for a decision to be made. For example, two young employees both approach their managers and ask if they can be supported to undertake Open University degree programmes. One is turned down flat, while the other is told that she will be reimbursed for the total cost of the tuition. Elsewhere in the organization, a third employee is half-way through a programme which he is paying a 50-per-cent contribution towards. He has also signed an agreement that he will return the other half of the costs should he leave the organization within two years of completing his course.

The fictitious example above could no doubt be topped by virtually all training professionals from their own experience. To avoid this sort of mess, it is necessary not only to have a policy, but to ensure that it is widely distributed and adhered to. A policy document lays down not only what the organization wants done, but also who has the authority to make decisions, who must be consulted and who must be informed.

It is a matter of opinion and judgement as to where a policy statement stops and a procedures manual starts. Sometimes the two are best combined, or may form part of a wider manual of personnel policies and practices. An example of how the question of the Open University courses might be covered is:

1 *Policy.* The company may provide support for employees who wish to pursue further education courses through open learning in their own time. The level of support given will be determined according to the following criteria:
   (a) The relevance of the proposed course to the individual's current work
   (b) The value of the education to the individual's long-term development
   (c) The costs involved

(d) The amount of money previously given in support of the individual concerned

(e) Availability of funds in the training budget.

2 *Guidelines.* In general, the company will consider providing support as follows:

(a) Tuition fees – usually a maximum of 80 per cent but in special circumstances up to 100 per cent

(b) Cost of books and materials – up to 100 per cent of cost subject to a predetermined limit

(c) Cost of residential workshops – up to 100 per cent.

3 *Authority.* Whether financial support is given, the level of support and any conditions will be determined by the training manager in consultation with the individual's department manager. Financial support likely to exceed £1,000 in any one year must be approved by the personnel director, who may also require the individual concerned to enter into a formal written agreement regarding reimbursement of any support given in certain circumstances.

What should a policy cover?

Any training issue that the management is concerned with should be treated in a consistent way. The following list is not exhaustive:

- Training for occupational competence
- Training for change
- Induction training
- Health and safety training
- Formal training schemes
- Training for people who become incapacitated
- An equal opportunities statement
- The aims and objectives of the training function
- Responsibility for identifying training needs and formulating plans
- Responsibility for deciding the training budget.

In all cases, it is important that the responsibility for ensuring training takes place is as clearly defined as possible, and authority levels are indicated.

The practice among some organizations is to keep the policy statements secret. One can only guess at the reasons for this, but it would seem to indicate a fear either that everyone would know that the policies were not being adhered to, or that if everyone knew what they were entitled to then the training function would be overwhelmed with requests! A well-constructed policy document should not support either of these fears. Organizations which claim to be committed to the concepts of training and development should be confident enough to publish their policies for all their employees to read.

The Formulation of Training Plans

Once a policy has been established and training needs have been determined, it becomes necessary to begin the process of meeting those needs by determining a plan of action. Plans are normally sorted out in terms of the following questions:

- Who is to be trained?
- How are they to be trained?
- When are they to be trained?

Who is to be trained?

Assuming that a totally comprehensive training needs analysis has been completed, the trainer will have a complete list of who needs training. It is rare that a training function will have the resources to address all the needs that it is aware of in a short period of time. Accordingly it must determine an order of priorities. Very often, there will be some urgent needs which will be obvious to all concerned, and effectively predetermined. For example, if a new factory is being built, it is often the case that security officers will be among the first to be recruited and trained. After the most obvious and urgent needs have been identified, the best way to proceed is to identify items of training which will themselves contribute to reducing the training need. For example, if it has been decided that a team of instructors needs to be trained, it is sensible to make that a priority.

After these two types of priority have been addressed, the training officer will be left with a range of training to be planned. Which should come first: management, supervisory, operative or technical training? This is a matter of judgement, but normally it is advisable to look at the top levels first. If you send a supervisor on a fairly progressive course, but the manager still believes in doing things in the old way, then the training of the supervisor will have been wasted. The key to this question is, of course, to involve line management in determining the priorities as much as possible. Managers vary in terms of how much they want to be involved in planning training, but the best will be committed enough to the process to give it serious attention.

How are they to be trained?

Should training be by:

- External courses?
- Internal courses?
- Planned experience?
- Coaching?
- Self-study/open learning?
- Day release?

The answer to many of these questions will be obvious. If a young office worker is in need of a comprehensive education with regard to business practices, then the local college will have the answer. If the assistant purchasing officer needs enhanced negotiating skills, then probably a short external course will be appropriate. There will, however, be some needs which are sufficiently widely distributed to make it worthwhile to consider internal or in-house training. For example, if there are twenty-four supervisors who all need a basic course in supervisory skill, it will be far cheaper to arrange for a training consultancy to run two or three in-house courses than to send all twenty-four away for training.

Arranging individual coaching, planned experience or simply informational sessions can often achieve results at little or no cost. Most organizations contain a wealth of experience and knowledge. It is silly to send someone away on a three-day course when the information they actually need might be acquired from a two-hour session with an experienced person in another part of the building.

When are they to be trained?

There are five factors which will influence these decisions:

1 The volume of training to be arranged
2 The cost of the training
3 The ability to the organization to release people for training
4 External resource constraints, such as college course availability
5 Internal resource constraints.

Taking all these factors into account, the training function must lay out a time-scale which is realistic and manageable. This may be in terms of a plan stretching five years ahead, or even longer. Normally, though, it is not feasible to do a detailed analysis more than twelve months in advance. Indeed, changing circumstances will almost always ensure that even a twelve-month plan is unlikely to survive the year intact.

It is not good practice to have very concentrated bursts of training followed by years of inactivity. Nor is it sensible for an individual to be sent on half-a-dozen one-week courses within a four-month period if he or she receives no training in the five years before or after this time. On the other hand, if the organization wishes to change its culture it is no use spreading 'customer care' over a ten-year period.

Ultimately, the pace and volume of training will be determined by senior management. Put forward an unrealistic timetable, and you will not get the support you need. Set out a sensible and cost effective strategy which you can defend, and you are likely to receive the backing you require. An example of a simple training plan for a small department is shown in table 9.1.

There is no one right format – each organization will have its own needs. It may be more sensible to categorize training functionally rather than by department (for example, supervisory training; technical training; operator training). Whatever format is chosen, the training function should use the plan as the basis for ensuring that the training needed actually takes place, and in a systematic manner.

Budget

The concept of a budget is one which causes newly appointed managers in all functions considerable difficulty. One of the reasons for this is that the term is used in a variety of different ways not only between organizations, but also within organizations. In most training contexts, budgeting is comparatively simple when considered against the complexities of line managers' budgets, which have to take account of very many variables.

The definition of budget which I personally find most useful is this: 'A training budget is a statement of what the organization intends to spend on training in a given period of time.' A key concept here is the intention of spending on training. Occasionally, organizations are able to make money directly through their training activities, but this is not normally the case. The money in the training budget is, therefore, the sum the organization has set aside for training activities. If more than this amount is spent, then the overspend will have to come from elsewhere. However, you would be wrong to think that accountants and directors are always pleased when a budget is underspent. If a budget is not fully used, then it means that an investment that the organization has wanted to make has not been made, and that money that could usefully have

Table 9.1 Training plan for a finished goods warehouse department

Trainee	Training required	Method	Timing
A Brown – warehouse manager	● Computerized stock control techniques ● New accounts procedures	● External course (5 days) ● Seminar with project accountant (½ day)	● By end June (to be arranged) ● By end August (to be arranged)
B White – warehouse foreman	● Supervisory skills ● New accounts procedures ● NEBSS course	● In-house course (3 days) ● Seminar with project accountant (½ day) ● Local college, evenings	● March (arranged) ● By end August (to be arranged) ● Ongoing
C Green D Black E Pink – truck drivers	● Operation of new forklift truck ● Use of fire extinguishers	● Manufacturer's training, in-house (one day) ● In-house by Fire Brigade (½ day)	● On delivery (c.July) ● 14 September (arranged)
F Blue G Red – warehouse workers	● Truck driving ● Use of fire extinguishers	● Internal training by D. Black (instructor) ● In-house by Fire Brigade (½ day)	● August–October ● 15 September (arranged)

been employed elsewhere in the organization has been tied up. In some instances, that money will be lost. Except when the organization has already signalled that it wanted to see savings on budget expenditure, it may also mean a lower budget henceforth. In general, therefore, a budget is there to be spent. But how is it derived?

There are two approaches to the allocation of a training budget. Either:

● Decide what training is needed
● Plan to meet those needs

- Cost the plan
- Allocate a budget to meet the plan;

or:

- Decide how much is to be spent
- Plan to spend that amount.

In practice, most organizations operate a hybrid approach. Some training needs have to be met for the organization to function, but organizations also realize that there must be a balance between training expenditure and other expenditure.

Accordingly, proposals for training budgets need to be prepared in a realistic manner, but in a way that makes investing in training seem worthwhile. We can consider three elements which go towards the overall training budget:

1 A *capital* budget. This covers expenditure on major (as defined by the organization) equipment or resources.
2 A *fixed cost operating* budget. This covers establishment costs, typically comprising such elements as:
   (a) Salaries, pension, costs etc.
   (b) Premises costs and associated overheads
   (c) Allocated general 'support overheads'.
3 A *variable cost/revenue* budget. This covers costs which vary according to the activities carried out, and revenues which may accrue either from external sources (such as grants) or from charging out training services within the organization. These may include:
   (a) External course fees
   (b) Outside consultants' fees
   (c) Consumable materials
   (d) External venue costs
   (e) Food, travel and accommodation costs.

Some organizations also choose to allocate the costs of trainees' wages, coverage costs, lost production and so on to the training budget. Where internal charging is introduced it is essential that other departmental budgets include provision for training expenditure, otherwise the exercise is a certain way of ensuring that little or no training takes place.

It will be readily appreciated that the relationship between the preparation of a training plan and the preparation of a budget proposal is extremely close. Training is essentially a service function, and effective planning and budgeting also depend on communication from other departments regarding their plans. Whenever a capital proposal for new equipment is put forward, the cost of training should be included. However, line operating departments may omit this element, either because they have not thought about it or because it will have the effect of making their proposed investment look too expensive.

The training budget should also include an element for contingencies. Not all training needs can be foreseen, and it is important that specific requests for immediate needs can be accommodated.

Records

There are many purposes to the keeping of training records. They are, on the one hand, part of the control mechanisms for monitoring the activity and effectiveness of the training function, and, on the other, a record of the formal learning that an individual has achieved. The design of any record system must, of course, reflect the needs that it is intended to meet.

Some records are necessary for statutory reasons (for example, to comply with safety legislation) or to prove that someone has been given the necessary training to comply with an organization's quality assurance system. In some instances, records may need to be kept indefinitely to prove, for example, that someone had attended a session on hearing protection before starting work in a noisy area – twenty years ago!

In most instances the training record is a record of learning that has been achieved – a statement that a specified learning objective has been met to a specified extent. As such, it should be signed by whoever is responsible for determining competence. All record keeping is tedious to most of us, and any paperwork should be kept to a minimum. If possible, design a system that serves more than one purpose. For example, a simple training programme can be laid out to serve as:

- A checklist of things to be learned
- A checklist of determinants of competence in these things
- A record of attainment

Computerized record systems tend to serve as a summary record rather than as a replacement for a paperwork system. If well designed, they can be used to provide statistical data regarding training or to enable rapid searches to be made to find individuals who possess certain skills. It should be possible for a training function to answer such questions as:

- Has anyone ever attended a course at Wolverhampton Polytechnic?
- How many people attended that?
- How many people attended that series on finance for non-financial managers last year?
- How many days off-the-job training does the average manager receive in this organization?
- What training has Sarah Smith had since she started?

One of the big gaps in most training records concerns the training which someone received before joining the organization. At the very least, new employees should be asked to provide details of the training they received – together with copies of any certificates or other documentation which is available. The current move to establish a nationally consistent system of recording vocational learning will take many years to provide a comprehensive 'portable' record system, and there will always be gaps.

Resourcing

The resources that a training function needs to manage are:

- *People*, such as training officers, instructors and support staff
- *Facilities*, such as training rooms and workshops
- *Equipment*, such as projectors and flip charts
- *Material*, such as videos, training packs and books
- *Cash* – the budget to spend on external courses, venues etc.

Like any other function, the training function should aim to achieve its objectives at the minimum cost compatible with maintaining quality standards. The level of expenditure on training is a senior management decision. Very few training functions consider themselves to be adequately resourced; even fewer consider that they have the resources they would like.

Although the overall expenditure on training is a senior management responsibility, the making of a case for extra resources is the responsibility of the function. When considering how to approach this, think about how the other functions construct their cases. They do not say, 'I'd like a new computer because the present one's really old-fashioned', or 'We need a new computer-integrated production line because that's what they have got next door', or, 'I'd like to spend £50,000 on advertising on television because it's a really exciting idea.' Rather, they have to make a case for an investment that will produce a return, in cash terms – the computer will produce tighter financial controls and pay for itself within a year; the new production line will mean greater output or lower costs; the advertising campaign will result in extra sales. And yet trainers seem reluctant to use the same approach. This is because of the difficulties of really identifying the cost benefit relationship between training and performance, which are almost unsurmountable if a really rigorous case has to be made in many circumstances.

Intelligent boards do, however, understand this and often do not require guarantees of a return on their investment in training. But they do value some sort of basis on which to make their decision. Sometimes the case for the investment is easy to make: for example, 'Last year we spent £10,000 on hiring hotel rooms for training courses. If we were to spend £8,000 equipping the empty offices in B wing, then we could run all the events there', or, 'Sending the new recruits to the computer training centre costs us £500 a time. We will take eighteen next year so it will cost us £9,000. We could buy suitable hardware for £4,000, and then we could hire a trainer for only £200 per trainee.' More often, the case for training is much harder to make to a cynical manager. However, which of the following is more persuasive?

- 'The junior management training course will be very enjoyable and we'll make sure everyone gets one of these lovely new folders. It'll only cost £4,000. We'd really like to get into that.'
- 'The Personnel department has put the cost of recruiting a new graduate at £5,000. Last year, we lost three of the twelve we took on within the first nine months. Two of them said that lack of management training was a significant factor in their decision to leave. If the proposed graduate development programme, which will cost £4,000, results in the retention of one extra person, then it will be cost effective. Additionally, we can anticipate that the programme will help the graduates achieve management posts more quickly than if they do not receive the training.'

The second argument is far from perfect. However, it contains several key features:

- There is factual evidence – even though some of it is only estimated.
- The case is put forward with the needs of the organization in mind, not the preferences of the training department.
- There is an estimate of the possible outcome and therefore saving to the organization.
- Other, less tangible benefits, are hinted at, but not overstated as they are impossible to defend if challenged.

Wherever resources must be argued for, a case must be made that allows the decision makers to feel that they can allocate expenditure on the basis of adequate information and with some idea of the value of the outcome. It is not difficult to anticipate some of the questions that might be asked and how your answers might be received:

'Can I have the money to buy this video?'
'Have you investigated whether there are any less expensive ones that would do the same job?'

'I want to send her on this rather expensive residential course in London.'
'Is there a similar but non-residential course available locally?'

Having successfully argued for the investment, spending the money effectively is just as important. Some organizations put great store on image, and want the training function to project a quality, sophisticated image – only the best is good enough. Others want the minimum expenditure possible, and lavish spending will attract lavish criticism. It all depends on the culture, and the perception the organization has of the role of training. Obtaining value for money is, of course, important. Getting quotations, asking for discounts and demanding demonstrations is part of the role. So is attending exhibitions of equipment, training providers and video producers. Perhaps your organization has a purchasing function. If so, remember that some purchasing officers seem to see their job as making sure that nobody gets exactly what he or she wants – so be prepared to justify your choice.

Selecting External Training Courses

Another part of the role is responding to questions like this: 'Can you find us a one-day course on statistical techniques for quality control staff within the next month or so? Not on a Monday or Friday, and not more than an hour's drive away.'

There is a wide range of organizations which provide training courses on an open basis. Some of these are purely commercial providers, some are attached to educational establishments, yet others are associated with professional institutes. Many organizations belong to group training associations, chambers of commerce, or other supporting agencies which offer training courses. The difficulty the trainer has is in finding out what is available. Various directories can be helpful in this respect, as can advertisements in the professional journals. Contact made with other training professionals, perhaps through a local ITD branch, can be an invaluable time-saver. There are even organizations which offer a database service, but they cannot be fully comprehensive.

If you are going to send people on external courses regularly, then you need to be on the mailing list of the training providers which are of interest to you. The reader enquiry services of professional journals can help you to build up the number of organizations that will send you details; or attend the major training exhibitions and conferences. Training organizations are very keen to get you on their lists. Some will try to arrange a visit to see you. If that suits you, fine; but do not be pushed into a meeting that you do not want.

Once you have identified a number of training providers, you need to choose one which offers the course you need. This is not easy, and there is no one approach which will guarantee that you select the best. However, you can narrow the odds:

- Read the course description very carefully. If you are not satisfied, ring the provider up. They should be happy and able to answer your questions.
- Beware false public courses which are really only a come-on to try to sell you in-house training.
- Date, duration and location are often important to the delegate.
- Involve the delegate and/or the line manager in selecting a course.
- Reputation and recommendation are worth a lot.
- You can visit the provider concerned.
- You can ask for references.
- You can ask to visit a course that is running – although you must be sensitive to the trainer's desire not to let that interfere with the course.
- If you have delegates with special needs, such as wheelchair access, make sure that the provider can accommodate them.

Many of the public courses that are advertised never actually run. Demand for places is often unpredictable and providers can rarely guarantee that a viable number of bookings will be received. However, a reputable provider should be honest with you if you ask as to the likelihood of a course running. If you pay for a course that is subsequently cancelled you should only accept a transfer if it suits you. If not, insist on a refund. Ensure that you know exactly what is included in the price. Examination fees, lunch and accommodation may or may not be included. You have every right to expect decent joining instructions for your delegate in ample time, complete with a map or directions, parking arrangements etc. Remember, the delegate and his or her manager will blame you if your selection is poor. However, if it is wonderful, do not expect any credit.

Using and Choosing Consultants

Many training professionals have, as part of their wider responsibilities, the task of deciding when outside help may be appropriate. There is usually no shortage of help available, but the selection of the right providers of training expertise is quite critical.

When to use consultants

There are many reasons why a training function may decide to seek outside assistance. These can include:

- *Expertise.* Consultants may possess expertise with regard to the subject matter to be delivered, techniques of analysis, or skills of delivery.
- *Volume.* The permanent training establishment may not be able to cope with the workload, even if they possess the expertise.
- *Cost.* In some circumstances it can actually work out less expensive to buy the services of an external agency than to resource, prepare and deliver training services internally.
- *Credibility.* Often the message can be delivered more effectively by an outside 'expert' than by the organization's staff.
- *Objectivity.* The outsider can give an unbiased view of the situation in the organization. Comparison with best practice elsewhere is possible, and there is less risk of internal politics.
- *Taking the heat.* Unpopular measures can be portrayed as being the recommendations of the consultants, and management does not have to defend its decisions.
- *Spending the budget.* There may be money left, so spend it quickly before the year end!

Some organizations use consultancy services extensively, some not at all, and others to provide an occasional contribution to the overall training activity. Using outsiders may be expensive, but many managements evolve a cost effective strategy which gives them access to skills and expertise when they need them, rather than having to carry the costs of retaining those capabilities on a permanent basis.

Before deciding to use outside training services, the organization should clarify exactly what help it needs. Ask yourself:

- What do we need to be done?
- Why do we need outside assistance to do it?
- How much are we prepared to pay?

- Do we need to learn to tackle this kind of problem ourselves?
- How will we know if we are getting a quality service at a fair price?

Choosing consultants

Once these questions have been answered, the next stage is to select a suitable consultant or consultancy organization. There are many organizations which offer training delivery and consultancy services. The usual ways of identifying possible providers are:

- Recommendations
- Professional institutes
- Governmental organizations
- Advertisements, mail shots etc.

In general, it makes sense to talk to a small number of possible providers. This in itself can be a time-consuming process, and a few consultancies tend towards high-pressure sales techniques. The consultants will want to ask you questions, but it is important to remember that you are in control – they must convince you of their competence, not vice versa.

The discussion with the consultant should aim to answer the following questions:

- What relevant experience does he or she possess?
- Will he or she be acceptable to our people?
- Is he or she really interested in understanding our problems, or more intent on selling us a standard solution?
- What will the cost be? What is included in the fees quoted?
- How solid and reliable is the consultancy?
- How likely is the consultancy to regard your contract as important?
- What depth of resources does the consultancy have?
- Could we develop a long-term relationship in a variety of areas?

The fees that are charged for training services vary very greatly. The quality of the service provided does not bear a direct relationship to the fees charged. Paying a lot does not guarantee high quality. On the other hand, paying well below the going rate should make you suspicious. Freelance trainers, who do not have high establishment overheads to support, are often considerably less costly than large training concerns. However, client organizations may find themselves doing 'a little typing' or 'a little photocopying', which soon grows into a considerable administrative burden. Also, consider what would happen if she or he fell ill half-way through a programme – is there any back-up?

Some consultancies employ separate sales and training staff. Is this acceptable to you? Or do you want to insist on meeting the trainers before deciding to commission the consultancy? Before agreeing to anything, check what you will be charged for. Is the offer of talking to your managers for a day a genuine one? Or will you be charged for it? Be wary.

Summary

Administration is about getting things done. Creative solutions are of no value unless they are translated into action, and this is particularly true in the field of training. Good administrative systems and procedures are a help to getting the right things done efficiently and consistently. They should not be obstacles to getting things done, nor should they become ends in themselves.

Do not underestimate the power of recommendation. Well-supported arguments assist the trainer in his or her role as an agent of change when seeking approval for a course of action, or when trying to influence others.

Further reading

Francis, D. and Woodcock, M. (1975) *People at Work: A Practical Guide to Organisational Change.* La Jolla: University Associates.

Lock D. and Farrow, A. (1988) *The Gower Handbook of Management.* Aldershot: Gower.

Pepper, A. (1983) *Managing the Training and Development Function,* Aldershot: Gower.

Phillips, K. and Shaw, P. (1987) *A Consultancy Approach for Trainers.* Aldershot: Gower.

10
National Training Policies in Britain

BOB HAMLIN

The past, at least, is secure.

Daniel Webster, 1830

Introduction

Industrial training is once again near the top of the political agenda in the UK, and is likely to remain there as long as politicians perceive skill shortage as the main factor inhibiting national economic performance and international competitiveness. The most recent attempts by government to reform radically the nation's training system are well on the way to full implementation. These include the setting up of a network of voluntary, employer-led training and enterprise councils (TECs) throughout England and Wales and an equivalent network of local enterprise companies (LECs) in Scotland, the establishment of a coherent, unified national framework of vocational qualifications and national standards administered through the National Council for Vocational Qualifications (NCVQ), and the piloting of a training credit (TC) scheme which enables young people to 'buy' approved training relevant to their employment and career aspirations.

To understand how and why the national training policy of the present government and the alternatives advocated by the various opposition parties are as they are, it is necessary to understand why all previous attempts to improve the nation's training system have failed. For over a hundred years the history of training in Britain has been one of persistent failure and recurrent periods of acute skill shortages. Whenever comparisons have been made between Britain's training practices and those of its Western European competitors, the general conclusion has been that countries such as Germany and France have had better national training systems, more capable of quickly responding to technological change and economic growth. In contrast the British training system, which has changed little over the past hundred years despite numerous attempts by successive governments, has failed to produce the quantity and quality of skilled labour required to meet national needs.

The factors that have prevented any fundamental transformation of British training practices stem from two deeply rooted nineteenth-century traditions, namely *apprenticeship* and *voluntarism*. Throughout the twentieth century right up to the present day these two time-honoured traditions have been strongly upheld by employer associations and trade unions alike. This twin fact has had a very strong influence on the thinking of successive governments of all political persuasions, and has largely determined the form and degree of state intervention in the nation's training system.

Since the early days of the Industrial Revolution the tradition of apprenticeship has been the predominant system for supplying skilled workers into the national labour force. Up until recent times entry into apprenticeship was restricted to boys leaving school, who would be indentured as apprentices with employers. Apprenticeship placed a contractual obligation on the employer to train the apprentice in a given trade. In the main it was custom and practice for the apprentice to work alongside a skilled craftsman, and it became the tradition for craftsmen to pass on the tools of the trade, albeit slowly. Typically an apprenticeship would last from five to seven years depending on the type of trade; during the early years of the apprenticeship very low rates would be paid. The quality of training received by apprentices would vary greatly from trade to trade and from employer to employer. The range and depth of skill acquired would be limited to those particular trade skills specifically and narrowly associated with the type of work performed at the particular place of employment. Upon completion the apprentice would be accorded trade *skilled status*, which gave eligibility for membership of the particular trade union. Employment in a given trade would be unobtainable without membership of the appropriate trade union.

Apprenticeships, therefore, had no national standard system of qualifications attached to the status of skilled worker other than being time-served. In many industries, such as printing, for example, apprenticeship became the only route to skilled status, with entry, content and duration controlled by the trade union, and with pay rates determined through collective bargaining. Hence apprenticeship became and remains to the present day an integral part of the British labour relations scene.

The tradition of voluntarism in state–industry relationships stemmed from the belief that such matters as labour relations, and therefore industrial training, were for industry alone and that government should not interfere or be involved. Hence apprenticeship was seen not as a concern of government but rather as a matter solely for industry itself. This voluntarist approach contrasts sharply with the corporatist approach applying in Germany, where there has been for decades a framework of nationally agreed training procedures, standards and systems that have been funded and administered jointly by industry and government. It also contrasts sharply with the interventionist approach in France, where public organization of industrial training funded through taxation has predominated. Throughout most of the twentieth century the traditions of apprenticeship and voluntarism have consistently been the underlying factors that have characterized the British training system and which, with hindsight, have contributed to its failure in providing the adequate supply of skilled workers necessary for national economic growth.

Another factor that has contributed to the endemic skill shortages in Britain has been the deeply rooted attitude of *short-termism*. Unlike their counterparts in competitor countries, particularly Japan, British management and British trade unions have historically conducted their affairs within very near time horizons. Open labour markets which render skilled workers a collective good have meant that employers have been uncertain about being able to recover the costs incurred in developing skills. Hence, over the decades, only the major employers have tended to train skilled workers in any significant numbers, and even these companies have usually cut back drastically on training during periods of economic downturn. Most other organizations have not trained at all, but instead have obtained their skilled labour by poaching. This has inevitably contributed to wage inflation and loss of competitiveness.

Traditionally, craft unions have also been very short-sighted in wage negotiations, using their power to grab as much jam today as possible for their members, including the apprentices, regardless of the longer-term economic consequences for the business. Employers, until recent times, have generally appeased the unions and passed on the extra wage costs to customers. This manifestation of short-termism has increasingly led to apprenticeships becoming much more costly than those in competitor countries. For example, in Germany trainees currently receive only 30–

40 per cent of a skilled worker's earnings averaged over the duration of a traineeship, whereas in Britain it is nearer to 75 per cent. Hence high cost has been a factor inhibiting employers from investing in skills training. However, it should also be borne in mind that the short-term evaluation criteria used by banks and the City have additionally had an inhibiting effect on British management. This has induced short-termism towards investment in skills.

National Training Policies, 1889–1959

At the latter end of the nineteenth century, industrial training was associated mainly with apprenticeship and two other very limited systems for producing skilled workers. *Learnership*, like apprenticeship, was for boys leaving school, but was limited to a narrow range of manual skills usually associated with a single machine or process only, it did not lead to skilled status or craft union membership. *Upgrading* was the mechanism for promoting unskilled adults who had acquired knowledge and practical experience of trade skills by working alongside skilled craftsmen. Upgradings were not common, and were often resisted by the relevant trade unions.

The emergence of new technologies and the impact of the 'scientific school' of management increasingly threatened certain traditional craft skills, and this led to protectionist and defensive strategies from the unions. Inevitably, this drive towards higher productivity through mechanization, mass production and the division of labour led to a contraction in the range and depth of craft skills required, and thereby undermined the control and influence that trade unions had over the processes of production.

Around this time, comparisons were made with other industrialized nations. Great dismay was expressed about the masses of young men who received no training at all and who ended up as unskilled workers plying a trade in the streets, unlike their counterparts in Germany who 'would be in the factory or the army either learning their trade or receiving good and wholesome discipline' (Sheldrake and Vickerstaffe 1987). The problem was perceived to be the inadequacy of the training system in Britain to provide proper industrial training for sufficient numbers of workers.

The belief that the state should ensure that training was provided led to the passing of the Technical Instruction Act of 1889, which resulted in the setting up of technical schools and colleges throughout the country, some modelled on the technical institutes in Germany. Technical eduation courses were developed in conjunction with particular local companies. In some industries, such as the gas industry, the courses of instruction were up to four years' duration and included both day release and examinations operated by the City and Guilds of London Institute. However, these technical education courses were primarily for supervisory and technical staff, rather than for manual workers. Nevertheless, they laid the foundations for a wider application of technical education in later decades. It could be said that the Technical Instruction Act was the first significant government intervention to have had an impact on industrial training in Britain.

The outbreak of the First World War in 1914 required both men and women to be trained to perform well-defined skilled and semi-skilled operative jobs. The traditional training systems were too slow and the Ministry of Munitions funded the setting up of three types of government-led schemes, namely:

● Training courses in technical schools
● Training courses in instructional factories that were under the direct control of the Ministry
● Training in instructional bays attached to certain works.

These schemes were primarily aimed at producing semi-skilled machine operators within three months. Towards the end of the war the emphasis changed to providing rehabilitation training for disabled ex-servicemen, to give them sufficient training to acquire skilled status and trade union membership as well as employment. These schemes, which were supposed to equate to apprenticeships, involved from 6 to 8 months at one of the technical schools or instructional factories, followed by 18 months inside a factory working as an improver.

By 1919 the Ministry of Labour took responsibility for all government-sponsored industrial training, and for the next five years focused on disabled ex-servicemen, leaving the traditional apprenticeship system to provide able-bodied skilled workers. The deepening depression of the 1920s resulted in widespread mass unemployment, and the craft trade unions pressured the Ministry of Labour to restrict the numbers of disabled ex-servicemen admitted on to the government training schemes. Difficulty was also experienced in getting employers to offer the 18-month placement for 'improverships', and ultimately the schemes were abandoned and replaced by courses for the unemployed which predominantly focused on handicraft skills.

During the Depression Years, the number of apprentices recruited into industry was very low, and by 1927 the government was again concerned about a possible shortage of skilled workers. Hence, as a temporary measure, it created the Interrupted Apprenticeship Scheme. This was designed to enable able-bodied ex-servicemen whose apprenticeships had been interrupted by military service to finish their training through a process of technical education funded by the government, but over a shorter time-scale.

To offset the worst effects of mass unemployment, the government also set up and funded a number of training schemes for the unemployed, the most important of which were:

- Government Training Centres (GTCs). These were for men to learn a trade in a 6-month course followed by placement in industry as an improver. The trade unions regarded this as a dilution of the traditional apprenticeship. 'Dilutees', as these workers became known, were not generally recognized as fully skilled by the trade unions.
- Instructional Centres. These aimed to provide 'physical and moral rehabilitation for the long-term unemployed' through 12-week residential courses comprising 'fairly hard work, good feeding and mild discipline' (Davison 1938). No wages were paid, and this led to many trainees refusing to work. The fact that centres were remotely situated, and refusal to attend could lead to unemployment benefit being withheld, caused the scheme to be highly unpopular and resented.
- Training Schemes for Women. These were to prepare unemployed women and girls for domestic service. Both residential and non-residential courses were run in a variety of centres throughout the country.
- Junior Instructional Courses. These were operated by local education authorities on behalf of the Ministry of Labour for unemployed young people under 18, with the aim of 'reducing the demoralising effects of long-term unemployment and of preparing young people for absorption into industry' (Sheldrake and Vickerstaffe 1987).

Of the 2 million people who received training under these schemes the vast majority (1.5 million) were unemployed young people who passed through the junior instructional centres. Hence the government's attempt to increase the number of adult skilled workers into the labour force through the 'dilutee' system had only a limited impact.

By 1935 the general upturn in the economy began to reduce unemployment and the Ministry of Labour's training schemes were progressively run down. However, with the outbreak of the Second World War more skilled labour was needed. The number of places available at the remaining government training centres was rapidly expanded and new centres opened up.

By 1941 many employers expressed concern about the courses being 'too long, too general and too theoretical' (Sheldrake and Vickerstaffe 1987), and hence the basic training courses were reduced in length from 16 weeks to 4–8 weeks. Only exceptional trainees were allowed to continue their training to develop 'high-grade skills', which were supposed to be equivalent to the trade skills acquired through a traditional apprenticeship. With the scope of the GTC courses being reduced, those in industry who had acquired skilled status through the traditional system perceived all training provided by government training centres as being of poor quality. They never seriously considered the GTC high-grade skill training as an acceptable substitute for traditional time-served apprenticeship training. Many GTC-trained people were unable to continue in employment after the war other than in semi-skilled jobs or in non-unionized workshops or companies. Hence the British training system was little changed after the Second World War.

In the immediate post-Second World War period industrial training slipped from the political agenda, but it re-emerged in the early 1950s when skill shortages again began to give cause for concern. The National Joint Advisory Council of the Ministry of Labour decided that a 'number of industries should be asked to review their training facilities' bearing in mind the fact that 'the implementation of nationally agreed training schemes for over 70 industries or sections of industries was less than extensive' (Sheldrake and Vickerstaffe 1987). Clearly industry was failing to recruit and train apprentices in sufficient numbers to meet the wider needs of the economy. However, government intervention was considered inappropriate as apprenticeship was still widely thought to be a matter solely for employers and trade unions. Neither side of industry desired any change in the voluntarist approach to the provision of skills training in the UK.

Apprenticeship schemes varied considerably industry by industry, with 5 years now being a typical time period. Day release for further education, which originated from the Technical Instruction Act of 1889, became part of many apprenticeship schemes during the 1950s, but was not universally so. Furthermore, there was still no standard system of qualifications attached to trade skilled status other than that of being time-served. The actual training received by apprentices in each industry would vary from company to company according to custom and practice, which amounted to a random and chaotic system.

By the mid 1950s there was widespread criticism of the British training system, with concerns being expressed once again by the government and others. The increasing shortages of skilled labour, the poaching of skilled workers, too specialized and company-specific training, the lack of nationally agreed syllabuses and formal qualifications, poor training methods, overlong apprenticeships and age restrictions on entry imposed by the trade unions were some of those concerns. Furthermore, the government was also concerned that very little other industrial training was being given outside the apprenticeship system.

The Carr Commission, set up in 1956 to investigate the adequacy of the British training system in light of the anticipated bulge in the number of school leavers resulting from the post-war baby boom, reported its findings in 1958. This led to both sides of industry ultimately accepting the need for a voluntary Industrial Training Council with the aim of encouraging and even exhorting industry to review and develop its training arrangements and to effect improvements.

At about this same time the Crowther Report (1959) highlighted the differences between the British training system and those of other Western European countries, and drew attention to the lack of a coherent national system of vocational training and practical education in this country. It highlighted also the lack of dialogue between education-ists and trainers which was peculiar to the British apprenticeship system. It appeared there was a tendency to see 'education' and 'training' as two radically distinct and unconnected activities, with much greater value being placed on education. In governmental and educational circles it was widely recognized that Britain lagged behind its main European competitors in terms of skill levels and technical education qualifications, and that the voluntarist approach to training was failing the nation. Even so, both employers and trade unionists chose to remain unconvinced that there was a major problem and were resistant to any increased government involvement in training.

National Training Policies, 1960–1979

In 1962 the Conservative government published the White Paper 'Industrial Training: Government Proposal', which highlighted the link between skill shortages and the national economic performance. It identified three objectives for a new national training policy, namely:

1 To link industrial training into the wider economic and technological needs of the nation so as to ensure industrial growth
2 To improve training standards
3 To spread the costs of training more evenly across companies.

The White Paper proposed setting up, under the auspices of the Ministry of Labour, a network of tripartite industrial training boards (ITBs) for all of the main industries (such as engineering, construction, chemical and allied products etc.), with board membership being made up of employers, trade unionists and educationists. These boards were to have statutory powers to raise annual levies, which were to be paid by all employers within scope of a particular ITB and subsequently disbursed back to companies in the form of grants, depending on the quantity and quality of training provided in any given year. Hence the government's intention was to administer a national training system comprising a stick-and-carrot mechanism, with the stick (the levy) inducing a degree of compulsion on employers to train their employees, and the potential carrot (the grant) spreading the costs of training across companies. It was hoped that the tripartite composition of the ITBs would help to break down some of the strength of trade unions over the existing traditional form, structure and workings of apprenticeships, and also to help bridge the schism between education and training within the British cultural consciousness.

The impetus behind the White Paper came mainly from Whitehall and from independent advisory organizations such as the British Association for Commercial and Industrial Education (BACIE), but not from employers nor from the trade unions, which were still strongly tied to the traditions of voluntarism and short-termism. However, hostility to the proposed state intervention was muted, due possibly to the increased recognition that economic planning and incomes policy might prove to be better alternatives to economic management in Britain than the stop-go policies of the past.

The White Paper had the widespread support of all of the opposition parties, and although it had been produced and published during the office of a Conservative administration, the Industrial Training Act was in fact enacted in 1964 by the newly installed Labour government of Harold Wilson. The 1964 Act had three main aims, namely:

1 To ensure an adequate supply of properly trained men and women at all levels in industry
2 To ensure an improvement in the quality and efficiency of industrial training
3 To share the cost of training more evenly among firms.

The primary means of achieving these aims was through a Central Training Council (CTC) and the network of ITBs.

The CTC was an advisory board to the minister and vetted all the proposals of the ITBs. It was also tasked to highlight and examine the needs of trainer training. Over twenty-five ITBs were ultimately established as statutory organizations under the Act, and a number of voluntary boards were also set up, such as the Local Government Training Board. Each ITB had the following functions:

- To provide or secure provision of sufficient training courses for all employees in its respective industry
- To make recommendations about the provision, length, nature and content of training and associated further education
- To pay grants to employers who provided training of an approved standard of quantity and quality
- To set and impose a statutory training levy on employers in order to fund the other functions and its own running costs.

The levy raised by some ITBs (such as the Engineering ITB) amounted to 2.5 per cent of a company's payroll. It was through the levy/grant incentive system rather than through a system of 'statutory rights and obligations', as existed in some other countries (such as France), that all employers were expected to contribute to their own and to national needs.

Besides introducing this new form of financial inducement/coercion of industry to extend and increase its industrial training, the number of government training centre places for accelerated adult training in certain key trades, namely in engineering and construction, was increased. While it had become evident by the late 1960s that the Industrial Training Act of 1964 had increased the amount of industrial training within the economy as a whole, the impact had differed greatly from industry to industry and from skill category to skill category. Whereas there had been significant increases in the number of craft and technician apprenticeships, there were only marginal increases in skill training for skilled and semi-skilled operatives, or for other categories of skilled worker in, for example, commercial and clerical occupations.

About this time the results of the Royal Commission on Trade Unions and Employment (the Donovan Commission, 1968) were published. The commission was highly critical of the traditional British craft training system, and claimed that in most industries apprenticeships were still based neither on standardized training programmes nor on formal qualifications, despite the existence of the ITBs. The commission strongly recommended that 'training standards and formal qualifications' should be introduced and that the traditional 'time-serving' and 'unofficial age-entry restrictions into skilled trades' should be abolished. Some ITBs had made significant progress towards improving the standards of training associated with an apprenticeship; for example, the first-year off-the-job and subsequent on-the-job module training schemes for craft and technician apprentices within the engineering industry. In many other industries, however, formal, standards-based training took place only during day-release at a college of FE, and even this tended to be more theoretical than practical. Progressive exposure to 'tool-skill' training on the job continued to be slow, unsystematic and totally dependent on the availability of suitable work, which was dictated by the size and type of employer.

Hence, contrary to the intention of the Act, the ITBs concentrated more on increasing the volume of what industry had already been doing, rather than on cultivating major reforms of the process of training skilled workers. ITBs were criticized for not questioning sufficiently the way industry deployed and utilized its skilled labour and for not effectively challenging the appropriateness of the traditional apprenticeship system for meeting the real needs of their respective industries.

Employers allowed the widespread deployment of craftsmen in jobs that required less skill, and also the craft unions insisted on the manning of new equipment by their members even though technically such equipment could be manned equally well by skilled operative labour. Trade unions fought hard to preserve the relative skill and wage differentials between the different categories of unionized labour. The rigid lines of demarcation between trades created a barrier to any notion of skill training for upward mobility, from unskilled to semi-skilled worker, semi-skilled worker to skilled operative and skilled operative to craftsman.

Trade unions had a powerful voice on the tripartite boards of the ITBs. Coupled with the vested interest of British unionism to retain control over the duration and content of apprenticeship, it was perhaps unrealistic of the government to have expected ITBs to have initiated radical changes to the British training system.

By 1970 many more criticisms were being voiced about the workings of the Industrial Training Act. Employers in general expressed unease over what they felt to be a high degree of state intervention, with too much power residing in the hands of government officials. Small firms argued that the ITBs favoured the large firms by being unrealistic in their expectations by putting too much emphasis on off-the-job training and by discounting the traditional, informal, on-the-job training methods that predominated within small businesses. They also criticized the ITBs for demanding too much paperwork. Educationists complained about being insufficiently represented on the boards of ITBs and of being treated as the 'poor relation' by the employer and trade union representatives. Other general criticisms stemmed from the belief that ITBs had become too bureaucratic, were focusing their resources too narrowly on the specialized skill needs of their own industries and were not giving attention to the retraining and redeployment of unemployed workers.

The ITB system had been the first serious attempt by government to effect a major reform of British training practices. It was a national mechanism designed not only to increase the quantity and quality of skill training within particular industries, but also to generate an across-industry approach with a focus on national needs.

Unfortunately the attempt failed, mainly because of what the Brooking's Institution study, entitled 'Britain's Economic Prospects' (Caves 1968), referred to as 'the bloody mindedness' of British unionism and the 'sleepy headedness' of British management, both being manifestations of short-termism. By the early 1970s training in Britain was still largely synonymous with the traditional forms of apprenticeship. The pattern of indentured apprenticeship remained essentially the same, with the average length now being 4 years, and with the retention of age-entry restrictions and time-serving as the main form of qualification.

The impact of the 1964 Act was formally reviewed in a government document entitled 'Training for the Future' (1972), which concluded that:

- The levy/grant system had provided a spur to training activity.
- A permanent system was not required, would be unfair to small firms and should be phased out over time.
- There would be a continuing need for financial incentives for particular training activities of importance to the economy.
- The advisory work of the ITBs had been beneficial and should be expanded.
- A national coordinating body was required to fill gaps not covered by the ITBs and to avoid duplication in areas of overlap.

The report recommended a continuing future role for the ITBs and the setting up of a central national organization. Whereas the Confederation of British Industry (CBI) feared a national training authority would take power away from industry, the trade unions argued the need for a central integrated manpower agency.

The report led directly to the Employment and Training Act of 1973, which became a compromise response to the conflicting demands within industry and the shift in trade union opinion over the issue of coordinating training nationally. The Act had two major elements; firstly it created the Manpower Services Commission (MSC) as the key organization for central employment and training policies outside of the then Department of Employment, and comprising both employer, trade union and education interests. Two executive arms were set up for the MSC, namely the Employment Service Agency, which was responsible for Job Centres, the Professional Executive Recruitment (PER) register and vocational guidance services, and the Training Services Agency (TSA), which took over responsibility for the existing Skillcentres (formerly GTCs), the Training Opportunities Scheme (TOPS) for the unemployed, the ITBs, and research, development and the quality of training. The second major effect of the 1973 Act was to set an upper limit of 1 per cent of emoluments for training levies that could be raised from employers by ITBs, and to provide a system of levy abatement and exemption, with the MSC financing the operating costs of the ITBs.

The MSC became the leading national voice in training matters and the primary mechanism for implementing national policies. It also played a major role, along with the ITBs, in gaining a wider acceptance for planned and systematic training, an achievement which contributed to the creation of a more receptive climate for radical change to the national training system in the following decade.

The 1973 Act tried to revamp the existing national training framework with the formation of the tripartite MSC, but it weakened the mechanism to pursue its aims successfully by minimizing the levy to 1 per cent of payroll. During the 1970s manufacturing industry began to cut back on the number of apprenticeships. Furthermore, the level of training in many industries in Britain continued to compare badly with its Western European competitors. The trends in the labour market were working against an increase in training. In fact, employment in manufacturing industry as a percentage of the total working population declined with the shift towards service industries where there was no tradition of apprenticeship, or for that matter any other type of industrial training system.

These factors led to increased pressure on the government to take a more active and direct role in training. This resulted in new major priorities being set for the national training policy, which were:

- To help prevent skill shortages
- To sustain opportunities for young people to acquire skills training
- To improve vocational preparation for the less qualified
- To increase training and retraining opportunities for adults
- To make training more responsive to real demands.

Various ad hoc measures were introduced by the government between 1973 and 1979 to counter the growing unemployment, and these ranged from support for training places in industry through to job creation programmes. Three early mechanisms used to meet the identified priorities were:

1 The Special Measures and Training for Skills programmes, which were designed to encourage greater recruitment and training of craft apprentices
2 The Unified Vocational Preparation (UVP) Scheme, which was aimed at young people below craft level
3 The Youth Opportunities Programme (YOP), which was aimed at subsidising employers to provide training and work experience for unemployed young people. There were two types of YOP, namely Work Experience on Employers' Premises (WEEP) and Short Training Courses (STC). The vast majority of YOP provision was through the WEEP programme.

By 1976 the lack of adult retraining opportunities, as well as the continued underdevelopment of adult skills training in companies, were being highlighted. Also fears were expressed that the state might be 'subsidising training in industry that would have happened anyway', and that the Special Measures might be 'leading to an actual reduction in the training effort of industry' (Sheldrake and Vickerstaffe 1987). By the end of the decade the MSC mainly focused on the Youth Opportunities Programme, a situation reminiscent of the 1930s.

National Training Policies, 1980–1991

On taking up office in 1979 the newly elected government of Margaret Thatcher inherited 'a set of training policies that were far from comprehensive, efficient or successful' (Sheldrake and Vickerstaffe 1987). Despite the abundance of schemes developed throughout the 1970s the number of apprenticeships continued to decline, adult retraining remained neglected and high youth unemployment persisted. Furthermore, little progress had been made in persuading industry to adopt any radical new approaches to skills training which would lead to an increase in the supply of skilled labour. Some minor modifications in apprenticeship arrangements to create extra job flexibility had taken place in some industries, such as engineering, but industry by and large had failed to reform the apprenticeship system or to amend the traditional restrictive practices. Indeed, employers had contributed to the creation of skills shortages by continuing to designate craft status to jobs that had been deskilled. This inevitably meant that trained craftsmen were grossly under-utilized and job vacancies could only be filled by fully trained apprentices, who were in short supply.

Two documents published around this time set the scene for the need for change in national training policies. The first, which was produced by the Central Policy Review Staff (CPRS) and entitled 'Education, Training and Industrial Performance', highlighted the importance of both vocational preparation and the setting of measurable standards in training. Specifically the report recommended that the British training system should be based on the following principles:

- Objective standards for qualifications should be laid down.
- A person who had attained those standards should be universally accepted as eligible to do the work.
- Apart from introductory training, the content and duration of training schemes (traineeships) should be determined by what was required to reach the set standards.
- No artificial barriers should be placed against access to training or retraining based either on age, sex or colour.

The report also recommended that the balance of resources should be shifted from initial craft apprenticeship training towards retraining and the vocational preparation of young people.

The second document, which was produced by the MSC and entitled 'Outlook on Training', contained detailed recommendations for:

- Converting the statutory ITBs into voluntary training organizations funded by industry
- Strengthening the role of the MSC so that it could exercise greater leadership and extend its activities in relation to the unemployed and other vulnerable groups
- Expanding the Unified Vocational Preparation (UVP) scheme
- Devising and implementing a strategy on adult training and retraining.

Following the publication of these two reports the MSC carried out a further review of the ITBs and in July 1981 submitted to the Secretary of State for Employment a 'Framework for the Future'. This initially led to nineteen of the twenty-four statutory ITBs being abolished and ultimately being replaced by over two hundred voluntary industrial training organizations (ITOs). As a result of these changes the MSC became the only body with responsibility for the implementation of national policies; the ITBs and ITOs were free, if they wished, to confine themselves to the specific needs of their own industries.

In December 1981 the government published the White Paper 'New

Training Initiative – A Programme for Action', which set out three primary objectives for a new national training policy:

1 To reform the apprenticeship system and improve training standards by developing skills training schemes that would allow people to enter training at different ages and with different levels of ability, to acquire agreed skill standards and qualifications appropriate to a job and subsequently to progress to higher levels of skill if they so wished.
2 To develop a permanent bridge between school and work by providing the opportunity for all young people under 18 years of age either to continue in full time education or to enter training and/or planned work experience.
3 To increase adult training by opening up widespread opportunities for employed or unemployed workers to acquire, increase or update their knowledge and skills.

The New Training Initiative (NTI) had emerged after almost twenty years of continuous policy changes and debate, and still many of the training problems remained the same, namely: skill shortage in key industries; inadequate levels of adult skill training; low levels of qualifications among the British workforce as a whole; and a separation in people's minds between 'vocational training' and 'education'.

Unlike earlier attempts to reform the British training system the NTI focused upon the content and process of training, not just the quantity of training. It 'was seen initially as a partial return to a voluntary system for getting industry to reform its training traditions and to embrace the need for adult retraining'. In the event NTI, through its heavy focus on the YTS, was to mark 'an unparalleled extension of State intervention in the nation's training system both in terms of form, content and funding' (Sheldrake and Vickerstaffe 1987). During the first five years of implementation only limited progress was made towards achieving the three main NTI objectives; unfortunately YTS also became the butt of much criticism and disillusionment.

Regarding NTI objective 1 (training standards), the five remaining statutory ITBs and many of the voluntary ITOs had either already introduced into their respective apprenticeship schemes, or were in the process of developing, procedures for skill testing to defined training specifications and standards. For example, 'Skill Testing in the Building Industry', which in fact was not introduced until 1986, had as its main objective the need 'to ensure that in future everyone officially recognised as a skilled worker could perform a defined group of basic skills to standards of quality and time prescribed by the industry'. However, as was shown by the experience of the construction ITB, the achievement of this objective was extremely difficult, with pilot runs of the skills tests giving high failure rates.

With regard to NTI objective 2, the Youth Training Scheme (YTS) was launched in September 1983. Unfortunately YTS was introduced during one of the deepest economic recessions of the century, with mass unemployment widespread and worsening. Coupled with the fact that the government had set the trainee allowances at levels which many thought very low compared to the first and second year wage rates enjoyed by apprentices in full time employment (this would be typically 50 per cent and 60 per cent of the craftworker's rate respectively,) the 'scheme' was widely criticized as being a sop to youth unemployment.

Many of the employer-based YTS programmes were accused of being no more than glorified systems of work experience with little training, and just a means of securing cheap labour. Even with apprenticeships in some industries, such as the building industry, the on-the-job (on-site) component was often unsystematic, uncoordinated or non-existent. The type of training experience given was still invariably dictated by the range of work which a particular employer was engaged upon at the time.

Concerning NTI objective 3, the adult training strategy received no major injection of funds and therefore was the least visible and weakest aspect of NTI. However, the MSC did fund various projects designed to raise awareness of the importance of adult training and retraining and to develop more positive attitudes on the part of employers and trade unionists. Two joint MSC and National Economic Development Office (NEDO) research reports are examples. The first, 'Competence and Competition', examined adult training arrangements in the UK as compared with the USA, Japan, West Germany and France. The second, 'A Challenge to Complacency', reported the lack of interest taken by British chief executives and senior managers in industrial training. Both reports revealed the shortcomings and inadequacies of industrial training in Britain compared to what happened in other countries.

In addition, a number of other schemes were set up, such as the MSC Community Programme (CP) directed at the adult unemployed, and the DES Pickup Programme aimed at identifying and meeting the training needs of local companies. Some initiatives, such as the MSC Training for Enterprise Scheme, were focused on small businesses and the self-employed.

The NTI perceived that vocational education and training needed to be improved, and it was recognized that there was a need for 'training standards of a new kind'. Progress in this direction was made subsequent to the publication of the White Paper 'Working Together – Education and Training (Employment Department and DES 1983). This ultimately led to the setting up in 1986 of the National Council for Vocational Qualifications (NCVQ) which, in hindsight, can be recognized as a landmark development in the British training system. Its development stemmed from the belief that countries such as West Germany had vocational education and training structures that were far better than those in Britain, and that these had been contributing to their superior economic performance.

The NCVQ was tasked to create a new coherent and unified national framework of *vocational qualifications* and *national standards* that:

- Were relevant and comprehensive
- Were easy to access, with no unnecessary barriers or constraints such as age limits, specified periods of training and experience or modes of learning
- Recognized competence and capability in the application of knowledge and skill
- Provided opportunities for progression to higher education and professional qualifications
- Allowed for certification of education, training and experience
- Secured the support of employers, examining and validating bodies, and others concerned.

It was envisaged that the framework would ultimately enhance different levels of award up to and including higher levels of professional qualifications. The first four levels of the framework would cover the range of achievements spanning qualifications from the most basic to those approximating to higher national awards, and the fifth level and above would cover professional qualifications. Further information on the way in which these are being developed is given in chapter 5.

The NCVQ was expected to secure agreement of the various professional bodies to fit all appropriate parts of their professional qualifications into levels I–IV of the NVQ framework by 1991. This was the target date when the government intended to reduce its funding of the non-statutory NCVQ and make it increasingly dependent upon funds raised from levies paid by the respective certifying bodies. As it has transpired the defining of national standards and the setting up of the NVQ system has proved far more arduous, protracted, contentious and administratively costly than had at first been anticipated. As yet it is too soon to assess the likely success of NVQs and the standards programme.

Nevertheless, the progress made to date has at least begun to change radically the whole approach to vocational education and training in the UK. However, the benefits will only materialize if the achievement of NVQs gains widespread credibility with employers and the cost of acquisition is deemed by them to be affordable.

In February 1988 the Government published the White Paper 'Training for Employment', which led to the launching later in that year of the 'New Adult Training Programme. The main features of this programme were as follows:

1 *Aims.* To secure the third objective of NTI by:
   (a) Giving adults the skills they need to get and keep jobs
   (b) Making opportunities available for 18–24-year-olds and those aged 18–50 who have been unemployed for more than two years
   (c) Providing a broad range of training and encouraging employers to play a greater part
   (d) Encouraging individuals to take a greater interest in their own development
   (e) Making a major strategic investment in the motivation, adaptability and skills of the British workforce.
2 *Principles.* The scheme to be a voluntary programme that assures high-quality training provision focused on the individual, provides real incentives for all concerned to take apart and is locally planned and delivered.
3 *Design.* The key elements in the design of the scheme to include:
   (a) Counselling, guidance and assessment by approved training agents (ATOs) who produce for each trainee 'a personal action plan'.
   (b) Structured programmes of directed training (minimum 40 per cent) and practical experience provided or organized by an appointed organization termed the training manager (TM)
   (c) Every trainee to receive a record of achievement, and wherever possible gain a vocational qualification or credit towards one with a national seal of approval, preferably within the NCVQ framework.
4 *Quality assurance.* Training quality to be assured through:
   (a) The establishment of quantifiable performance indicators (such as recruitment rates after training)
   (b) The awarding of 'approved status' to training agents and training managers (providers)
   (c) The provision of funds for training staff within the ATOs and TMs
   (d) The establishment of an adult training board
   (e) Monitoring of the scheme.

The New Adult Training Programme, subsequently called Employment Training (ET), replaced all of the then existing adult training schemes such as the Job Training Scheme (JTS), Community Programme (CP),

Voluntary Projects Programme (VPP) and some employment rehabilitation schemes. Its design and arrangements for delivery were similar to those of the YTS and, like the YTS, the successful achievement of its aims required great commitment and involvement of employers.

Towards the end of the 1980s it had become evident that the NTI had only been partially successful in changing the British training system. Hence in its White Paper, 'Employment for the 1990s' (December 1988), the government identified lack of skills as the most significant barrier to job growth and proposed to establish a 'training and enterprise framework that would meet Britain's key employment needs and increase its international competitiveness'. It provided a major role for employers, not just at the national level but more importantly at the local level. The White Paper set out a range of objectives to be achieved over a 3-year time-scale, which included:

- Establishing a national network of training and enterprise councils (TECs) through England and Wales and an equivalent network of local enterprise companies (LECs) in Scotland, designed to plan and deliver training and promote the development of small businesses at the local level. Interestingly this network was modelled partly on the German Chambers of Craft Industries, which have had the responsibility for locally based training delivery systems in Germany, and partly on the American 'free-trade' model.
- Setting up a National Training Task Force comprising eminent industrialists and others to assist the Secretary of State in establishing and developing the LECs and TECs and promoting greater investment by employers in the skills of the British workforce.
- Launching a Business Growth Through Training Programme designed to unify the help available to companies in developing training strategies to meet their business objectives.
- Consulting with the then seven remaining statutory industrial training boards with a view to drawing up agreed programmes and timetables for becoming independent non-statutory bodies.
- Privatizing the Skills Training Agency (STA) so that it would become a profit-making organization with a 'clear commercial focus able to compete on level terms with other providers'. (The STA was responsible for the remaining skill centres, which had had their origins as government training centres during the Depression years of the 1920s.)

It was the government's aim to build on the existing involvement and commitment of business by inviting local groups led by top local employers and community leaders to form the TECs, the four key functions of which were:

1 To examine local labour markets by assessing the key skill needs, the prospect for expanded job growth and the adequacy of existing training opportunities
2 To draw up plans for securing quality training and enterprise development that would meet both government guarantees and local community needs
3 To manage training programmes for young people, for unemployed people and for adults requiring retraining
4 To provide support services for small businesses, including training, which were relevant to local needs.

At least two-thirds of the membership of each TEC/LEC had to be chief executives from local private-sector organizations, with the other third of the membership comprising senior figures drawn from local education, training and economic development organizations, voluntary bodies and trade unions. The TECs and LECs were expected to evolve gradually over a period of 3–4 years; in fact it took until the end of 1991 before the completed network of 82 TECs within England and Wales, and the equivalent network of 22 LECs in Scotland, had become fully operational.

Under the new system, LECs and TECs were made responsible for the government's major new ET scheme, which, at the time it was launched, was claimed to be the largest and most ambitious training programme for unemployed people in the world. The scheme provided up to 12 months' training for those taking part; an expectation was placed on TECs and LECs to involve employers in the ET programme so that training was relevant to the jobs into which trainees might move and was of the right quality. There was a time lag between the start of ET and the time when TECs and LECs could take operational responsibility. When they did so most TECs and LECs drastically reduced the ET programme provision through lack of government funding. TECs and LECs were also made responsible for running the Youth Training Scheme (YTS), subsequently called Youth Training (YT), and the Business Growth Through Training (BGT) programme.

In response to an original suggestion by the Confederation of British Industry in its 1989 report 'Towards a Skills Revolution', the government revealed in October 1990 details of a training credit (TC) scheme. The training credits represented an entitlement to school leavers between 16 and 17, including those with special needs, to 'buy' approved training relevant to their employment and career aspirations. TECs/LECs were given the task of administering the scheme, with training provision being delivered only by approved training organizations (ATOs) to at least level II of the standards set by the NCVQ. Most TECs/LECs saw the

TC scheme as a major initiative by government that would assist them in achieving their strategic objectives; they interpreted their main role as being that of marketing the training credits, monitoring the quality assurance and auditing the outcomes.

Eleven TECs/LECs were selected to develop practical plans for piloting the scheme, taking into account their local circumstances. The result of these pilots, which commenced in April 1991, were not available to us at the time of writing and therefore we do not yet know how successful they have been. Even so, it has been widely reported that entitlements to training credits will most probably be extended to all school leavers. Although the TC scheme has been warmly welcomed, a cautionary note is called for because, as the Department of Employment concedes, there is a disturbingly low enthusiasm for self-improvement among school leavers, so it is by no means certain that the training credits will be spent. Indeed, it was reported in December 1991 that less than 45 per cent of the training credits given to school leavers through the pilot schemes had in fact been used. Hence the success of the scheme will very much depend on the ability of the TECs/LECs to market the credits to young people, and also on the quality of the advice and counselling given.

In December 1990 the government initiated another important change in the British training system by making TECs/LECs responsible for the budget associated with work-related further education, which up until then had been managed by the Department of Employment. This change of funding arrangement, which directly affected colleges of further education (FE) and higher education (HE), enabled TECs/ LECs to become directly involved with local education authorities in shaping the local provision of work-related FE. This further increased the influence of TECs/LECs on vocational training in their areas. At the time of writing it was also being reported that responsibility for the Careers Service would probably become shared between local education authorities and their respective local TECs/LECs, thereby effecting a further fundamental transformation in the vocational education and training system of the country.

Observation and Comment

The voluntarist training policies adopted by the Conservative government from 1988 onwards, which have led to the final dismantling of the ITBs and the creation of TEC and LEC networks throughout the UK, have quietly revolutionized the way Britain trains its workforce; this has resulted in a dramatic change in the training role of government. The way the MSC was organized during the 1970s and early 1980s and all of the programmes it initiated were top-down, having been designed and funded centrally, as also were the various eligibility rules and regulations. The philosophy behind TECs/LECs has turned this on its head and created a bottom-up framework, where local rather than national needs determine government funding and provision. State intervention in the nation's training system has been drastically reduced. Post-1988, only remnants of the old MSC have remained, firstly in the guise of the Training Commission, then of the Training Agency and latterly as the Training Education and Enterprise Directorate (TEED) of the Department of Employment. The role of TEED has been limited to that of mainly supporting TECs/LECs with information about what each has been up to, conducting research and development into training technologies, generally helping the networks of TECs/LECs, and initiating national training innovations as appropriate. The TECs and LECs are contracted to the TEED.

Although TECs/LECs have been asked to implement the government's YT, TC and ET programmes for young people and unemployed adults respectively, their primary role has been to get employers to invest more in skills training and in the development of their own workers. This is of paramount importance if Britain is to match the level of skilled workers produced by competitor countries. But as this chapter reveals, despite all of the efforts of successive governments throughout this century, whether Conservative, Labour or Coalition, the level of skills training provided in Britain except during the two periods of world war has persistently been much lower than that achieved by other nations. Recent research has revealed that in Germany the number of skilled workers qualifying in, for example, mechanical engineering trades has been five times higher than in Britain, and for those qualifying as electricians it has been four times higher. Then again, in office work and in the clothing industry Germany has produced ten times more skilled workers than Britain. The link between skills training, economic growth and international competitiveness appears to have been well understood by employers in other countries, but in Britain the problems of skill shortages have not yet been resolved successfully.

Whether the newly created TECs/LECs will be successful in radically transforming British training practices and overcoming skill shortages as the government intends, only time will tell. Many doubt whether the TECs and LECs can succeed without some form of compulsion being applied to force employers to train their employees. Even the commitment to training of some of the leading industrialists who head the TECs themselves has been brought into doubt; the findings of recent research have revealed 'a lack of emphasis of training in the companies of TECs' board members' (Kraithman et al. 1991).

The Conservative government's reliance on the voluntarist approach to industrial training and upon market forces and free trade in training have been widely criticized as being fragile and unlikely to succeed. In the policy document 'Modern Manufacturing Strength', which was published in March 1991, the Labour party outlined its approach to reforming the nation's training system. When in government it would make it illegal to employ 16-year-olds without giving them training, and would introduce a training levy on employers. It would also set up a new national body to work alongside the TECs/LECs and to provide more support for the non-statutory industrial training organizations (ITOs), whose records of achievement have been somewhat dismal to date. The proposed training levy would be set initially at 0.5 per cent of payroll but ultimately increased 'to a level more acceptable to the training world'. Tax incentives would be introduced for companies spending more than 0.5 per cent of payroll on training as a means of encouraging them to upgrade their training programmes. This approach appears to be based on various aspects of both the French and German national training systems.

From this brief history of national training policies adopted by Britain over the past hundred years it will be appreciated that there have been certain factors outside the industrial training context, but concerned with labour relations and the British industrial culture, which have thwarted the various attempts of successive governments to reform radically the nation's training practices. These factors, which still persist in the 1990s, stem from short-term thinking in the part of all of the main stakeholders in British industry, namely the employers, the trade unions, the employees and the shareholders. They have led to:

- Skilled workers being deployed in jobs that require less skill than they possess (for example, graduate engineers in technician jobs, technicians in craft jobs and craftworkers in skilled operative jobs etc.), which has created artificial skill shortages
- Skill status being relatively undervalued, with pay differentials between the unskilled and the skilled being narrow, which has reduced any incentive for workers to aspire to the acquisition of higher-level skills other than for reasons of personal job satisfaction. Why should young school leavers offer

themselves for skills training when they can earn more money in unskilled occupations?

- Apprenticeships having become very costly systems of training compared to comparable traineeships in competitor countries
- Managers being ambivalent about skills training, thinking of it more as a short-term cost to be avoided if at all possible than as a long-term investment vital for future business success
- Companies adopting accounting systems and bankers using evaluation criteria that force line managers to operate within near time horizons
- The city demanding maximum dividends today at the expense of encouraging sufficient plough-back investment in the skills required for tomorrow to sustain long-term profit growth.

Summary

Unless those aspects of the British industrial culture which induce short-termism towards investment in skills training can be reduced or eliminated, then it is unlikely that current or future national training policies, whether based on variants of the voluntarist, corporatist or interventionist approaches, will have any more success in resolving the nation's skill shortages than those policies of the past. If Britain is ever to achieve the goal of producing the best-trained workforce in Europe, it seems that combined, concerted action by government, employers, trade unions and city institutions will be required in order to recast the British industrial culture, not just the British training system.

Acknowledgement

For the early parts of this chapter the author has drawn heavily on the work of John Sheldrake and Sarah Vickerstaff.

Further reading

Burke, John W. (1989) *Competency Based Education and Training*. Lewes: Falmer.

Caves, R.E. (1968) *Britain's Economy Prospects – A Brooking's Institution Study*. London: Unwin.

Davison, R. (1938) *British Unemployment Policy since 1930*. London: Longman.

Jessup, G. (1991) *Outcomes: NVQs and the Emerging Model of Education and Training*. London: Falmer.

Jones, O. and Smith, P. (1990) *A Strategic Evaluation of Youth and Employment Training*. Manchester: Manchester Business School.

Kraithman, D., Wall, A., Bowles, T., Adams, J. and Rainnie, A. (1991) Can TECs Cope with Recession? *Employment Institute Economic Report*, vol. 5, no. 1, January.

Sheldrake, J. and Vickerstaff, S. (1987) *The History of Industrial Training in Britain*. Aldershot: Avebury.

Steedman, H. (1990) Improvement in Workforce Qualification: Britain and France 1979–88. *National Institute Economic Review*, August 1990.

Steedman, J. and Wagner, K. (1989) Productivity, Machinery and Skills: Clothing Manufacture in Britain and Germany. *National Institute Economic Review*, May 1989.

Stevens, J. and Mackay, R. (1991) *Training and Competitiveness*. London: Kogan Page.

11
Developing Employees

STEVE TRUELOVE

Success nourished them; they seemed to be able, and so they were able.

Virgil

Introduction

Most of us happily use the phrase 'training and development' without much thought. What, then, is the difference between 'training' and 'development'? Come to that, what is the difference between 'training' and 'education'? The following definitions should not be taken as absolutes, but as working definitions for the way the terms are used in this chapter:

- *Education* is a process whose prime purposes are to impart knowledge and develop the way mental faculties are used. Education is not primarily concerned with job performance.
- *Training* endeavours to impart knowledge, skills and attitudes necessary to perform job-related tasks. It aims to improve job performance in a direct way.
- *Development* is a process whereby individuals learn through experience to be more effective. It aims to help people utilize the skills and knowledge that education and training have given them – not only in their current jobs, but also in future posts. It embodies concepts such as psychological growth, greater maturity and increased confidence.

It can readily be appreciated that many 'educational' courses include elements of training; that some training courses have large educational components; and that all these processes contribute to the unlocking and nurturing of the potential within people. Education, training and development are not sequential or hierarchical; rather, they are interlinked and interdependent.

For many people, personal growth experiences occur without any planning or influence from training professionals. Many managers and supervisors have an intuitive understanding that allowing someone to have a go at something will be good for them. Others, however, fail to recognize the ability and potential in their subordinates and much talent remains forever untapped. The trainer's role is to encourage, perhaps even to organize, managers and supervisors to develop their subordinates as fully as possible.

One common way for people to be developed is the 'in-at-the-deep-end' method. This involves giving an employee a difficult and demanding assignment without adequate preparation, guidance or assistance. He or she will either 'sink or swim', says the manager. Very often, we can look back at our own careers and remember being dropped in at the deep end. If we were lucky, we learned to swim quickly enough to cope with the situation and came out of it exhausted, but knowing that we had survived. Next time, it would not be so bad. However, suppose that we had failed. Perhaps we would react by taking the view that, 'I can't do that: please never put me in that position again.' Of course, if the manager who put us in that position in the first place viewed the failure as evidence of intrinsic weakness in us, then we might not be given a second chance anyway – 'I let her tackle it once. She was hopeless.'

The problem with the in-at-the-deep-end, sink-or-swim approach is that it has a high casualty rate. Many people who could be taught to swim fail and (metaphorically) drown. So what constitutes a better approach? As in any other training situation, we start by looking at needs. However, here we are focusing on longer-term needs than is usually the case, and we are looking at the organization's needs and the individual's needs at the same time.

The Individual's Needs

Other chapters in this book deal with the identification of training needs in some detail. When considering development needs, the key aspects of using these techniques is to consider various elements at the same time.

Firstly, people vary in their needs and drives. Some want to grow and develop, to achieve great things, to realize their potential to the full.

Others prefer not to take risks. They do not want to be constantly tackling new things, but are content to do their current jobs well.

Secondly, people vary greatly in their abilities. There often seems a reluctance among trainers to acknowledge this. Personnel specialists have no such difficulty, and readily reject applicants who they believe do not have the right abilities to succeed in a particular job. Trainers sometimes seem to be committed to the idea that anyone can learn anything, given a well-designed training programme. This is clearly not the case.

Thirdly, the organization may or may not be able to provide the development the individual wants and is capable of benefiting from. Giving inexperienced people opportunities to learn and to make mistakes can be very disruptive and costly, and is not always practicable.

For example, a company employed a capable and conscientious instrument engineer in charge of a small team of technicians. A vacancy arose which involved being in charge of a number of sections, coordinating a multidisciplinary workforce and several professional engineers. The instrument engineer was offered the promotion. He declined it, because he did not want the extra pressure and stress that the job would bring. The company did not accept this view, and brought various pressures to bear on him to accept the promotion. Reluctantly, he did so. But within weeks of taking the job, he handed in his notice. He had managed to find a position elsewhere that would allow him to function at the level he was comfortable with.

Key techniques to identify aspirations are:

- Structured interviews
- Appraisal systems which particularly address this aspect
- Observation – does the individual seek out development opportunities? Does she or he push for involvement whenever possible?
- Personality questionnaires or other specifically designed instruments which look at the need to achieve.

Key techniques to identify abilities are:

- Psychometric tests which measure aptitudes
- Assessing current performance through an appraisal scheme or by other performance indicators
- Using simulations, exercises or small assignments to test ability without undue risk
- Temporary promotion or assignment to a different job.

The Organization's Needs

No organization should believe that it really knows what its future needs will be with any degree of accuracy. We live in a dynamic time when organizations are having to respond to change at an ever-increasing rate. None the less, it is part of the job of the human resource function to try to predict and prepare for needs as well as possible. Note the term 'human resources' rather than 'training': preparing for such future needs requires a coordinated approach from both personnel and training specialists. Talented people need to be recruited before they can be developed.

In order to anticipate our organizations' future needs, we need to think about what forms of organization we will have in the future, and what kinds of people we will need. This is a complex issue, but we can see quite clear trends emerging:

- Organizations are less prepared than they used to be to carry surplus employees. This is particularly true for service organizations, whose workload fluctuates rapidly. Anyone who is not versatile is vulnerable to redundancy.
- Even if someone is versatile, talented and hardworking, the organization may not require his or her services all of the time. New patterns of employment are evolving whereby people become self-employed, or set up businesses to serve their previous employer for some of the time and to look for other opportunities at other times.
- Few people can safely assume that they will have a single career. More frequently than ever before, people will pursue two or more careers during their working lives. The pace of technology change will require the learning of new skills and knowledge on a continuing basis.
- Traditional organizational command structures are being replaced by more loosely defined organizational forms. Inherent in these is the requirement for people to make decisions as to how they go about their jobs – either independently, or as part of small teams. The new organization is more interested in results than in how the job is done.
- Work groups and teams are beginning to select their own leaders and will not accept inappropriate management techniques forced on them from above.

Organizations are learning to value key people as assets to be nurtured and developed. At the same time, they must allow people to consider their careers outside the organization. It should not be unthinkable for employees to discuss leaving the organization, becoming self-employed, or taking a year or so off work. It may suit the organization to encourage such thinking so that its staff are employed truly voluntarily.

Too often, organizations are clogged up with disaffected time-servers – men and women who joined ten, twenty or thirty years ago and who occupy positions that they once dreamed of attaining, but which now bore them. They feel trapped. The reason is that they *are* trapped. Most organizations allow progression along conventional career paths, but have no or limited mechanisms for someone to say 'I'd like a change, please', or, 'My job no longer gives me feelings of satisfaction.' And so talented, ambitious and hardworking employees are slowly, often imperceptibly, turned into sour, bored and resentful employees. The damage this does is enormous. Not only do we make their lives miserable, but we make the whole organization inefficient and unresponsive. Development opportunities become fewer, and the young, hopeful newcomers are warned of the inevitable dreariness that the future holds for them.

Why does this happen? Often it is because the organization pays too little attention to the needs of the people it employs. It is, of course, concerned with its own needs; with getting the job done effectively and well. Individuals' needs are not its prime concern. Yet many analysts repeatedly find that successful organizations are so successful mainly because the people in them are 'turned on'. They are doing a good job because they *want* to do a good job; because they get feelings of achievement and accomplishment from what they are allowed to do at work.

This message is not only propounded by current writers such as Tom Peters (Peters 1987) and Charles Handy, but has also been advocated by 'classic' management theorists such as Douglas McGregor and Frederick Herzberg (Herzberg 1966). Time and again, it is recognized that the development of individuals is a function of providing 'an organisational climate conducive to growth' (McGregor 1960) and of allowing people the opportunity to do work they regard as meaningful and worthwhile. 'Every job should be a learning experience', said Herzberg in a 1973 interview, and that is a useful principle to remember when thinking about development. Yet many managers reject that concept. They insist on recruiting fully experienced people who require no training at all. They can look at a subordinate who has been doing exactly the same job for the last five years, as he or she is expected to do for the next ten, and not think anything is wrong. They believe that their subordinates come to work for the lowest of motives.

McGregor termed them 'Theory X' managers, and there are still plenty of them around. 'Theory Y' managers, on the other hand, believe in creating such conditions that the members of the organization can achieve their own goals best by directing their efforts towards making the organization successful. In those conditions, people will constantly be striving to use their potential fully: to learn, to take responsibility, to advance. This does not mean that an organization with a 'Theory Y' philosophy is the soft option. Far from it – for employees are expected to strive harder and achieve more on their own initiative. Those who have to be bullied and chivvied along are not welcome.

The organization cannot make people learn, but it can provide opportunities for learning.

Opportunities for Learning

Opportunities for learning may be put into three categories:

1 Learning deliberately initiated by someone else to develop the individual
2 Learning that occurs as a consequence of the demands that the job makes
3 Learning deliberately initiated by the individual

Learning deliberately initiated by someone else includes 'formal' development interventions, such as:

- *Coaching* – taking someone through the experiential learning cycle in a systematic way with the intention of improving the capability to apply specific skills or deal with problematic situations
- *Mentoring* – assigning a respected and competent individual (other than the direct boss) to provide guidance and advice in order to help someone cope with and grow in the job
- *Counselling* – helping someone clarify her or his own position with regard to job performance, career path or other issues by facilitating self-analysis
- *Training* – specific off-the-job inputs which are designed to meet other short-term or long-term needs, and which can be as brief as a one-day seminar or as major as a full MBA programme
- *Planned experience* – promotion, job rotation, job enlargement, job enrichment, secondment; one way or another, arranging for the person to tackle new areas of work
- *Projects* – responsibility for achieving something outside the normal activities of the job; sometimes with the individual in charge of the project, at other times as a member of a task force or project team
- *Committees* – perhaps internal, perhaps external; often allowing an increase in the breadth of perception of the organization or the environment in which it operates.

Learning that occurs as a consequence of the demands the job makes includes:

- *Covering* – for the boss or others when they are on holiday, sick or otherwise absent
- *Crisis* – coping with exceptional workload or difficulties because there is no option
- *Organizational growth* – growing organizations almost automatically develop people by requiring more of them as new ventures become operational, new markets are entered and new levels of activity achieved.

Learning initiated by the individual includes:

- *Volunteering* – consciously and willingly taking on tasks which will be a learning experience. This involves not only extra effort, but also a degree of risk, because failure is possible. Some organizations have a climate which encourages and applauds risk taking, others suppress such actions.
- *Reading* – textbooks, journals and newspapers are all readily available. Yet it is astonishingly easy to find talented people who have not read a textbook for years, and do not even bother to leaf through the professional journals that arrive on their desks every month.
- *Education* – evening classes, Open University, distance learning etc. Few organizations allow time off for full-time study, but it is not unknown. In deciding whether or not to support someone who is interested in furthering his or her education the direct relevance of the subject matter to the individual's job is often considered to be important. Yet for many people, it is the skills such as analysis, research, persuasive writing and critical thinking that the educational process gives them that prove to be valuable, rather than the knowledge of the subject matter being studied.
- *Outside activities* – practising skills through taking responsibility in organizations such as the Junior Chamber of Commerce, local ITD branch, charities or youth organizations.

However opportunities for learning arise, real learning does not happen automatically. For an experience to result in a permanent change in someone, that experience has to be analysed and related to previous knowledge. People often have to be helped to gain the most from their experiences, and it is the role of the trainer to encourage this.

Job Design

The concept of job design is an intriguing one. The vast majority of employees take for granted that their jobs exist and that their activities and responsibilities are natural component parts of a meaningful whole.

It is often considered to be important that these component parts are itemized in a document such as a job description, which as clearly as possible draws boundaries around the job. People then know what they have to do in order to fulfil the requirements of the job.

There are two questions that arise here:

1 What is the extent to which it is necessary or desirable to specify what someone must do in his or her job?
2 How can we build opportunities for achievement, satisfaction and development into everyone's work?

Why have job descriptions?

Some organizations are beginning to abandon the use of formal job descriptions altogether. This is particularly so in small, dynamic companies, but may well become a more common trend in the future. Other organizations view the job description as a bedrock component of professional human resource management, without which little can be achieved.

Arguments in favour of job descriptions are that they:

- Help people know what they are supposed to do
- Identify what needs to be learned
- Are necessary to ensure a just payment system through job evaluation
- Are an essential aid to effective recruitment
- Help managers to monitor and control their subordinates.

Arguments against job descriptions are that they:

- Create barriers which limit people's contributions artificially
- Obstruct change – particularly if a change in the job description can result in a change in pay
- Focus on what people do and the methods they use, rather than on what they are required to achieve
- Are costly to prepare and maintain in an up-to-date condition.

It is probable that most large organizations will continue to find job descriptions of value. However, the way they are written, and the extent to which they try to cover everything that the job holder does, will probably change to allow for greater scope for the individual to grow and develop his or her own job. Perhaps the much-loved little phrase 'any other duties as required' will be replaced by a statement such as 'any other activities that contribute to the achievement of the organization's goals'. While we will continue to need some jobs to be tightly defined as to their role and scope, others will need to be much looser in nature so that individuals can directly, and of their own initiative, contribute to the continual improvement of the organizations within which they work, with personal and organizational development thereby becoming inseparable.

Building in opportunities

Many of the readers of this book will be employed to perform jobs designed by someone else. That is to say, one or more people, probably higher up in the organization have decided to create a job with an appropriate job title to perform certain activities. Sometimes this process produces interesting and rewarding jobs, at other times routine, boring and frustrating jobs. In time, the job may change or disappear. It may be split into two or more component parts, or it may absorb part of one or more other jobs. All too frequently, this process goes on with inadequate regard for the quality of working life that the job holder will experience.

We need to organize work, as far as possible, so that everyone is able to experience feelings of satisfaction and achievement through what they do. This is not an altruistic view. People will not give their best performance if they are required to perform boring, routine and undemanding work. Nor will they be able to develop in such jobs. Rather, they will become frustrated, then may quit the organization, become a troublemaker, or give up and become passengers, doing as little as they can get away with.

Motivation is a complex subject, but increasingly, people want to achieve personal growth and development through their work. They expect to be allowed to prove themselves through their jobs, to tackle new problems, to learn new skills. Talented people want to know more about the training and development that the organization will provide for them, and rate this as an important factor when selecting which organization to join. For some jobs, it will be possible to lay down what must be learned. But for many, the individual will have a degree of choice. The motivational power of freedom of choice must not be undervalued. We will all apply ourselves more rigorously to tasks we have chosen than to those forced upon us. This includes the task of learning new things.

Outdoor Development

Many organizations focus their development efforts on outdoor development. There are many variations of the approach, including the use of sailing boats, canoes or other items requiring physical involvement. The idea is that the immediacy and reality of the situation is more effective in producing learning than are classroom-based situations. While outdoor-based activities sometimes aim to teach specific skills, the usual emphasis is on the importance of teamwork, the development of leadership, or building confidence. Whether outdoor development is effective or not is, frankly, a matter of opinion. As with most attempts to produce lasting change, evaluation is very difficult. Notwithstanding the lack of solid evidence as to its effectiveness, training and development in the outdoors has established itself as a major sector of the UK training scene. Many organizations believe that their commitment to outdoor development is fundamental to their success, and the fact that it is so popular with many 'blue-chip' companies give some evidence to that proposition.

The supporters of outdoor training believe that the process very much enhances learning according to Kolb's four-stage cycle of learning:

1 Concrete experience is followed by;
2 Observation and reflection, leading to;
3 The development of abstract concepts and frameworks, enabling;
4 Hypotheses to be tested in future action.

It is argued that in a classroom situation success or failure in a game or exercise may matter little to the participants: 'Oh, so I did it wrong. It's a stupid game anyway.' By comparison, the activity in an outdoor setting may have fairly strong implications for the participants: 'We got lost and walked for miles and miles in the rain because our leader didn't listen to us.' So the concept is that because the 'concrete experience' is more real and significant, the learning will also be more real and significant.

Some would argue that the learning tends to produce better canoeists and abseilers than it does managers or employees; that effective leadership in an outdoor situation does not necessarily translate into effective leadership in, say, a data-processing situation. Its supporters, however, assert that managing an outdoor situation is a powerful way of simulating real life; that because the projects are not directly work-related, the principles are highlighted and available to be reapplied back at work.

One very real problem with using the outdoors is that it discriminates in favour of the younger and more active people in the organization. Imagine that everyone in your office except you goes on a team-building event. You did not go because you were disabled, overweight, unfit, scared of heights or pregnant. You would feel very isolated from the rest of them because they would have shared a common experience which you missed out on. A course delegate once told me that her company had recently run a series of outdoor events. Attendance was not compulsory, but when redundancies were announced, all those who had opted out of the events lost their jobs.

Whatever the merits or pitfalls of using the outdoors to help people develop, choose your training company with care. Check that they know what they are doing from a training viewpoint as well as an outdoor viewpoint. Ask them how they cope with delegates who display anxiety, or who want to quit half-way through. Also remember that accidents can and do happen. Check on the medical back-up and the insurance situation. Think through how you will handle the logistics of getting people to the event with the appropriate clothing and equipment.

Self-development

Some training professionals have job titles which indicate that they are in charge of 'management development'. Yet it is impossible for any individual to control the development of others. They can help, they can provide resources, and they can encourage. But they cannot force people to learn. More and more it is recognized that individuals have to be responsible for their own development, and that they can do a lot for themselves. Some self-development techniques, such as those described by Boydell and Pedler, concentrate on increasing self-awareness and insight. They include consciously analysing the attitudes and feelings of those you interact with at work in order to develop your sensitivity. They also encourage in-depth analysis of your own abilities and motivations in order for you to be able to focus your development efforts where they will be most effective.

The concept of self-development can also include managing your own career. At one time, large, successful organizations would try to take the responsibility for career development from individuals. The organization would map out career paths and help guide employees through the necessary stages to achieve their potential. There can be some merit to this approach in stable environments, but the rate of change in organizations now means that we all have to manage (as well as we can) our own careers. This, again, includes self-analysis in order to be able to make informed choices about what learning we need and to achieve positions that will meet our needs.

We do not all want the same things out of our jobs. Helping someone to manage his or her own development, and thereby his or her own career, is often a matter of assisting in the analysis of possibilities and evaluating options. While predicting career paths is becoming less easy, many people feel a need to have some sort of plan to follow. Talking them through possibilities allows them to construct an internal 'road map' of career paths for themselves, which can result in reduced anxiety and greater determination, yet does not delude them. They become aware that they will face choice points, and that there are many routes from A to B, and still more from A to F, G, H and so on. See figures 11.1 and 11.2.

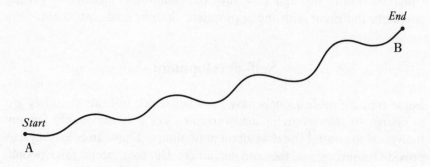

Figure 11.1   Traditional career path

Please note that whatever mental road map anyone makes for themselves, it will be wrong. The purpose is to help give a sense of direction in a world full of ambiguity and change. The map must be redrawn from time to time whenever a career choice is made, or whenever a chosen path does not seem to be as rewarding as was anticipated.

The Peter Principle

To conclude this chapter on employee development on a cautionary note: one of the best-known concepts in the language of management is

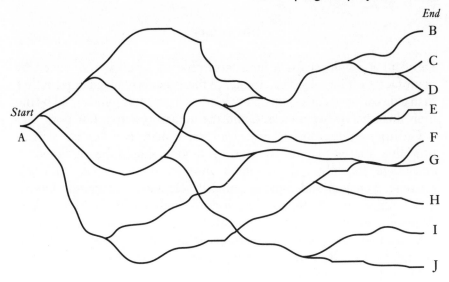

Figure 11.2   Road map of career paths

'The Peter Principle', an idea coined by Dr Laurence Peter and popularized in the best-selling book of the same name. It is still worth considering what Peter said with regard to development.

The Peter Principle is this: 'In a hierarchy every employee tends to rise to his or her level of incompetence.' The basis of this statement is that hierarchical organizations tend to reward competence in a job by (eventual) promotion to the next level. Only when someone is promoted to a job at which he or she is incompetent does this process end for the individual. Eventually, therefore, every post tends to be occupied by an incompetent person. The work of the organization is accomplished by those employees who have yet to reach their level of incompetence.

One of the important questions that arises is, 'Who defines competence?'. Very often, it will be the individuals' superiors. If they are already at their own level of incompetence, then either they will apply the wrong criteria for competence, or they will deliberately suppress talent so that their own mediocre performance is not shown up. Through these mechanisms, the best people may easily be overlooked and their careers frustrated.

The other key message that Peter put across is that each of us must consciously judge our own competence and try to avoid taking on jobs that will produce stress and misery simply because they are available. Increased responsibility, status and pay may or may not make us happier. We must think about these questions for ourselves and make our own judgements.

Summary

Developing employees is a long-term process which is influenced by many factors. The role of the trainer in this process is a facilitative rather than a directive one. Responsibility for development is jointly held by the individual, his or her manager, and the human resource function.

Creating an appropriate organizational climate is a key element in providing for employees to grow, and jobs should be designed to encourage individual development through more or less constant learning. Personal and organizational development are closely linked, and training interventions often address both needs simultaneously. Although much of the development process is informal, progressive organizations take positive steps to maximize opportunities for learning and growth by setting up monitoring systems and showing an interest in individuals' development.

Outdoor development and self-development are two approaches that are currently popular. As part of your self-development, make sure you read some of the books listed at the end of each chapter. *The Peter Principle* is a good one to start with.

Further reading

Boydell, T. and Pedler, M. (1981) *Management Self-development: Concepts and Practices*. Farnborough: Gower.

Francis, D.L. (1985) *Managing Your Own Career*. London: Collins.

Handy, C. (1989) *The Age of Unreason*. London: Business Books.

Herzberg, F. (1966) *Work and the Nature of Man*. Cleveland, Ohio: World Publishing.

Honey, P. and Mumford, A. (1986) *Manual of Learning Styles*. Maidenhead: Peter Honey.

Kolb, D.A., Rubin, I.M. and McIntyre, J.M. (1984) *Organisational Psychology: An Experiential Approach to Organisational Behaviour*. 4th edn. Englewood Cliffs, N.J.: Prentice-Hall.

McGregor, D. (1960) *The Human Side of Enterprise*. New York: McGraw-Hill.

Mumford, A. (ed.) (1986) *Handbook of Management Development*. 2nd edn. Aldershot: Gower.

Peter, L.J. and Hull, R. (1969) *The Peter Principle*. London: Souvenir Press.

Peter, T. (1987) *Thriving on Chaos*. New York: Harper and Row.

Wood, S. (ed.) (1988) *Continuous Development: The Path to Improved Performance*. London: Institute of Personnel Management.

Index